THE TOLL OF
INDEPENDENCE

Clements Library Bicentennial Studies

This study and publication were made possible by a grant from
Lilly Endowment, Inc.

THE TOLL OF INDEPENDENCE

Engagements & Battle Casualties of the American Revolution

Edited by
HOWARD H. PECKHAM

THE UNIVERSITY OF CHICAGO PRESS
Chicago   *London*

HOWARD H. PECKHAM is director of the William L. Clements Library and professor of history at the University of Michigan. He is the author of many books, including *The War for Independence* and *The Colonial Wars.* [1974]

THE UNIVERSITY OF CHICAGO PRESS, CHICAGO 60637
THE UNIVERSITY OF CHICAGO PRESS, LTD., LONDON

© *1974 by The University of Chicago*
All rights reserved. Published 1974
Printed in the United States of America

International Standard Book Number: 0-226-65318-8
Library of Congress Catalog Card Number: 74-75615

CONTENTS

INTRODUCTION

☆

Certain basic statistics about the American Revolution—frequency of engagements, casualties in battle, deaths in camp, prisoners of war, size of the army at any given time, total number of participants, geographical spread or concentration of its actions—have never been compiled. In consequence the dimensions of that war have always been hazy. The names of a few generals and of a few big battles or campaigns are the chief legacy. Yet it was a long war, full of wearing, small actions, its theater stretching from the St. Lawrence River to the Gulf of Mexico and inland to the Mississippi River, and the fortunes of the combatants rising or falling, though most of the major battles went against the Americans.

For a century and a half the story of the Revolutionary War persisted as a frequent topic of Fourth of July orations, usually delivered in the open under sunny skies. It should be a winter's tale, told around a hearth on blustery nights when there are no distractions, when images rise easily in the flames, and logs crackle like musket shots, and when the comfortable warmth contrasts with that chilled, ill-equipped, determined band of men trying to be an effective army.

This volume offers two kinds of information. It presents the most complete list ever attempted of military and naval engagements involving Americans. Each engagement is briefly described in chronological order. Enough information is provided to identify the location, the date, the opposing units and their commanders, and what happened, so that laymen may understand the actions. Little attempt has been made to determine the size of the opposing forces; when such figures were mentioned, they frequently were wildly unreliable.

We have not hesitated to refer to the Americans at times as rebels, as the word carries no pejorative connotation in our minds. We have tried to indicate whether they were militia or regulars in state regiments or in the Continental Army. We have not used the word *Whig* as a label. Similarly, we have not used *Tory*, but *Loyalist*, to identify British-allied Americans. Otherwise, we have called the enemy British or German, not Hessian. Although the majority of German soldiers were Hessians, the rest were from other German provinces. No attempt has been made to indicate Scottish or Irish regiments.

vii

Opposite each descriptive entry is the classification of American casualties suffered according to killed, wounded, captured, missing, and deserted, indicated by their initial letters. *Missing* is a temporary status. Such soldiers either had been captured, or had run away and returned, or had deserted. Of course, there was not always agreement on those figures, and our procedure in making judgments and evaluations is explained farther on. Those persons wounded who died within a day or two have been removed from that column and added to the column of killed. Enemy casualties are indicated in the text where readily found, but they were not the object of our search; besides, such figures were endlessly complicated by the custom of the British commanders of not reporting German or Loyalist casualties.

In some instances only total figures were reported by American commanders, such as "30 casualties." This is true even of such an important battle as the American defeat on Long Island in August 1776. In such cases we have ventured to break down the total into its probable components from our familiarity with the percentages of killed, wounded, and captured in similar circumstances, or in deference to historians who have studied particular battles in detail. These are guesses, of course, and such figures are enclosed in parentheses to show that they represent the editor's estimate. More exasperating were the reports that simply said "our casualties were light." How many is "light"? In other instances the enemy suffered considerable losses, but none are reported on the American side — a highly unlikely circumstance, yet we felt we could not invent a number. We confess to bafflement in these two types of examples and have left the casualty columns blank. Therefore, our totals each year and for the whole war must be accepted as *verifiable minimums*, not complete accountings.

At the outset some decisions had to be made as to what constituted a military action. A clear implication is that there was resistance. Full-scale battles were obvious, but other operations were less easy to define. Thus Howe's evacuation of Boston and Clinton's departure from Philadelphia were important moves in the war, but they were not engagements. Neither was Montgomery's capture of Montreal without opposition. The seizure of a fort from which the defenders had fled without firing a shot might be a victory, but was it much different from a march? A foraging expedition that met nothing but cries of protest from civilians was not a military action according to our definition. Resistance, in our view, might be slight and ineffectual, but it ought at least to endanger the attackers.

Sieges running for days or weeks were admittedly awkward to fit into our chronology. Casualties usually were reported for the whole period, not on a daily basis. Therefore, unless there were particularly active days of assaults or sorties, we entered long sieges on the date they ended and listed the total casualties for the period. There was no easy alternative. It was also difficult to separate civilian captures from military after a city surrendered, but we tried to limit ourselves to the military personnel. We do not record civilian casualties at any place.

Frontier Indian raids posed a special problem. Indian attacks on exposed cabins of western settlers would have occurred at this time, war or no war. Civilians often retaliated. In that sense these actions bear no relation to the American Revolution. However, Indian raids led by British officers or agents, or clearly inspired by them, or raids by tribes allied with the British, or attacks by Indians on American militia are counted as incidents of war and listed here. Similarly, attacks by other Indians under American officers are also counted. Civilians, especially women and children, who fell before enemy Indians are not counted as casualties of war, simply because they were civilians. It proved impossible to separate Indian casualties from white when they jointly participated with American forces.

Negroes, like Indians, participated on both sides of the Revolution. Slaves were promised their freedom if they would serve the British Crown, and naturally some of them did. After the war they were relocated in Florida, the West Indies, or transported to Halifax and thence to Sierra Leone in Africa. Many free Negroes and slaves were enlisted on the American side, and numbers of them were killed, wounded, or captured, and as such they are included in the figures given here, but it is impossible to identify them separately. We can only refer the reader to Benjamin Quarles's carefully researched study, *The Negro in the American Revolution* (Chapel Hill: University of North Carolina Press, 1961). He offers an estimate of about 5,000 Negroes who served the American cause, but he cannot even guess the number of Negro casualties.

We have listed battles on North American land between Spanish and British, and French and British, although we do not count the losses of our allies with American casualties. Some West Indian islands changed hands or were attacked, but such hostilities bore little relation to the American Revolution beyond the fact that our allies exploited opportunities to advance self-interest.

Our military chronology includes actions in which British naval ships fired on shore installations, towns, houses, or American troops on land. Such ship firing almost always elicited American replies, feeble though they might have been. American attacks on enemy watering parties or other landing parties were also considered to be land actions. The reader may be as surprised as we were at the number of times British warships fired on American troops and towns in the early years of the war. They reveal how busy the British navy kept itself. Although these were indecisive, minor clashes, they do emphasize the dangers faced by American residents along coastal waters, harbors, and islands, and by troops moving within sight of enemy ships.

British ships are identified by name, preceded by the initials HMS for His Majesty's Ship, but no attempt was made to identify the type of ship. The captain's name follows immediately where known. The initials USS are used before the names of American ships. Actions on inland lakes or bays, where fought by soldiers turned seamen, are still listed with land engagements rather than with naval conflicts. Thus, the gallant action of Arnold's quickly built, pathetic fleet that delayed Carleton on Lake Champlain in 1776 is found among military battles. Landings of United States crews to attack forts, as in the Bahama Islands, are also considered land actions.

A separate section has been provided for genuine naval battles, and types of naval engagements included are explained at the beginning of that list.

We should point out also that the status of some local actions as war measures seemed questionable. In the intense hostility between rebels and Loyalists, as in New Jersey or South Carolina, for instance, a few persons on one side might seize an opponent in his house and jail him or contrive to kill him. Such actions border on kidnapping or premeditated murder rather than a military engagement. We have used discretion in listing such dubious incidents.

In editing the battle reports we have become aware of two geographical areas in relation to which information is fragmentary, vague, or conflicting. One is the frontier on the west, north (Maine–New Brunswick), and south (Georgia–East Florida). The other is comprised of the Carolinas and Georgia; it became the main theater of war after mid-1780 and was the seat of much irregular and guerrilla warfare. It is easier to understand the failure of historians to concentrate on the frontier than the neglect of proud Southerners to exploit in accurate detail the Revolutionary War in their own states.

Battle deaths do not account for all loss of life attributable to the war. There were also those who died in camp, either of wounds or of disease. A second statistical study is being prepared at the Clements Library — *The Sinews for Independence: Monthly Reports of the Continental Army*, edited by Charles H. Lesser — to be published later as a companion volume to this one. From it we have culled the few figures that are available on the nonbattle-related mortality of soldiers in service. They are far from complete, but the estimate they suggest is explained in the final section, "Summations and Implications."

Another category of loss is deaths among prisoners of war. These were not counted, of course, among battle casualties or among deaths in camp. In fact, they were never counted. All we have are estimates, as explained in "Summations and Implications."

Interest in the casualty figures and actions of the Revolution goes back to such members of the war generation as Thomas Jefferson. The future president sent to the Italian scientist Giovanni Mattia Fabroni a fantastic estimate of British losses up to November 1777 that showed 8,894 killed, 11,023 wounded, and 10,046 captured, and then guessed that American losses were half those amounts.[1] Contemporary newspaper readers could have perused the figures Jefferson quoted in *The Maryland Journal* for February 10, 1778.[2]

A British periodical of this time, apparently in criticism of government policy, projected similar figures on British losses during the first three years of the war. It estimated that 8,848 men had been killed, 9,785 wounded, 10,161 captured, and 1,100 deserted, for a grand total of 29,494 British casualties. The figures, of course, are wildly exaggerated, made up of such losses as 900 killed in seizing Fort Washington, 800 killed at Brandywine, and 2,100 of Burgoyne's army killed. They cannot be taken seriously. *The American and British Chronicle of War and Politics* (London, 1783) listed the main actions of the Revolution, but rarely mentioned casualties.

Even more unbelievable are the figures of Dr. James Thacher, a

1. Jefferson to Fabroni, June 8, 1778, Sol Feinstone Collection, Military History Research Collection, Carlisle Barracks, Pa. The original letter was reported as missing in *The Papers of Thomas Jefferson* (Princeton: Princeton University Press, 1950), 2: 195–98, where a draft and transcript were used.

2. There are some small errors in the various transcriptions of the figures from *The Maryland Journal.*

surgeon in the Continental Army, who estimated total American deaths in the war at 70,000![3]

Since Thacher's time amateur historians and others have continued to evince interest in casualty figures and lists of engagements. Henry B. Dawson included the Revolution in his two-volume *Battles of the United States* (New York: Johnson, Fry, and Co., [1858]), although he recounted only the major campaigns. Incidental to compiling a roster of Revolutionary War officers in 1893, Francis Heitman added a list of battles arranged alphabetically and then chronologically. This appendix to the *Historical Register of Officers of the Continental Army* (1893; 2d ed. Washington: Rare Book Shop Publishing Co., 1914) listed 335 military engagements. (Our total is 1,331.) Small clashes were omitted, along with all naval actions, and there are numerous errors. No casualty figures or descriptions of battles were provided. Nevertheless, it has been a useful work for identifying officers, although we have uncovered errors there, too. A slightly revised version of Heitman's list of battles was reprinted in the *Army Almanac* (Washington: Government Printing Office, 1950), and the list has been utilized elsewhere, since it was the best available. The more important actions have also been included in Stetson Conn's *An Army Chronology of the American Revolution*, OCMH Monograph no. 160 (Washington: Office of the Chief of Military History, 1971).

For decades the Department of Defense has given out the figures 4,435 killed and 6,188 wounded in the Revolution, and these have been cited in *The World Almanac* repeatedly. The source for that total is the records of the Adjutant General's Office as prepared at the Armed Forces Information School with the warning that the "total number undoubtedly is much larger." The killed figure was made up of 4,044 from the army and 391 from the navy and marines. The wounded total was composed of 6,004 from the army and 184 from the navy and marines. Our totals (see "Summations and Implications") are much higher. The late antiquarian Clarence S. Peterson, for his mimeographed "Known Military Dead during the Revolutionary War, 1775–1783" (Baltimore, 1959), managed to list *by name* approximately 9,500 soldiers and sailors who were killed or who died sometime during the war years. Some of the deaths occurred after a soldier returned to civilian life, so not all the deaths reported in Peterson are attributable to

---

3. James Thacher, *A Military Journal during the American Revolutionary War. . . .* (Boston: Richardson and Lord, 1823), p. 426.

the war. *The Dictionary of American History* (New York: Charles Scribner's Sons, 1940) 1: 322, quotes from the Adjutant General's Office: "4044 killed and 6004 wounded, considerably below the real numbers." Using enlistment figures and total population, the contributor also estimated that a maximum of 250,000 men bore arms in the Revolution. In our opinion, this total is too large, but as yet it is only an opinion.

A word should be said about our investigative procedures. Each of the original thirteen states has made an effort, with varying success, to collect and preserve its records of the Revolutionary War. Such records may be in the form of archives in public depositories, private manuscripts in historical societies, publications by the state or by a historical society, or carefully researched monographs on battles or regiments, or biographies. With a grant from Lilly Endowment, Inc., we were enabled to orchestrate a vast search of eastern state archives and libraries and the National Archives. To each state we assigned a graduate student in history recommended by a university there, and we asked the student to confine his or her investigation to engagements and attendant casualties in that state. Since Maine was part of Massachusetts until 1820, and the pertinent records for Maine have been printed in full, no assignment was made in Maine. However, a researcher was active in Vermont, and two more worked in the Office of Naval History, Washington, recording naval engagements. Another worked in the National Archives. Preprinted 4-by-6 card forms were supplied each investigator, and a card was filled out on every engagement from every source. Consequently several cards were prepared on most of the battles.

The result was receipt at the Clements Library of more than 4,250 cards. Here four more researchers were at work on this volume and another to follow. They examined certain microfilm sources and various secondary general works we considered reliable, making additional cards amounting to over 1,000. A bibliography is found at the end of this volume.

Casualty figures usually differed in different sources. It was the editor's responsibility to reconcile the differences, make further research, and determine which figures were most accurate, using the recognized rules of historical evidence: Was the reporter in a position to know what happened? Did he see or have knowledge of the whole battle or only part of it? Did he report promptly? Was he likely to minimize or exaggerate losses? And so on. It was clear at once that no reliance could be placed on British reports of American casualties, or vice versa, except that the British were likely to be accurate on the number of American prisoners they had taken. Sometimes, in the absence of an official letter, we accepted reports in a newspaper, allowing for its Loyalist or rebel bias. Again we felt that at least the number of American prisoners reported in a Loyalist paper was likely to be correct because the editor probably obtained his figure from the British officers involved in the engagement. To reconcile disparate figures, recourse was occasionally had to secondary studies by reliable historians. Where the only reference to an engagement was found in a later, secondary account, we have cited it in a footnote to warn the reader.

It was not possible to cite the source we finally used for each engagement without overloading the book with footnotes. Our sources remain on file in the Clements Library. Fortunately for our main purpose of counting casualties, the most obscure actions were the small ones that were least likely to have cost any lives. However, local historians may dispute a date or an exact location with us, or even add a forgotten encounter or casualty. Corrections and additions are welcome. At least now we have a list that aims at completeness and accuracy. Heretofore there was no publication to which such information might be appended. Heitman's list was so selective as to render additions pointless.

We start our list of engagements and casualties with the familiar encounter on Lexington Green the morning of April 19, 1775. We are not unaware that efforts have been made to persuade the United States Congress to recognize the battle of Point Pleasant on the Ohio River, October 10, 1774, as the first battle of the Revolution. This engagement was part of a punitive expedition against Ohio Indians by some militia units under the command of Governor Dunmore of Virginia. No one would be more astonished then Lord Dunmore to find himself regarded by anyone as having started a revolt against British authority. Of all the colonial governors, he was, a few months later, the most vigorous in trying to subdue the American rebels.

As for the last engagement of the war, Kentucky, Ohio, and South Carolina have put forward claims to it. Actually, it appears to have occurred in, of all places, what is now modern Arkansas. We say "appears" because again some definition must be agreed upon. Does one mean the last action on land or at sea? Must American rebels be involved, or can it be an engagement between one of our allies and

Britain? We leave the reader to draw his own conclusion after examining the several 1783 engagements on land and water.

After all the work was done, there remained incomplete and vague reports on half a dozen possible engagements. If they could be roughly located, they could not be dated, and what happened was not always clear. Perhaps they refer to actions already listed. In all of them only four or five men were killed or wounded. We hope we may be forgiven for reluctantly omitting them, as we did not know where to place them in our listing or precisely how to interpret the scanty evidence.

In grateful acknowledgement of services rendered, we thank the following holders of Lilly Endowment fellowships in 1972 and 1973: Martha Blauvelt working in New Jersey, Harriet Bloomberg in Vermont, David K. Bowden in South Carolina, James E. Brady in New York, Joseph J. Casino in Pennsylvania, John J. Fowler, Jr., in Rhode Island, James M. Grant in Georgia, William C. Heimdahl in Washington, D. C., Ivan J. Kaufman in New Hampshire, Ross M. Kimmel in Maryland, John D. McBride in Virginia, Catherine M. Rottier in Washington, D. C., Randall Schrock in North Carolina, Donna Spindel in Connecticut, Deborah Waters in Delaware, J. Todd White in Washington, D. C., and George Wise in Massachusetts.

Researchers who worked with devotion on this volume at the Clements Library were Jo Ann Staebler, who also typed the columnar forms with precision, made the elaborate index, and kept tabs on the bibliography; and David Whitesell, a student volunteer who searched our newspapers for naval engagements. Professors John Shy and James Vann of the Department of History have been especially helpful as advisers to the project in terms of treatment of the data and general policy. Above all I am indebted to Charles H. Lesser, who with an invaluable sense of organization prepared instructions for the fellowship holders, visited them on location, kept track of their incoming reports, and showed great insight into the constant problems that plagued this compilation.

MILITARY ENGAGEMENTS
AND CASUALTIES

DATE	ENGAGEMENT	AMERICAN LOSSES				
		K	W	C	M	D
Apr. 19	LEXINGTON, MASS. After a musket was discharged by someone not identified, British troops under Maj. John Pitcairn fired on the 70 Minute Men under Capt. John Parker. Some of those moving off the Green returned the fire and wounded 1 British soldier.	8	10	4[1]		
	CONCORD, MASS. Militia under Maj. John Buttrick fought British regulars under Capt. Lawrence Parsons. British losses were 3 K and 8 or 10 W.	2	2			
	CONCORD TO CHARLESTOWN, MASS. Retreating British regulars were under fire by militia under Gen. William Heath, especially at Menotomy. The British lost 70 K, 182 W, and 22 C.	(39)[2]	(27)[2]		5	
Apr. 20	HANOVER, MASS. British party fired on Col. Theophilus Cotten's Mass. militia.	1	1			
May 10	FORT TICONDEROGA, N.Y. Fort was captured by troops under Cols. Ethan Allen and Benedict Arnold. 48 British prisoners were taken.					
	FALMOUTH (PORTLAND), ME. Militia under Col. Thompson seized Capt. Mowat of HMS Canceau ashore but failed to capture his ship.					
May 11	CROWN POINT, N.Y. Fort was captured by troops under Lt. Seth Warner; 13 British prisoners were taken.					
May 16	LAKE CHAMPLAIN, N.Y. Some Va. militia who joined N.Y. and Conn. militia at Lake Champlain seized Maj. Skene's ship.					
May 17	FORT ST. JOHN'S, QUE. Col. Benedict Arnold with 36 troops rowed from Ticonderoga to St. John's, captured the garrison of 22 and a sloop, and returned.					
May 18	FORT ST. JOHN'S, QUE. Col. Ethan Allen took a detachment to the empty fort, but retreated when a British force appeared.			3		
May 21	GRAPE ISLAND, MASS. Mass. militia under Gen. Joseph Warren drove off a British foraging party.					
May 27	HOG AND NODDLE'S ISLANDS, MASS. British marines attacked militia under Gen. Israel Putnam who were driving off cattle. The British had 2 K and 2 W.			4		
May 31	PETTICK'S ISLAND, MASS. Foraging party under Col. Lemuel Robinson was attacked by British.					
June 2	DEER ISLAND, MASS. Foraging party under Maj. John Greaton drove sheep and cattle from island in Boston harbor and took several British prisoners.					

1. Paul Revere and 3 others were captured before engagement at Lexington.

2. Figures arrived at by deduction of Lexington and Concord losses from reported day's total of 49 K and 39 W and 5 M.

DATE	ENGAGEMENT	AMERICAN LOSSES				
		K	W	C	M	D
June 2	PISCATAQUA RIVER, PORTSMOUTH, N.H. Shots were exchanged between Americans on shore and British in guard boats of HMS Canceau and Scarborough. British had 3 W.					
Before June 6	NEW CASTLE, N.H. Shots were exchanged between Americans on shore and a British ship.		3			
June 8	BOSTON AREA, MASS. Shots were exchanged between Americans on shore and HMS Glasgow, Lt. Howe.					
Before June 11	BOSTON AREA, MASS. British schooner was grounded and burned after being fired on by Americans on shore. British suffered 2 K and several W.					
June 17	BUNKER HILL, MASS. Connecticut troops were bombarded at daybreak while building breastworks.	1				
	BUNKER HILL, MASS. Mass., N.H., and Conn. troops under Col. William Prescott were attacked three times by British under Gen. William Howe and finally driven from the hill. British lost 226 K and 828 W.	140	271	30[1]		
June 18	MARBLEHEAD HARBOR, MASS. Shots were exchanged between Americans on shore and HMS Merlin, Capt. Burnaby.					
June 21	BOSTON, MASS. Two Indians killed 4 British soldiers in raid on outposts.					
June 23	CHARLESTOWN, MASS. Three Indians killed 3 British sentinels.					
June 24	ROXBURY, MASS. British bombarded American camp.	2				
	BOSTON NECK, MASS. Skirmish occurred at the Brown house.	2				
June 26	BOSTON NECK, MASS. British attacked American sentries.					
July	LYME, CONN. Shots were exchanged between Americans on shore and HMS Kingsfisher, Capt. Graeme.					
July 8	BOSTON NECK, MASS. Mass. volunteers under Maj. Benjamin Tupper and Capt. John Crane attacked British guardhouse at Brown's house and burned it.					
July 10	WEYMOUTH, MASS. Men from 6th Conn. regiment seized 40 whale boats and 19 prisoners.					
	OFF CHELSEA, MASS. Americans who went to burn hay on an island were fired on by British marines.	1	1			
	BRANFORD HARBOR, CONN. Seven men in boat from HMS Kingsfisher, Capt. Graeme, were seized on shore.					
July 11	LONG ISLAND, MASS. Americans under Col. John Greaton in 47	1	1			

1. Casualty figures vary from 60 or 70 K and 100 W, to 165 K and 304 W. Washington, who wasn't there, reported to his brother in July 138 K, 276 W, and 36 M.

DATE	ENGAGEMENT	AMERICAN LOSSES				
		K	W	C	M	D
July 11	LONG ISLAND, MASS. (cont.) whale boats took 15 civilian prisoners and burned hay intended for the British.					
c. July 12	COCKSPUR ISLAND, GA. HMS Phillippa, Capt. Maitland, was boarded while unloading and all its gunpowder seized.					
July 12	ROXBURY, MASS. Conn. troops were fired on from British lines.	1				
c. July 15	MAJOR-BIGUYDUCE (CASTINE), ME. Inhabitants captured 5 sloops sent by Gen. Gage for wood.					
July 16	MACHIAS, ME. HMS Diligent and Tatamogouche were seized by inhabitants.					
July 18	ROXBURY, MASS. Exchange of cannon fire occurred between British and American lines.	2				
July 20	NANTASKET, MASS. American party under Maj. Joseph Vose burned lighthouse and took 5 prisoners.		2			
	LONG ISLAND, MASS. Americans under Col. Christopher Greene on a foraging expedition were fired on.	1				
July 29	CHARLESTOWN NECK, MASS. York County, Pa., riflemen under Capt. Michael Doudel attacked a British sentry post, killed 5 and captured 2.			1		
July 30	NANTASKET, MASS. Several companies under Maj. Benjamin Tupper burned buildings, killed 7, wounded 5, captured 40.	1	2			
July 31	CHARLESTOWN NECK, MASS. Americans attacked British guard post; 3 or more British killed.	1				
Aug. 1	CAMBRIDGE, MASS. Skirmish took place "without much damage done on either side."					
Aug. 2	BUNKER HILL, MASS. Another skirmish, in which some British were killed, 3 taken prisoner.	2				
Aug. 3 or 4	ROXBURY, MASS. Attack made by Americans on lighthouse; 45 casualties to the British.	1				
Aug. 6	CHARLESTOWN NECK, MASS. While burning several buildings, Americans were fired on from British ships.					
	PENNY FERRY, MYSTIC RIVER, MASS. Artillery shots were exchanged between a Capt. Lyndly's company and the British.					
c. Aug. 6	MACHIAS, ME. Seventeen British seamen taken prisoner; 30 more captured at Cape Ann, Mass.					
Aug. 8	GLOUCESTER HARBOR, MASS. Americans under Maj. Coffin recaptured two schooners from boats of HMS Falcon, Capt. J.	2	1			

DATE	ENGAGEMENT	K	W	C	M	D
Aug. 8	GLOUCESTER HARBOR, MASS. (cont.) Linzee. <u>Falcon</u> guns bombarded Gloucester, and Linzee sent a party ashore to burn the town. Party was repulsed with 3 K, 1 W, 35 C.					
Aug. 11	PLUM ISLAND, MASS. Americans in 3 boats made unsuccessful attempt to prevent British from stealing cattle.					
Aug. 13	CHELSEA, MASS. Two British barges and 2 boats exchanged fire with soldiers under Lt. Col. Loammi Baldwin. Several British were wounded.					
Aug. 15	CHARLESTOWN RIVER, MASS. HMS <u>Fowey</u>, Capt. G. Montagu, exchanged shots with Americans on shore.					
Aug. 17	ROXBURY, MASS. British fired on Col. Joseph Spencer's 2nd Conn. regiment.		1			
Aug. 19	ROXBURY, MASS. British fired on the same regiment again.					
Aug. 22	LAKE CHAMPLAIN, QUE. American Capt. Remember Baker made an unauthorized raid northward with 6 men in a boat, met another boat containing 6 Caughnawaga Indians and killed 2.	1				
Aug. 24	NEW YORK, N.Y. HMS <u>Asia</u>, Capt. Vandeput, fired on Americans who were moving cannon from Battery. 1 British sailor killed.		3			
Aug. 27	PLOUGHED HILL, MASS. British on Bunker Hill cannonaded American works on Ploughed Hill occupied by troops under Gen. John Sullivan.	3	2			
Aug. 28	ROXBURY, MASS. Col. Joseph Spencer's 2nd Conn. regiment fired on British.					
	CHARLESTOWN RIVER, MASS. HMS <u>Fowey</u>, Capt. G. Montagu, fired on Americans and their boats.					
	WINTER HILL, MASS. British ships fired on N.H. troops in fortifications.	3				
Aug. 30	STONINGTON HARBOR, CONN. HMS <u>Rose</u>, Capt. Wallace, chased American boats that were moving cattle and fired on town. British suffered some casualties.	1	1			
Aug. 31	ROXBURY, MASS. British cannonaded the American camp.	2				
Sep.	ST. MARY'S RIVER, FLA. Jermyn Wright's fort was attacked by 20 Ga. militia under Capt. John Baker.					2
Sep. 1	ROXBURY, MASS. British fired on American lines.	2				
Sep. 3	ROXBURY, MASS. Americans attacked British line and killed or captured 15.					

6

DATE	ENGAGEMENT	AMERICAN LOSSES				
		K	W	C	M	D
c. Sep. 3	NEW YORK, N.Y. Americans captured and burned a sloop with 12 Tories on board.					
Before Sep. 4	ST. JOHN, N.B. Sloop from Machias, Me., burned fort and barracks and captured British brig.					
Sep. 4	NEAR ST. JOHN'S, QUE. American scouting party under Capt. Noble Benedict came upon Mohawks in a boat, and killed 2 to 6.					
Sep. 6	NEAR ST. JOHN'S, QUE. American troops under Gen. Richard Montgomery were routed by 60 to 100 Indians under Capt. Tice, N.Y. Loyalist. Enemy had 5 K and 5 W.	8	9			
Sep. 10	NEAR FORT CHAMBLY, QUE. Gen. Richard Montgomery led 800 troops northward who were attacked from boats and breastworks. They killed 2 enemy and sank a boat with 35 aboard.					
Sep. 15	CHARLESTON HARBOR, S.C. Militia under Col. Isaac Motte captured Fort Johnson and its garrison.					
Sep. 16	BOSTON NECK, MASS. Exchange of fire took place between British and Americans.	(2)	(5)			
	MARTHA'S VINEYARD, MASS. Tender from HMS Swan, Capt. Ayscough, fired on the inhabitants.					
Sep. 17	BOSTON NECK, MASS. Further exchange of fire occurred between two lines.					
	TARPAULIN COVE, ELIZABETH ISLANDS, MASS. HMS Swan, Capt. Ayscough, seized whaling brig in Cove and was fired on from shore.					
Sep. 18	CHARLESTOWN RIVER, MASS. HMS Fowey, Capt. G. Montagu, fired on Americans, and those on Winter Hill replied.					
	FORT ST. JOHN'S, QUE. American Gen. Richard Montgomery laid siege to fort and sent out Maj. John Brown who engaged the enemy, killing 8 Indians.		2			
Sep. 22	FORT ST. JOHN'S, QUE. British garrison fired on American camp.	1				
Sep. 23	ROXBURY, MASS. British fired on American camp.					
Sep. 25	MONTREAL, QUE. Col. Ethan Allen was leading 110 Canadians and Conn. troops when attacked by 500 regulars and militia sent out by Gen. Guy Carleton. Enemy lost 3 K and 2 W. Allen was captured and most of his Canadians deserted.		7	46		(55)
Sep. 26	GOVERNOR'S ISLAND, BOSTON HARBOR, MASS. Americans under Lt. Benjamin Tupper seized livestock and burnt buildings.					
Sep. 27	FORT ST. JOHN'S, QUE. Brisk exchange of fire between Americans and fort.	1	1			

7

DATE	ENGAGEMENT	AMERICAN LOSSES				
		K	W	C	M	D
Sep. 28	TARPAULIN COVE, ELIZABETH ISLANDS, MASS. HMS Viper, Lt. Graves, was fired on by inhabitants ashore.					
	OFF CUMMINGS POINT, S.C. HMS Tamar, Capt. Thornbrough, fired on armed Americans in 3 canoes.					
Before Sep. 29	MARBLEHEAD, MASS. Local residents boarded and captured British merchantman and carried her to Salem.					
Oct. 2	PORTSMOUTH HARBOR, N.H. HMS Prince George, Capt. Emms, blundered into harbor and was captured.					
Oct. 3	FORT CHAMBLY, QUE. Skirmish occurred between French Canadians on either side.	(5)				
Oct. 4	FORT ST. JOHN'S, QUE. Two British vessels and fort cannon fired on Col. Bedel's party of Americans and Canadians.		1			
Oct. 6	BOSTON NECK, MASS. Exchange of fire left one British soldier killed.	1				
Oct. 7	BRISTOL, R.I. Four British ships under Capt. Wallace fired on the town for 2 hours.	2				
Oct. 9	JAMESTOWN, R.I. HMS Glasgow, Capt. Howe, fired on the town.					
Oct. 10	BEVERLY, MASS. HMS Nautilus, Capt. Collins, fired on citizens and militia under Col. Henry Herrick, and received fire from Hannah, U.S. privateer. British had 2 W.		1			
Oct. 11	FORT ST. JOHN'S, QUE. British fired on the American besiegers.	1				
Oct. 16	PLOUGHED HILL, MASS. British fired on Americans on the hill.					
Oct. 17	CHARLES RIVER, MASS. Two American gondolas fired on British on Boston Common. One cannon burst.	2	6			
	FORT CHAMBLY, QUE. 50 Americans under Maj. John Brown and 300 Canadians under Capt. Henry B. Livingston forced surrender of fort, taking 82 prisoners under Maj. Stopford.					
Oct. 18	ROXBURY, MASS. Gen. Putnam's American troops were firing on Boston when a cannon burst.	2	4			
	FALMOUTH (PORTLAND), ME. Crews of 4 British ships under Capt. Mowat went ashore and burned 2/3 of town. Inhabitants fled.					
Before Oct. 20	FORT ST. JOHN'S, QUE. While American troops under Col. Seth Warner met an enemy party from Montreal, taking 5 and killing some, Gen. Montgomery sank a schooner.	1				

8

DATE	ENGAGEMENT	AMERICAN LOSSES				
		K	W	C	M	D
Oct. 15 -21	NORFOLK, VA. Royal Governor Dunmore led 5 raids from his ships on Oct. 15, 17, 19, 20, 21 and seized arms.			7		
Oct. 25	FORT ST. JOHN'S, QUE. Garrison fired on the American besiegers.	1				
Oct. 26	HAMPTON, VA. HMS Otter, Capt. Squire, fired on town, but landing party was repulsed by militia under Col. William Woodford. British lost 2 K and 2 W.					
Oct. 30	LONGUEIL, QUE. American Col. Seth Warner repulsed a large force of Canadians and Indians. Enemy suffered heavy casualties.					
Nov. 1	JAMESTOWN, VA. Two British tenders fired on town from the river.					
	CONANICUT ISLAND, R.I. Boats from HMS Bolton exchanged shots with Americans on shore.					
Nov. 2	CONANICUT ISLAND, R.I. Boats from HMS Bolton, Glasgow, and Rose exchanged shots with inhabitants.					
	PLOUGHED HILL, MASS. Cannon on floating batteries in Mystic River fired on American positions.					
	LONGUEIL, QUE. Col. Seth Warner's troops repulsed British attempt to land. Latter lost several killed, 4 captured.					
	FORT ST. JOHN'S, QUE. Garrison commanded by Maj. Charles Preston surrendered to Gen. Richard Montgomery. British had lost under 25 K during siege.					
Nov. 3	NINETY-SIX DISTRICT, S.C. Loyalists captured a wagon of ammunition intended for Cherokees which was guarded by S.C. Rangers.			(22)		
Nov. 8	NEAR SOREL, QUE. British ships fired on Major John Brown's troops on shore.					
	NEWPORT, R.I. British ships fired on the town.					
Nov. 9	LECHMERE POINT, MASS. Large British raiding party was repulsed by 2 regiments under Cols. William Thompson and Benjamin Woodbridge.	1	2			
	PHIPP'S FARM, MASS. British force under Lt. Col. George Clerk went ashore from boats and removed livestock under fire.	(6)				
	BURWELL'S FERRY, VA. Boat from HMS Kingsfisher, Capt. J. Montagu, fired on by rifle guard.					
	CHARLESTOWN, MASS. Large British foraging party was driven off by American riflemen; maybe 5 enemy killed.		1	3		

DATE	ENGAGEMENT	AMERICAN LOSSES				
		K	W	C	M	D
Nov. 9	WOLF'S COVE, QUE. HMS Hunter, Capt. Mackenzie, exchanged fire with Americans on shore.					
Nov. 13	(MONTREAL, QUE. Town surrendered to Gen. Richard Montgomery.)					
Nov. 14	JAMESTOWN, VA. Two sentinels from Capt. John Green's company repulsed British boat attempting to land, wounded one man.					
	KEMP'S LANDING, VA. Enemy force under Royal Governor Dunmore defeated 150 militia under Cols. Joseph Hutchings and Anthony Lawson.	9		14		
Nov. 16	JAMES RIVER, VA. HMS Kingsfisher, Capt. J. Montagu, exchanged fire with Americans on shore, and continued next 3 days.					
Nov. 17	CHARLOTTETOWN, PRINCE EDWARD ISLAND. Two American privateers raided town, captured 2 officials.					
Nov. 18	QUEBEC, QUE. Gen. Benedict Arnold's besieging force was fired on.	1				
Nov. 18 -22	NINETY-SIX, S.C. Militia under Maj. Andrew Williamson was besieged by larger force of Loyalists under Gen. Patrick Cunningham. Enemy lost 52 K and W.	1	11			
Nov. 22 -29	GREAT BRIDGE, VA. British garrison in fort resisted attacks by Americans under Lt. Col. Charles Scott.	2	1			
c. Nov. 29	NEAR NORFOLK, VA. American militia under Col. William Woodford captured some of Gov. Dunmore's troops.					
Dec. 4	GREAT BRIDGE, VA. American militia under Col. Edward Stevens attacked Negro guards, killed 2 and captured 2.					
Dec. 9	GREAT BRIDGE, VA. Militia under Col. William Woodford engaged Loyalists and British sailors, killed 13 and captured 17, all wounded.		1			
Dec. 10	CONANICUT ISLAND, R.I. Capt. Wallace of HMS Rose led landing party of 200, burned houses, skirmished with militia, carried off livestock.	2	7	2		
	QUEBEC, QUE. HMS Hunter fired again on Gen. Arnold's troops.					
Dec. 13	QUEBEC, QUE. HMS Hunter fired again on Gen. Arnold's troops.					
	PRUDENCE ISLAND, R.I. British troops driven off after fight with local militia and loss of 14 K and 1 C.					

DATE	ENGAGEMENT	AMERICAN LOSSES				
		K	W	C	M	D
Dec. 14	NORFOLK, VA. American troops under Col. William Woodford took possession of the town.					
	QUEBEC, QUE. Gen. Benedict Arnold's troops were fired on.	2	5			
Dec. 16	BRENTON'S POINT, R.I. HMS Rose, Capt. Wallace, sent marines ashore for hay, but they were driven off by local militia.					
	QUEBEC, QUE. Gen. Benedict Arnold's troops were fired on.	1				
Dec. 17	LECHMERE POINT, MASS. HMS Scarborough, Capt. Barkley, fired on the Americans.		2			
Dec. 19	SULLIVAN'S ISLAND, S.C. American rangers under Lt. William Withers raided island, burned buildings, captured 8, killed 3 or 4.					
	LECHMERE POINT, MASS. Americans sustained cannonade from Boston and Bunker Hill.		1			
Dec. 22	GREAT CANE BRAKE, ANDERSON CO., S.C. Rangers and militia under Lt. Col. William Thompson defeated Loyalists under Capt. Patrick Cunningham, killing 5 and capturing 130.		1			
Dec. 23	ELIZABETH RIVER, NORFOLK, VA. Shots were exchanged between HMS Otter, Capt. Squire, and militia on shore.					
Dec. 29	ELIZABETH RIVER, NORFOLK, VA. Shots were exchanged between boat from HMS Otter and militia on shore. Repeated 2 days later.					
Dec. 31	QUEBEC, QUE. Assault made on town by troops under Gens. Richard Montgomery and Benedict Arnold at night. Montgomery was killed; Arnold was wounded and reported 73 K and W, all but 210 C. British loss was 7 K and 11 W.	51	36	387		
	TOTALS for the year 1775:	323	436	519	5	57

11

DATE	ENGAGEMENT	AMERICAN LOSSES				
		K	W	C	M	D
Jan. 1 -2	NORFOLK, VA. Three British ships fired on town, then a landing party set fire to it, at Gov. Dunmore's direction. British had 6 K, several wounded. Two or 3 women killed in Norfolk.	1	5			
Jan. 2	FORT ISLAND, NEWPORT, R.I. Americans burned buildings before being driven off by guns from HMS Bolton, Lt. Graves.					
	CONANICUT ISLAND, R.I. Later that day HMS Bolton exchanged fire with Americans on shore.					
Jan. 5	SULLIVAN'S ISLAND, S.C. HMS Cherokee, Capt. Fergusson, exchanged shots with American battery.					
Jan. 8	CHARLESTOWN, MASS. Americans under Maj. Thomas Knowlton burned several houses, killed one enemy, captured 5.					
Jan. 9	WARWICK NECK, R.I. HMS Bolton, Lt. Graves, exchanged shots with Americans on shore.					
c. Jan. 10	NEAR HAMPTON, VA. American guard at a lighthouse drove off British in boats.					
	NEAR HAMPTON, VA. British tender landed a party that suffered 6 K and 1 C from American defenders.					
Jan. 12	SAVANNAH HARBOR, GA. Nine American volunteers burned 3 British ships and damaged 6.					
	PRUDENCE ISLAND, R.I. Fifty militia under Capt. Job Pearce retreated before 250 British marines landed from ships under Capt. Wallace. Three enemy wounded.	2	2			
Before Jan. 13	NORFOLK, VA. British fired on town to cover a landing in which they had several wounded.	3				
Jan. 13	NARRAGANSETT BAY, MASS. Landing party from HMS Swan, Capt. Ayscough, was engaged by Americans. Enemy lost 3 K and 1 C.					
Jan. 20	ANDREW SPROWLE'S PLANTATION, VA. British landing party was beaten off by Col. William Woodford's militia, with one enemy killed.					
Jan. 21	ELIZABETH RIVER, VA. Landing party from HMS Otter and Liverpool burned buildings before being forced off by Col. William Woodford's militia. Three enemy killed.	3	1			
Jan. 22	NORFOLK, VA. Americans, firing on British transporting tobacco, were dispersed by guns of HMS Liverpool, Capt. Bellew.					
Jan. 27	CAPE FEAR, N.C. HMS Scorpion, Capt. Tollemache, exchanged fire with Americans in Fort Johnston. HMS Cruizer, Capt. Parry, did the same and repeated next day.					
Jan. 30	BOSTON HARBOR, MASS. Americans on Thompson's Island					

DATE	ENGAGEMENT	AMERICAN LOSSES				
		K	W	C	M	D
Jan. 30	BOSTON HARBOR, MASS. (cont.) fired on HMS Halifax, Capt. Quarme, till ship's cannon drove them off.					
Jan. 31	NORTH RIVER, MASS. HMS Hope, Capt. Dawson, tried to burn USS Hancock, Capt. Manley, aground, but was driven off by Mass. militia.					
Early Feb.	GUILFORD COUNTY, N.C. Militia under Capt. William Dent tried to stop Loyalists heading for Cross Creek (Fayetteville).	1				
Feb. 3	ELIZABETH RIVER, VA. Four Americans on shore exchanged shots with men in a boat from a British tender.					
Feb. 7	POINT COMFORT, VA. Shots exchanged between Americans on shore and HMS Kingsfisher, Capt. J. Montagu.					
	NORFOLK, VA. Md. militia under Capts. James Kent and William Henry drove HMS Otter, Capt. Squire, and two tenders away from American schooners.					
Feb. 13	DORCHESTER NECK, MASS. British detachment under Lt. Col. Alexander Leslie destroyed buildings before being repulsed.			6		
Feb. 14	DORCHESTER NECK, MASS. British surprised an American guard post.			2		
Feb. 18	NEWPORT, R.I. Shots exchanged between Americans on shore and HMS Rose, Capt. Wallace, when latter captured an American brig.					
Feb. 20	BRUNSWICK COUNTY, GA. Party of Americans under Capt. Dupre routed 50 men from HMS Cruizer, Capt. Parry, who were pillaging John Ancrum's plantation.					
Feb. 25 -26	CONANICUT ISLAND, R.I. American militia drove off British marines from HMS Rose, Capt. Wallace, with 30 enemy casualties.					
Feb. 27	MOORE'S CREEK BRIDGE, CAPE FEAR RIVER, N.C. Nearly 1200 Loyalists under Col. Donald McLeod were routed by 1000 militia under Col. Richard Caswell. Loyalists lost 30 K and W, 850 C.	1	1			
Early Mar.	FORT BARRINGTON, GA. Lt. Col. Thomas Browne and East Fla. Rangers seized American garrison on Altamaha River.			23		
Mar. 1	COCKSPUR ISLAND, GA. Action between local militia and British sailors wounded 4 of latter.		1			

13

DATE	ENGAGEMENT	AMERICAN LOSSES				
		K	W	C	M	D
Mar. 2 -4	NEAR CAMBRIDGE, MASS. Americans on Cobble Hill, Lamb's Dam, Lechmere Point, and Roxbury kept up fire on Boston while Americans occupied and fortified Dorchester Heights.	6	5			
Mar. 3	NEW PROVIDENCE, BAHAMAS. 270 American marines under Capt. Samuel Nicholas took Fort Montague. Next day they seized Fort Nassau without resistance.					
	SAVANNAH HARBOR, GA. Troops under Col. Lachlan McIntosh bombarded 300 British under Maj. James Grant when the British landed on Hutchinson's Island. British had at least 6 casualties. Actions on Skidaway and Cockspur islands ended the day.	2	3			
Mar. 4	DORCHESTER HEIGHTS, MASS. Occupied and fortified by 3000 Americans under Gen. John Thomas, but under fire.	2				
Mar. 7	MARTHA'S VINEYARD, MASS. Militia under Capt. Richard Wallen recaptured American ship Francis, wounded British captain.					
Mar. 9	NOOK'S HILL, DORCHESTER, MASS. American troops fortifying hill were bombarded by British in Boston.	4				
Mar.	CAPE FEAR RIVER, BRUNSWICK, N.C. HMS Scorpion, Capt. Tollemache, fired on Americans and sent boat to reduce breastworks.					
Mar. 13	QUEBEC, QUE. Party from HMS Hunter, Capt. Mackenzie, attacked Americans near Cape Diamond.	3				
Mar. 15	PLYMOUTH HARBOR, MASS. HMS Niger, Capt. Talbot, exchanged shots with Americans at lighthouse in Sawquish Cove.					
Mar. 16	NOOK'S HILL, DORCHESTER, MASS. British cannonaded American fortifications.		1			
Mar. 20	BOSTON HARBOR, MASS. Following evacuation of Boston Mar. 17, British sent watering party to Thompson's Island which was fired on.					
Mar. 25	COCKSPUR ISLAND, GA. Watering and woodcutting party from HMS Cherokee, Capt. Fergusson, attacked by Ga. militia and Creeks, who killed 3 and captured 13.					
	TYBEE ISLAND, GA. Ga. troops and Creeks under Col. Archibald Bullock burned Loyalists' houses and fought British marines, killing 3 and capturing several.					
	BELOW QUEBEC, QUE. Maj. Lewis DuBois led 100 from N.Y. regiment to attack Canadian force. He inflicted several casualties, captured 30, routed rest.					
c. Mar. 27	ST. PIERRE PARISH, QUE. Canadian force under Couillard was attacked by Americans, suffered 3 K, 11 W, and about 36 C.					

DATE	ENGAGEMENT	AMERICAN LOSSES				
		K	W	C	M	D
Mar. 28	LEWES, DEL. Troops under Col. John Haslet attacked boat's crew from HMS Roebuck, Capt. Hamond, and killed 2, captured 4.					
End of Mar.	SAVANNAH HARBOR, GA. Americans boarded captured Georgia Packet and tried to retake it.	(2)	(5)	4		
Apr. 3	BEDLOE'S ISLAND, N.Y. HMS Asia, Capt. Vandeput, fired on Americans who were burning buildings.					
Apr. 5	NORFOLK ROAD, VA. HMS Otter, Capt. Squire, fired on Americans who were firing on a canoe from Portsmouth.					
	NEWPORT, R.I. Americans on shore fired on HMS Rose, Capt. Wallace, and Swan, Capt. Ayscough.					
Apr. 7	NEAR CAPE HENLOPEN, DEL. After boats from HMS Roebuck, Capt. Hamond, chased schooner Farmer ashore, Capt. Charles Pope's Del. troops prevented the capture and drove off the boats.					
	STATEN ISLAND, N.Y. Capt. Hugh Stephenson with 3 companies drove off watering party from HMS Savage and James, killing 3, capturing 10.					
	CAPE FEAR RIVER, N.C. Shots were exchanged between HMS St. Lawrence, Lt. Graves, and Americans on shore. Firing was repeated on Apr. 9.					
Apr. 11	NEWPORT, R.I. American battery fired on HMS Scarborough, Capt. Barkley, and captured a brig and sloop.		1			
Apr. 12	BRINTON'S POINT, R.I. Americans fired on HMS Scarborough, Capt. Barkley, at anchor.					
	NANTASKET ROAD, BOSTON, MASS. HMS Orpheus, Capt. Hudson, exchanged fire with Americans on shore. Firing continued next 2 days.					
	CAPE FEAR RIVER, N.C. HMS Scorpion, Capt. Tollemache, exchanged fire with Americans on shore. Firing continued next 2 days.					
	COCKSPUR ISLAND, GA. Americans who attacked British on island were cut off by HMS Cherokee, Capt. Fergusson, and Raven, Capt. Stanhope. Action concluded next day.	1	2	15		
Apr. 13	CONANICUT ISLAND, R.I. Americans fired on HMS Scarborough, Capt. Barkley.					
Apr. 14	STATEN ISLAND, N.Y. American riflemen exchanged fire with HMS Asia, Capt. Vandeput, in the Narrows.					

DATE	ENGAGEMENT	AMERICAN LOSSES				
		K	W	C	M	D
Apr. 14	BRENTON'S POINT, R.I. Americans exchanged shots with HMS Scarborough, Capt. Barkley.					
Apr. 16	SWAN POINT, CHESAPEAKE BAY. Capt. Robert Harris and Md. militia captured British boat's crew who had come ashore to destroy boat being built.					
	CAPE FEAR RIVER, N.C. HMS Scorpion, Capt. Tollemache, fired on Americans on shore. Firing repeated next 2 days.					
Apr. 18	SANDY POINT, MD. Americans prevented capture of a grounded U.S. vessel by the crew of 2 British tenders, and killed 3.	1				
Apr. 19	NORFOLK, VA. HMS Otter, Capt. Squire, fired on Americans on shore, and repeated it 3 days later.					
Apr. 21	CAPE FEAR RIVER, N.C. HMS Scorpion, Capt. Tollemache, fired on Americans on shore, and repeated it next day.					
Apr. 22	CAPE FEAR RIVER, N.C. HMS St. Lawrence, Lt. Graves, exchanged shots with Americans on shore; repeated next day.					
Apr. 23	SANDY HOOK, N.J. Americans captured 35 of a watering party from HMS Asia, Capt. Vandeput.					
	HOBBS HOLE (TAPPAHANNOCK), VA. Militia retook a vessel from a British ship.	1				
Apr. 24	SANDY HOOK, N.J. Another British watering party fled into lighthouse and was captured by Americans.					
Apr. 25	ST. CATHERINE ISLAND, GA. HMS Hinchinbrook, Lt. Ellis, was fired on by Americans on shore.					
Apr. 26	CAPE FEAR RIVER, N.C. HMS Scorpion, Capt. Tollemache, fired on Americans on shore, and repeated it next day.					
May 1	FORT JOHNSTON, WILMINGTON, N.C. Shots were exchanged between Americans and HMS Cruizer, Capt. Parry. Firing repeated 2 days later.					
May 2	CAPE FEAR RIVER, N.C. HMS St. Lawrence, Lt. Graves, fired on Americans on shore.					
May 3	QUEBEC, QUE. American battery opened up on British in town.					
May 4	QUEBEC, QUE. Americans sent ship to burn Lower Town, while Gen. Wooster made ready to attack; but fireship failed.					
May 5	QUEBEC, QUE. HMS Hunter, Capt. Mackenzie, dispersed some Americans on shore and captured their guns.					
	WILMINGTON, DEL. HMS Roebuck, Capt. Hamond, was attacked in Delaware River by row galleys and launches but beat					

DATE	ENGAGEMENT	AMERICAN LOSSES				
		K	W	C	M	D
May 5	WILMINGTON, DEL. (cont.) them off.					
May 6	TINDALL'S ISLAND, N.J. British foraging party was attacked by militia.					
	QUEBEC, QUE. Gen. Guy Carleton with help from navy ships led attack on Gen. John Thomas' besieging troops and forced them to retreat upriver.	1		100		
May 7	ABOVE QUEBEC, QUE. HMS Martin, Capt. Harvey, and HMS Surprize, Capt. R. Linzee, fired on retreating Americans and on 3 U.S. ships.					
c. May 10	BRUNSWICK, N.C. British attacked Americans and lost 1 K.			(5)		
May 11	PORT NEUF, QUE. Americans fired on barge from HMS Surprize, Capt. R. Linzee, which answered attack next day.					
May 12	POINT PLATOR, QUE. HMS Martin, Capt. Harvey, fired on Americans on shore.					
	WILMINGTON, N.C. British force under Gens. Clinton and Cornwallis landed at Robert Howe's plantation and marched to surprise Maj. William Davis, who escaped. British lost 2 K, 1 C, and several wounded.					
May 13	SANDY HOOK, N.J. HMS Phoenix, Capt. Parker, fired on American troops who were attempting to seize watering boat from HMS Asia.					
May 16	CAPE FEAR RIVER, N.C. HMS Falcon, Capt. J. Linzee, and St. Lawrence, Lt. Graves, exchanged shots with Americans on shore.					
May 19	THE CEDARS, QUE. 600 British-allied Canadians and Indians under Capt. George Forster attacked about 400 troops under Col. Timothy Bedel. British lost 1 K, 2 W.	2	1	390		
May 20	QUINZE CHENES, QUE. 100 American reinforcements under Maj. Henry Sherburne were taken on their way to The Cedars.	(5)		95		
May 24	CAPE FEAR RIVER, N.C. HMS St. Lawrence, Lt. Graves, fired on Americans on shore, and repeated 3 days later.					
	LA CHINE, QUE. British pressed Gen. Benedict Arnold's retreating troops.			2		
May 27	GWYNN'S ISLAND, CHESAPEAKE BAY. Three British ships seized island and began building a fort, which drew American fire.					
May 29	LA CHINE, QUE. British-allied Indians fired on 3 American boats.					

DATE	ENGAGEMENT	AMERICAN LOSSES				
		K	W	C	M	D
Late May	ST. MARY'S RIVER, FLA. Loyalist William Chapman's plantation was raided by Americans.					
June 8	MANASQUAM, N.J. After British captured an American sloop, militia fired on British boarders and forced them from the sloop.					
	THREE RIVERS, QUE. About 2000 troops under Gen. William Thompson were attacked by British, who lost 12 or 13 K and W.	50		236		
	OFF POINT BATTI, QUE. HMS Martin, Capt. Harvey, fired on American troops on shore.					
June 10	DOVER, DEL. Loyalist light horse under Capt. Richard Bassett plotted revenge, but word got out and Bassett was captured in bed.					
June 11	HAMPTON, VA. Shots exchanged between HMS Otter, Capt. Squire, and Americans on shore.					
June 13	NANTASKET, MASS. Militia under Cols. Marshall, Whitcomb, and Whiting engaged in artillery duel with British ships.					
June 14	BOSTON HARBOR, MASS. Americans on harbor islands exchanged shots with HMS Renown, Capt. Banks, and Hope, Cdr. Dawson.					
c. June 20	LEWES, DEL. Loyalists under Thomas Robinson cut off garrison at Lewes until Col. Samuel Miles with 3000 militia dispersed them.					
c. June 21	NANTASKET, MASS. HMS Queen of England, Capt. Arnout, was fired on from the fort and captured.					
June 21	SANDY HOOK, N.J. Lt. Col. Benjamin Tupper's troops fired on British in the lighthouse.					
	SULLIVAN'S ISLAND, S.C. Fire exchanged between Americans on island and HMS Lady William.					
June 24	ISLE AUX NOIX, QUE. British and Americans engaged during American retreat from Canada.			8		
June 25	SULLIVAN'S ISLAND, S.C. American battery on island fired on British ships in creek. British regiment landed and returned fire.					
June 26	CHEROKEE TOWN, S.C. Carolina and Georgia rebel volunteers under Capt. James McCall attacked Cherokees.	4		2		
June 28	SULLIVAN'S ISLAND, S.C. British ships under Sir Peter Parker and 3000 troops under Sir Henry Clinton attacked Fort Moultrie under command of Col. William Moultrie and Gen. Charles Lee.	10	22			

MILITARY ENGAGEMENTS AND CASUALTIES

DATE	ENGAGEMENT	AMERICAN LOSSES				
		K	W	C	M	D
June 28	SULLIVAN'S ISLAND, S.C. (cont.) British lost 64 K, 141 W, 5 D, and withdrew.					
July	CAPE FEAR, N.C. British officer reported one of his sentinels wounded by rebels.					
	ST. JOHN RIVER, N.B. HMS Rainbow, Capt. Collier, drove off American force raiding settlements.					
Early July	ISLE AUX NOIX, QUE. Retreating American troops were attacked by British-allied Indians.	4		5		
July 2	FORT TONYN, ST. MARY'S RIVER, FLA. Col. John McIntosh led raid on Loyalist post, killed 1, captured 9. Fort was burned.					
	STATEN ISLAND, N.Y. Four British ships cannonaded American troops on shore.					
July 3	LONG ISLAND, N.Y. British detachment attempted to land but was ambushed by Americans, who killed several, captured 4.					
	STATEN ISLAND, N.Y. Three British ships fired on Americans and made a landing.		1	30		
July 4	ELIZABETHTOWN, N.J. British armed sloop attacked by American cannon.					
	THE NARROWS, N.Y. HARBOR. Shots exchanged between HMS Asia, Capt. Vandeput, and Americans on shore.					
	NEW YORK, N.Y. American sentinel at Upper Barracks Guard wounded by someone in the city.		1			
July 5	NEW YORK, N.Y. Another Barracks sentinel was shot.		1			
July 6	MACHIAS HARBOR, ME. HMS Viper, Capt. Graves, seized 5 American fishing boats despite rebel firing from shore.					
July 9	GWYNN'S ISLAND, CHESAPEAKE BAY. Gen. Andrew Lewis led attack on British, seized unfinished fort, burned several ships, forced other British ships to move down the bay. Enemy lost 2 K, 3 W.	1				
July 11	ST. MARY'S RIVER, FLA. Americans on shore fired on Loyalists in cutter from HMS St. John, Lt. Grant, killed 1, wounded 1, captured 5.					
July 12	NEAR JUNCTURE OF BROAD AND SAVANNAH RIVERS, GA. Col. Elijah Clarke led Ga. militia in attack on Cherokees, killing 4.	3	4			

DATE	ENGAGEMENT	AMERICAN LOSSES				
		K	W	C	M	D
July 12	HUDSON RIVER, N.Y. Extensive exchange of fire made between American batteries and HMS Phoenix, Capt. Parker, and Rose, Capt. Wallace.	6	3			
July 13	ELIZABETHTOWN, N.J. American fire from shore prevented British ship from capturing American boat. British had 2 W.					
July 13 or 14	CHESAPEAKE BAY. Americans surprised a Loyalist boat, killed 5.					
July 15	LYNDLEY'S FORT, LAURENS CO., S.C. American fort was attacked by 190 whites and Indians, who lost 2 K, 13 C.					
July 16	ST. GEORGE'S ISLAND, POTOMAC RIVER, MD. Gov. Dunmore's ships and troops were repulsed by Md. militia under Capts. Rezin Beall and John Barnes.		1			
	HAVERSTRAW, N.Y. Americans fired on a British tender and she fell down river after her sailors plundered a house.					
July 18	HAVERSTRAW, N.Y. Shots were exchanged between HMS Rose, Capt. Wallace, and Americans on shore.					
July 19	NEW YORK, N.Y. American batteries firing on enemy suffered an accident.	4				
July 20	LONG ISLAND FLATS, TENN. Va. militia under Col. William Russell battled Cherokees, killed 13 and wounded Chief Dragging Canoe.		4			
July 21	SPENCER'S INLET, S.C. HMS Glasgow Packet, Capt. Campbell, caught on a bar, was set afire by Americans.					
	CEDAR POINT, CHESAPEAKE BAY. HMS Roebuck, Capt. Hamond, fired on a Md. house.					
	BERGEN POINT, N.J. Americans fired on a British landing party, killed 3.					
	FORT CASWELL, WATAUGA, TENN. Cherokees under Old Abram unsuccessfully attacked American fort commanded by Capt. James Robertson.	2	3	1		
July 22	PAULUS HOOK, N.J. HMS Halifax, Lt. Quarme, exchanged fire with Americans on shore.					
	BIG SHOALS, OCONEE RIVER, GA. 20 Virginians under Capt. Thomas Dooley on way to join a Continental brigade were attacked by Cherokees.	4				
July 23	STATEN ISLAND, N.Y. Americans tried to capture 2 British sentries.	1				
	BRENT'S HOUSE, POTOMAC RIVER, VA. British ships under Capt. Hamond sent a landing party to Brent's house, where Capt.	3				

DATE	ENGAGEMENT	AMERICAN LOSSES				
		K	W	C	M	D
July 23	BRENT'S HOUSE, POTOMAC RIVER, VA. (cont.) James' militia were sleeping after a drinking bout. 2 British were wounded.					
	ST. GEORGE'S ISLAND, POTOMAC RIVER, MD. Md. militia beat off British attempt to land and burned 8 ships.					
July 24	BLACK'S FORT, VA. Militia ambushed some hostile Indians, killed 11, and Indians retaliated.	1	3			
	ELIZABETHTOWN, N.J. Lone American rifleman crossed river and attacked enemy post.	1				
July 25	HAVERSTRAW, N.Y. HMS Phoenix, Capt. Parker, exchanged fire with Americans on shore.					
	NEAR FISHKILL, N.Y. Five boats of British exchanged fire with Americans on shore.	1	2			
	ST. GEORGE'S ISLAND, POTOMAC RIVER, MD. HMS Fowey, Capt. G. Montagu, fired on Americans on shore. Maj. Thomas Price led Md. militia in attack on British watering party, killed about 10.					
c. July 25	BEAVERDAM CREEK, GA. American troops under Capt. John Pulliam skirmished with Cherokees.	1	1			
July 27	ST. GEORGE'S ISLAND, POTOMAC RIVER, MD. Maj. Thomas Price's Md. militia fired on HMS Roebuck, Capt. Hamond, and Fowey, Capt. G. Montagu.					
	SINGSING, N.Y. HMS Phoenix, Capt. Parker, fired on Americans on shore.					
Late July	HOLLAND STRAITS, MD. Maj. Daniel Fallen sent party to capture Loyalist schooner, took 4 men.					
Aug. 1	ESSENECCA, PICKENS CO., S.C. Col. Andrew Williamson led militia against Cherokee town, was ambushed but drove off Indians and burned town.	3	14			
	TAPPAN MEADOWS, N.Y. Fifteen Americans in a fishing hut fired on 5 boats trying to land, wounding some British.					
Aug. 3	OFF TARRYTOWN, N.Y. HMS Phoenix and Rose were attacked by several row gallies.	2	12			
Aug. 8	OCONORE, OCONEE CO., S.C. Col. Andrew Williamson continued offensive against Cherokees and killed several.					
Aug. 11	TOMASSEE, OCONEE CO., S.C. Col. Andrew Williamson attacked and burned another Cherokee town, killed 16 Indians.	6	17			

DATE	ENGAGEMENT	AMERICAN LOSSES				
		K	W	C	M	D
c. Aug. 15	ROANOKE INLET, N.C. Capt. Dennis Dauge's company drove off a foraging party from a British ship.					
Aug. 16	HUDSON RIVER, N.Y. HMS Phoenix and Rose were boarded by American seamen who tried to burn them.				1	
Aug. 18	HUDSON RIVER, N.Y. Americans fired on several British ships and were cannonaded.	1	2			
Aug. 22	FLATBUSH, LONG ISLAND, N.Y. Minor skirmish occurred between some of Gen. John Sullivan's troops and the British.		2			
Aug. 24	MARBLEHEAD, MASS. HMS Milford, Capt. Burr, chased American ship into harbor and was fired on from fort.					
Aug. 25	LONG ISLAND, N.Y. Another skirmish between Americans and British occurred.					
	BRACE'S COVE, MASS. HMS Milford, Capt. Burr, chased Diana into a cove. Diana's crew landed and fired on Milford, which towed Diana away.					
Aug. 26	LONG ISLAND, N.Y. Skirmish took place between Gen. Stirling's American troops and possibly Hessians, several of whom were killed.	2	3			
	LONG ISLAND SOUND, NEAR KILLING, N.Y. HMS Niger, Capt. Talbot, sent barge after American sloop, but it ran ashore and fired on the barge.					
Aug. 27	NEW CITY ISLAND, N.Y. Col. Morris Graham's two companies routed cattle stealers from 3 British ships.			1		
	LONG ISLAND, N.Y. About 17,000 British and Germans overran positions of 7000 Americans under Gens. Putnam and Washington. Total British casualties: 932. Total American casualties: 1097, 67 of those captured being wounded.	(200)		(897)		
Aug. 28	JAMAICA, LONG ISLAND, N.Y. Militia Gen. Nathaniel Woodhull, left with a few troops, was captured by British unit under Gen. Sir William Erskine and died of wounds.	1				
	THROGG'S POINT, N.Y. HMS Halifax, Lt. Quarme, fired on house on shore.					
Aug. 30	LONG ISLAND, N.Y. Gen. Thomas Mifflin's rear guard was attacked as he left the island.		4			
Late summer	ST. MARY'S RIVER, FLA. Americans overran plantation of Loyalist Benjamin Dodd, burned buildings, captured 6 men.					

MILITARY ENGAGEMENTS AND CASUALTIES

DATE	ENGAGEMENT	AMERICAN LOSSES				
		K	W	C	M	D
Sep.	WESTERN N.C. American Col. Andrew Williamson's continuing campaign against the Cherokees reported an ambush and other attacks. Indians lost at least 35.	15	21			
Sep. 3	BLACKWELL'S ISLAND, N.Y. British seized island despite American fire; HMS Rose, Capt. Wallace, also under fire.					
Sep. 4 -5	HUNT'S POINT, N.Y. Americans exchanged fire with HMS Halifax, Lt. Quarme, until the Americans were driven off.		1			
Sep. 5	YORK ISLAND, N.Y. HMS Rose, Capt. Wallace, exchanged fire with the Americans.					
c. Sep. 5	RAHWAY, N.J. Capt. Benjamin Cory's company skirmished with the British, took 1 prisoner.	2				
Sep. 6	GOVERNOR'S ISLAND, N.Y. Seven American boats beaten back from landing by British sailors and Germans.					
	FORT GEORGE, N.C. Col. Thomas Polk's N.C. detachment attacked British fort but was repulsed.	1	1			
Sep. 7	MT. INDEPENDENCE, VT. Skirmish with enemy near breastworks built by Americans; 3 K and 6 W of enemy.					
	SETAUKET, LONG ISLAND, N.Y. Americans in 60 whale boats and schooner Spy, Capt. Niles, landed and killed 13 Loyalists, captured 40.	1				
Sep. 10	MONTRESOR'S (RANDALL'S) ISLAND, N.Y. British landed and suffered 2 wounded before 20 American occupants escaped.					
Sep. 12	HORN'S HOOK, N.Y. In cannonade British attackers lost 1 K and 3 or 4 W.					
Sep. 13	EAST RIVER, N.Y. Four British warships and cannon on Governor's Island shelled Americans on lower Manhattan, who returned fire.	3				
Sep. 14	EAST RIVER, N.Y. American batteries fired again on 4 British ships.					
Sep. 15	KIP'S BAY, EAST RIVER, N.Y. After an hour's bombardment of Conn. militia, British landed 13,000 men in two waves. Militia fired a few rounds before fleeing.	(50)		(320)		
Sep. 16	HARLEM HEIGHTS, N.Y. Washington attacked British and drove them a mile south, inflicting 14 K and 154 W, which figures may not have included German casualties.	(20)	(40)			
	PAULUS HOOK, N.J. Regiments under Cols. Durkee and Duyckinck exchanged fire with British ships.					
Sep. 17	AMBOY, N.J. Americans fired on HMS Tamar's boats which had taken 4 prisoners.			4		

DATE	ENGAGEMENT	AMERICAN LOSSES				
		K	W	C	M	D
Sep. 18	PAULUS HOOK, N.J. HMS Phoenix, Capt. Parker, and Rose, Capt. Wallace, exchanged fire with batteries on Hudson River.					
	HARLEM HEIGHTS, N.Y. Scouting party of 200 met a superior British force and inflicted a few casualties.		(5)			
Sep. 20	PAULUS HOOK, N.J. Col. Durkee's regiment exchanged fire again with HMS Renown, Capt. Banks.					
	ISLE LA MOTTE, LAKE CHAMPLAIN. Gen. Benedict Arnold's protective ship Liberty attacked by British, Indians, and Canadians. British reported on American casualties.		7			
Sep. 23	MONTRESOR'S (RANDALL'S) ISLAND, N.Y. Lt. Col. Michael Jackson led 240 Americans in surprise attack on island, but when lead boat was fired on others turned back.	(2)	(4)	(28)		
Oct. 3	HARLEM HEIGHTS, N.Y. Party of Rangers sent out to drive away British reconnoitering party.					
Oct. 9	FORT LEE, N.J. Fort guns fired on HMS Phoenix, Capt. Parker, and Roebuck, Capt. Hamond, and 2 other ships, inflicting 27 casualties.					
	NEAR DOBBS FERRY, N.Y. Two American gallies ran aground under fire and crews escaped.					
Oct. 11	MOUTH OF HOCKHOCKING RIVER AT OHIO RIVER, O. Party of 7 militia was surprised by Indians.	2	3			
Oct. 11 -13	LAKE CHAMPLAIN, N.Y. Building his own fleet, manned by 820 men, Gen. Benedict Arnold battled Gen. Guy Carleton's naval invasion off Valcour Island and stopped it, but lost over half of his ships in running fight and second battle. British loss was about 40.	(20)	(60)			
Oct. 12	THROGG'S NECK, N.Y. Col. Edward Hand and 25 Pa. riflemen prevented Howe's troops from landing.					
Oct. 14	STATEN ISLAND, N.Y. Gen. Nathanael Greene took 600 men to raid small fort on island; killed 5 of enemy, took some prisoners.	2	4			
Oct. 18	PELL'S POINT, N.Y. After British landed, Col. John Glover's brigade of 750 tried to stop them moving toward Eastchester, killed at least 4, wounded at least 20.	8	13			
Oct. 19	HUNT'S POINT, N.Y. Americans tried to take a passing boat but were repulsed by guns of HMS Niger, Capt. Talbot.					
Oct. 21	MAMARONECK, N.Y. Col. John Haslet led 600 Va. and Del. troops against Col. Robert Rogers' Rangers and skirmished with	2	8			

DATE	ENGAGEMENT	AMERICAN LOSSES				
		K	W	C	M	D
Oct. 21	MAMARONECK, N.Y. (cont.) pickets, killing several, capturing 36.					
Oct. 23	NEAR WHITE PLAINS, N.Y. Minor skirmish of Conn. troops with British took place.	1				
Oct. 25	NEAR DOBBS FERRY, N.Y. American battery exchanged fire with HMS Tartar, Capt. Ommanney.					
Oct. 27	WHITE PLAINS, N.Y. British advanced on Gen. Alexander McDougall's brigade, which was reinforced by Col. John Haslet's Del. regiment.	15	15			
	FORT LEE, N.J. Two British frigates were driven away from Forts Lee and Washington by cannon fire.					
Oct. 28	FORT LEE, N.J. British ship bombarded the fort while land forces attacked it and lost several men.	1				
	WHITE PLAINS, N.Y. Gen. Howe led 8000 British and nearly 5000 Germans under Gen. Knyphausen against an equal number of regulars and militia under Gen. Washington. Although victorious after losing 214 British killed and 99 Germans killed and wounded, Howe withdrew to N.Y.C.	(25)	(125)			
Late Oct.	WESTERN N.C. American Capt. Moore reported to Gen. Griffith Rutherford he had killed 2 Cherokees in their deserted town.					
Nov. 1	NEAR LIBERTY POLE, N.J. British cannonaded the Americans.					
c. Nov. 3	LONG ISLAND, N.Y. Three to four hundred R.I. militia crossed sound and engaged British troops under Smith, killed 5 or 6, captured 24.	1	1			
Nov. 4	WHITE PLAINS, N.Y. American scouting party was in a skirmish with British.					
Nov. 5	OFF FLETCHER'S ISLAND. HMS Milford and George exchanged fire with Americans on shore.					
	HUDSON RIVER, N.Y. HMS Pearl, Capt. Williamson, exchanged fire with Americans on both shores and suffered several casualties. Same action repeated on Nov. 8.					
Nov. 7	NEAR FORT LEE, N.J. American boats filled with flour chased ashore, but they prevented British pursuers from landing.					
	CUMBERLAND CREEK, N.C.? American soldiers in boats captured a British schooner and sloop.					
Nov. 9	FORT LEE, N.J. Skirmish between Americans and Germans left 14 enemy killed and as many hurt.					

DATE	ENGAGEMENT	AMERICAN LOSSES				
		K	W	C	M	D
Nov. 12	FORT CUMBERLAND, N.B. Col. Jonathan Eddy led 80 militia in an attack on the fort.		1			
	SANDY HOOK, N.J. HMS Perseus, Capt. Elphinstone, exchanged fire with Americans on shore.					
Nov. 13	HUNTINGTON BAY, LONG ISLAND, N.Y. HMS Senegal, Capt. Curtis, exchanged shots with Americans on shore after running a privateer ashore and burning it.					
Nov. 16	FORT WASHINGTON, N.Y. Garrison under Col. Robert Magaw surrendered to Gen. William Howe's superior forces. British losses were 67 K, 335 W, 6 M.	54	100	2858		
Nov. 20	FORT LEE, N.J. When the British under Gen. Cornwallis crossed the Hudson, Gen. Nathanael Greene evacuated the fort, but lost as prisoners what he called skulkers in the neighborhood.	(8)		(100)		
Nov. 29	LONG ISLAND SOUND, N.Y. Landing party from HMS Halifax, Lt. Quarme, was fired on from shore.					
Nov. 30	FORT CUMBERLAND, N.B. British sallied out and counter-attacked Col. Jonathan Eddy's force.	1				
Dec. 1	BRUNSWICK, N.J. Gen. William Stirling's brigade was cannonaded by the enemy.	2	2			
Dec. 6	LONG ISLAND SOUND, N.Y. HMS Halifax, Lt. Quarme, exchanged fire with Americans on shore.					
Dec. 7	NAUSHON ISLAND, MASS. Seamen from HMS Diamond and Ambuscade plundered the island and burned houses, despite American fire. British lost 1 K and 1 W.	4	(6)			
Dec. 8	NEWPORT, R.I. A British landing under Gen. Henry Clinton drove off Gen. William West's militia detachment.					
	NEAR TRENTON, N.J. Gen. William Stirling's brigade in skirmish with Gen. Cornwallis' advance troops inflicted several casualties.					
Dec. 9	NEAR NEW BRIDGE, N.J. A raid by Col. William Malcolm's militia on Loyalist troops captured 2.					
Dec. 10	BAY OF FUNDY, N.B. Jolly boat of HMS Diligent, Lt. Farnham, was surprised by a party of rebels, who seized its ammunition.					
Dec. 11	BURLINGTON, N.J. Pa. galleys in Delaware River under Cdr. Thomas Seymour shelled town on seeing German troops enter it.					
Dec. 13	BASKING RIDGE, N.J. British Lt. Col. William Harcourt with 30 horsemen raided Gen. Charles Lee's headquarters, captured him and 4 others.	2	2	5		

DATE	ENGAGEMENT	AMERICAN LOSSES				
		K	W	C	M	D
Dec. 13	SANDY HOOK, N.J. Marines from HMS Syren, Capt. Furneaux, boarded schooner that had run ashore.			27		
Dec. 15	HACKENSACK, N.J. Gens. William Heath and George Clinton raided Loyalist storehouses, captured 8.					
Dec. 17	SPRINGFIELD, N.J. Skirmish occurred between Americans and enemy troops.		1			
Dec. 17 -18	VESSEL'S (McKONKEY'S) FERRY, N.J. German dragoons skirmished with American troops.					
Dec. 19	NEAR TRENTON, N.J. American detachment captured 3 Germans.					
Dec. 20	FOUR MILES ABOVE TRENTON, N.J. Lt. Friedrich von Grothausen led party of 25 Germans in attack on Americans who crossed river.		1			
	NORTHEAST OF TRENTON, N.J. In another skirmish 1 German was killed.					
	ENGLISH NEIGHBORHOOD, N.J. Gens. George Clinton and Samuel Parsons led 500 troops against Lt. Col. Abraham Van Buskirk's Loyalist regiment, captured 23.					
	LONG ISLAND SOUND, N.Y. HMS Halifax, Lt. Quarme, exchanged fire with Americans on shore.					
Dec. 21	NEAR TRENTON, N.J. Lt. Abraham Kirkpatrick's Va. troops fought with Germans, killed 1, captured 1.					
Dec. 22	MOUNT HOLLY, N.J. Americans were driven out of town by British and Germans.					
	RANCOCAS BRIDGE, N.J. American force attacked pickets guarding bridge, wounding 3.					
Dec. 25	LOWER BLUE LICKS, KY. American Col. John Todd and militia seeking powder brought to Ky. were attacked by Mingoes under Chief Capt. Pluggy.	2	2			
	NORTH OF TRENTON, N.J. German patrol chased 30 rebels back to their boats.		(3)			
c. Dec. 25	PORTSMOUTH HARBOR, N.H. Two tenders and HMS George, Capt. Burke, were driven into harbor by storm; their crews of 51 were taken prisoner by American soldiers.					
Dec. 26	TRENTON, N.J. Washington led 2400 across Delaware River Christmas night and surprised German garrison in Trenton, killed Col. Rall and about 22 others, took 918 prisoners, 84 of them wounded.	4	8			
Dec. 28	BEARD'S BLUFF, GA. American Lt. William Bugg took men out of the fort to reconnoitre and was attacked by Indians; fort was	4	1			

DATE	ENGAGEMENT	AMERICAN LOSSES				
		K	W	C	M	D
Dec. 28	BEARD'S BLUFF, GA. (cont.) abandoned.					
Dec. 29	McCLELLAND'S STATION, KY. Capt. Pluggy and his Mingoes attacked settlement, but withdrew after Pluggy was killed.					
	TOTALS for the year 1776:	604	562	5165	1	

DATE	ENGAGEMENT	AMERICAN LOSSES				
		K	W	C	M	D
Jan. 1	WARWICK NECK, R.I. HMS Diamond, Capt. Fielding, ran aground and was fired on by American battery and damaged before it could be refloated.					
Jan. 2	FIVE MILE RUN (ABOVE TRENTON), N.J. Skirmish occurred between Gen. Cornwallis' advance troops and those of Col. Edward Hand. One Hessian was killed.					
	STOCKTON HOLLOW (NEAR TRENTON), N.J. Second skirmish between Col. Hand's troops and Gen. Cornwallis' advance. Enemy lost at least 10 K, 20 W, 25 C.	(6)	(10)			1
	NEAR MONMOUTH COURT HOUSE, N.J. Maj. John Mifflin commanding 120 Pa. troops scrapped with 200 N.J. Loyalists under Lt. Col. John Morris, killed 4 and captured 23.					
Jan. 3	PRINCETON, N.J. Clash between Gen. Washington's army and 1200 British under Lt. Col. Charles Mawhood resulted in British losses of 28 K, 58 W, 129 C or more.	23	(20)	1		
Jan. 4	MAIDENHEAD (LAWRENCEVILLE), N.J. Three British soldiers and numerous wagons were captured by Capt. John Stryker and 20 cavalry.					
Jan. 5	SPANKTOWN (RAHWAY), N.J. Militia of N.J. clashed with a British foraging party, killed 1, wounded 3.					
Jan. 6	ELIZABETHTOWN, N.J. Gen. William Maxwell led N.J. militia in attack on a party of British and Waldeckers, killing and wounding 8 or 10, capturing 40.					
Before Jan. 10	FROG NECK, OFF NEWPORT, R.I. Hessian riflemen came to aid of Capt. William Dansey's company and fought off R.I. militia.	(5)				
Jan. 10	FOGLAND FERRY, EAST SIDE OF R.I. HMS Cerberus, Capt. Symons, was driven from its mooring by attack of R.I. militia. The crew suffered 6 K, several wounded.		1			
c. Jan. 15	CONNECTICUT FARMS, N.J. Three hundred N.J. militia under Col. Oliver Spencer fell on less than 100 Germans, killed 1, captured about 70.					
Jan. 16	NEAR BONHAMTOWN, N.J. Detachment of 350 Americans attacked a superior British force, killed 21, wounded 30 to 40 others.					
Jan. 17	NEW BRUNSWICK, N.J. Detachment of 200 Americans struck at a picket guard and was repulsed.	(3)		(30)		
Jan. 20	NEAR SOMERSET COURT HOUSE (MILLSTONE), N.J. Four hundred N.J. militia under Gen. Philemon Dickinson defeated enemy foraging party of similar size, killed and wounded some, captured 9 plus 40 wagons and 100 horses.	(4)				

DATE	ENGAGEMENT	AMERICAN LOSSES				
		K	W	C	M	D
Jan. 23	NEAR WOODBRIDGE, N.J. Detachment of 300 Americans attacked two British regiments, killed 7, wounded several.			2		
	NEAR MORRISTOWN, N.J. Detachment under Lt. Col. Josiah Parker scrapped with British and inflicted several casualties. Later Col. Charles Scott led 200 Virginians to same area and engaged British and Germans.	8				
Jan. 24	QUIBBLETOWN (NEW MARKET), N.J. 350 Va. troops under Col. Mordecai Buckner attacked about 600 enemy, inflicted heavy casualties.		4			
Jan. 18 -25	FORT INDEPENDENCE, N.Y. Gen. William Heath besieged the fort near Kingsbridge unsuccessfully during which a couple skirmishes occurred.	2	5			
Jan. 30	NEAR QUIBBLETOWN (NEW MARKET), N.J. Three hundred Va. troops under Lt. Col. Josiah Parker engaged a British foraging party and inflicted several casualties.	7				
Jan. -Feb.	ASH SWAMP (PLAINFIELD), N.J. Militia under Capt. McCoy was involved in skirmish with the enemy.	2	1			
Feb. 1	NEAR BRUNSWICK, N.J. Six to seven hundred Virginians under Col. Charles Scott attacked a foraging party under Lt. Col. Sir William Erskine.	9	15			
Feb. 8	QUIBBLETOWN (NEW MARKET), N.J. American detachment attacked a British foraging party. (Possibly the same skirmish as Jan. 30 above.)	12		6		
	HUDSON RIVER, N.Y. HMS Dependence, Lt. Clark, fired on 5 American boats which fled to Jersey shore and were burned.					
Feb. 9	HUDSON RIVER, N.Y. HMS Dependence, Lt. Clark, drove off a boatload of Americans who were pursuing a watering party from HMS George.					
Feb. 12	SANDY HOOK, N.J. British troops under Maj. Gordon attacked an American force.	(10)		70		
Feb. 15	NEAR BRUNSWICK, N.J. American scouting party engaged British and inflicted 7 or 8 casualties.					
Feb. 16	NARRAGANSETT BEACH, R.I. Capt. Clay's ship was driven on the beach by 2 British frigates, but people on shore fired and drove them off.					
Feb. 18	FORT McINTOSH, GA. Capt. Richard Winn and garrison of 75 was attacked by Lt. Col. Lewis Fuser's large British force; the fort was taken and burned.	4	3	68		

DATE	ENGAGEMENT	AMERICAN LOSSES				
		K	W	C	M	D
Feb. 20	NEAR QUIBBLETOWN (NEW MARKET), N.J. A skirmish resulted in 2 British killed.					
Feb. 22	NEWPORT, R.I. American galley Spitfire, covering a foraging party, engaged a British shore battery.	2				
	PAULUS HOOK, N.J. HMS Dependence, Lt. Clark, tied up to avoid ice, but when Americans tried to cut lines firing ensued.					
Feb. 23	PEEKSKILL, N.Y. Four British transports escorted by 3 warships landed to destroy American magazine. It was set fire by Americans before they retreated; 2 British were killed.					
	NEAR SPANKTOWN (RAHWAY), N.J. Troops under Gen. William Maxwell attacked a large British foraging party and inflicted over 100 casualties.	5	9			
Mar.	MIDDLESEX, CONN. A British boat crew landed and captured militia guard.			15		
	BELOW TICONDEROGA, N.Y. Party of American Rangers was surrounded by Indians under Capt. McCoye.	4				
Mar. 5	NEAR BRUNSWICK, N.J. Americans drove in a German picket guard.					
	HARRODSBURGH, KY. Forty-seven Shawnees under Chief Blackfish attacked an American surveying party and settlement.	2	4	1		
Mar. 6	ELIZABETHTOWN, N.J. N.J. Loyalist detachment under Maj. Robert Timpany attacked an American party.	2		4		
Mar. 8	PUNKHILL, AMBOY, N.J. A large British force under Gen. William Howe was attacked by Americans under Gen. William Maxwell.		3			
	SANDY HOOK, N.J. American party was beaten off in attack on British-held lighthouse.					
	FISHER'S ISLAND, LONG ISLAND SOUND, N.Y. Three Americans collecting corn were chased off by the enemy.					
Mar. 9	SAMPTOWN, N.J. Maj. Butler led an American detachment against a British picket guard and killed 4.					
Mar.12	CRANBURY, N.J. A party of Middlesex militia drove off an enemy plundering party.					
Mar.14	JERSEY SHORE. Maj. Robert Timpany led 40 Bergen County Loyalists in a skirmish with Americans.					
Mar.16	SPANKTOWN (RAHWAY), N.J. Gen. John Vaughan led British			15		

31

DATE	ENGAGEMENT	AMERICAN LOSSES				
		K	W	C	M	D
Mar. 16	SPANKTOWN (RAHWAY), N.J. (cont.). troops in an attack on Americans.					
	WESTCHESTER COUNTY, N.Y. N.Y. militia under Maj. Brinton Pain and Capt. Samuel Delavin were surprised at Stephen Ward's house by Loyalists under Capts. John Branden and Archibald Campbell. The Loyalists suffered 7 K, 5 W.	6		27		
Mar. 18	BRUNSWICK, N.J. Skirmish between British and Americans occurred.	4		8		
Mar. 20	ENGLISH NEIGHBORHOOD, N.J. Col. Joseph Barton led some Loyalists against a post held by Col. Levi Pawling.			4		
Mar. 21	NEAR NORWALK, CONN. Loyalists from Long Island invaded the area for plunder and a fight.			(8)		
Mar. 22	NEAR WOODBRIDGE, N.J. Maj. Joseph Bloomfield's N.J. regiment was involved in sharp action with a large British force, allegedly inflicting over 150 casualties and suffering "inconsiderable" losses.	(5)	(5)			
Mar. 23	PEEKSKILL, N.Y. Five hundred British landed from 8 flat boats to destroy stores. Gen. Alexander McDougall sent for Col. Marinus Willett at Fort Constitution who with 80 men drove off the enemy, which suffered 15 casualties.	2	5			
Mar. 24	NORTHERN N.J. Lt. Col. Henry Hollingsworth with Md. militia and Maj. Ritney with other troops skirmished with the British, inflicting some casualties.					
Mar. 28	STRAWBERRY HILL, WOODBRIDGE, N.J. Skirmish between British and Americans took place.					
Late Mar.	POWELL'S VALLEY, VA. Va. militia detachment was attacked by Indians in Virginia's westernmost valley.	2	1			
	NEAR TICONDEROGA, N.Y. Indians led by a British officer attacked a party of 32 Americans.	(5)		26		
Apr. 4	QUIBBLETOWN (NEW MARKET), N.J. A skirmish resulted in apparently 5 British killed.		1			
Apr. 6	NEAR WHEELING, W. VA. After Indians killed 10 settlers along the Ohio River and captured 3 children, militia under Lt. Mason pursued and killed one Indian.					
Apr. 10	WASHINGTON COUNTY, VA. Capt. James Robertson and 9 Va. militia pursued marauding band of Indians and killed one.		2			
Apr. 11	WEST JERSEY. A force of 50 British skirmished with some Americans.	5				

DATE	ENGAGEMENT	AMERICAN LOSSES				
		K	W	C	M	D
Apr. 12	BRUNSWICK, N.J. Gen. Benjamin Lincoln with 500 troops clashed with Gen. Cornwallis' British and Germans, wounding 5 of the enemy.	2		20		
Apr. 15	BONHAMTOWN, N.J. A Pa. detachment under Capt. Alexander Paterson attacked a British picket guard of 25, killed 8, captured 16.	1	2			
	BOONESBOROUGH, KY. Indians made an unsuccessful attack on the fort, commanded by Daniel Boone.					
Apr. 16	SWAN POINT, CHESAPEAKE BAY. A British raid on a ship building site led to their capture by Marylanders.					
	NEAR NEWARK, N.J. Clash occurred between some Americans and N.J. Loyalists, who had 3 K.					
c. Apr. 20	NEAR PISCATAWAY, N.J. Two hundred Americans were in a fight with British troops.	6	16			
	HACKENSACK, N.J. Loyalist raiding party was in action against some Americans.		1			
Apr. 21	BONHAMTOWN, N.J. Some Pa. troops under Lts. Benjamin Lodge and John McCabe drove in a British picket guard, killing 1, wounding 2.					
	NEAR CLOSTER, N.J. Fifty Bergen County Loyalists under Capt. Van Allen raided an American position.			3		
Apr. 22	NORTHERN N.J. Capt. Combs led a force against a British picket guard, killed 16 and captured 16.		3			
Apr. 23	NEAR MORRISTOWN, N.J. Lt. Col. Charles Mawhood's British brigade was in a skirmish with Americans and lost 5 K, perhaps 40 W.					
Apr. 24 -27	BOONESBOROUGH, KY. Fort was besieged by 40-50 Indians for 3 days.		7			
Apr. 25	AMBOY, N.J. Skirmish between British and Americans occurred.	4		26		
Apr. 25 -27	DANBURY, CONN. Col. William Tryon led 2000 British and Loyalists in landing at Westport and marched to Danbury, where he destroyed army stores and burned numerous houses before retreating to ships via Ridgefield. During the retreat he was attacked by Americans under Gens. Wooster, Silliman, and Arnold. The British lost 25 K, 117 W, 29 M.	20	75			
Apr. 26	HOPPERTOWN, N.J. Loyalists under Col. Barton raided an American camp.			5		

DATE	ENGAGEMENT	AMERICAN LOSSES				
		K	W	C	M	D
May 1	EGREMONT, MASS. In a clash between Loyalists and rebels, 3 enemy were killed.					
May 4	ALTAMAHA RIVER, GA. Col. John Baker led 109 Ga. militia against British-allied Indians.		2			
May 10	NEAR BONHAMTOWN, N.J. Gen. Adam Stephen's division skirmished with British 42nd, 71st, and 33rd regts. The British suffered 70 casualties.	7	15	5		
May 12	PARAMUS, N.J. Maj. Peter Fell's militia picket was attacked by Lt. Col. Joseph Barton's N.J. Loyalists and retreated into the woods.					
	SLOTTERDAM, N.J. Lt. Col. Edward Dongan with a small party of Loyalists attacked a post held by Capt. David Marinus.			6		
May 15	ST. MARY'S RIVER, FLA. Col. John Baker was in a skirmish with a party of E. Fla. Loyalist Rangers and Indians.		(5)			
May 17	NASSAU RIVER, FLA. Col. John Baker's troops were drawn into ambush and routed by Lt. Col. Thomas Brown's Loyalist Rangers.			11		
	NEAR METUCHEN, N.J. Gen. William Maxwell's brigade clashed with a British force and inflicted heavy casualties.	2	1	23		
May 18	AMELIA ISLAND, FLA. Lt. Col. Samuel Elbert's American troops attacked Lt. Ward's party.	1				
May 20	LOGAN'S FORT, KY. Garrison under Col. Benjamin Logan was besieged by British-encouraged Indians.	1	2			
May 23	SAG HARBOR, LONG ISLAND, N.Y. With 225 men from Conn. Lt. Col. Return J. Meigs led a raid on a British supply depot, killed 6, captured 90, burned 12 ships and forage.					
May 23 -25	BOONESBOROUGH, KY. Fort was attacked by Indians again. (See April 24.)		3			
May 25	PHILLIPSBURG, N.Y. HMS Dependence, Lt. Clark, fired on boats carrying troops across Hudson and burned 14 of them.					
May 26	NORTHERN N.J. Gen. Benjamin Lincoln with about 700 troops engaged a British force of similar size, killed 7.	1	2			
May 31	FALL RIVER, MASS. British raid to destroy sawmills resulted in 5 K, 6 W.					
Early June	BOONESBOROUGH, KY. Maj. Smith led 17 Americans north in pursuit of an Indian band and killed one.		1			

DATE	ENGAGEMENT	AMERICAN LOSSES				
		K	W	C	M	D
June 1	NEAR MIDDLE BROOK, N.J. Lt. Martin led 10 men from Capt. David Lyons' company in skirmish with a small party of British and German light horse, and killed one.	2				
June 2	ST. JOHNS, N.S. Capt. West led 16 men in a raid and captured 2 British.					
June 3	PHILLIPSBURG, N.Y. HMS Dependence, Lt. Clark, fired on rebels who were trying to burn the houses of some Loyalists.					1
June 6	WHEELING, W.VA. Fishing party from Capt. Vanmeter's Va. militia company was surprised by Indians.	1				
June 10	HACKENSACK, N.J. Americans skirmished with over 200 British green coats.					
	MIDDLETOWN, R.I. Americans fired on the British, killing 3, wounding 1.		1			
June 12	MIDDLETOWN, R.I. Another skirmish between Americans and British. (See above.)		2			
June 13	ELIZABETHTOWN POINT, N.J. A dozen British soldiers from Staten Island made a raid, lost 1 K and 3 W also.	1	3			
June 14	PHILLIPSBURG, N.Y. HMS Dependence, Lt. Clark, dispersed a party of rebels robbing Col. Phillip's house.					
	BRUNSWICK, N.J. Americans harassing Gen. Cornwallis' rear guard killed 2 and wounded 13.	9	30			
	BORDENTOWN, N.J. N.J. militia fired on British boats on the Delaware River.	1				
June 16	PHILLIPSBURG, N.Y. Watering party from HMS Dependence, Lt. Clark, was fired on by rebels, to which the ship replied.					
June 17	PHILLIPSBURG, N.Y. HMS Dependence, Lt. Clark, exchanged fire with rebels advancing on British lines.					
	NEAR GUILFORD, CONN. Landing party from 3 British ships burned house and 2 barns at Sachem's Head until repulsed by militia.					
June 18	CAPE COD HARBOR, MASS. HMS Juno, Capt. Dalrymple, was prevented from taking a brig that had gone aground by fire from American cannon and muskets.					
June 20	ENGLISH NEIGHBORHOOD, N.J. Scouting party of 30 N.J. troops skirmished with a British party.					
June 21	NEAR FORT PITT, PA. Mingoes from Pluggy's town engaged Americans in a fight.	2				
	NORTHERN N.J. N.J. Loyalist Col. George Taylor lost 4 men in a skirmish with rebels.					

DATE	ENGAGEMENT	AMERICAN LOSSES				
		K	W	C	M	D
June 22	NEAR BRUNSWICK, N.J. Large British force under Gen. William Howe was attacked by 4 brigades and Morgan's riflemen under Gen. Nathanael Greene.	3	3			
June 23	MACHIAS, ME. Two boats containing 40 men from HMS Vulture, Capt. Young, tried to land, but were driven off by rebels with several killed.					
June 25	NEAR AMBOY, N.J. Col. Theodorick Bland's Continental dragoons attacked the British.	(5)				
	NEAR FORT STANWIX, N.Y. Col. Peter Gansevoort's American garrison lost two officers in attack by Indians.	1	1			
June 26	BETWEEN METUCHEN AND SCOTCH PLAINS, N.J. Gen. William Stirling's division was attacked by British and Germans under Gen. Cornwallis, who suffered 6 K and 30 W.	(30)		50		
June 27	CAPE COD HARBOR, MASS. HMS Juno, Capt. Dalrymple, returned to get grounded brig and succeeded, but failed to take off a sloop because of fire from shore.					
June 28	EGG ISLAND, N.J. Watering parties from 3 British ships were fired on by Americans on shore, and one warship returned fire.					
June 30	MACHIAS, ME. Local militia party was attacked, perhaps by British marines.	(2)	(3)			
Late June	ST. JOHN, N.B. Rebels under Capts. Reuben Dyer and Jabez West were attacked by a British landing party under Maj. Studholm, who lost 9.	3	2			
July	NEAR FORT HOWE, GA. Twenty Ga. recruits led by Lts. Brown and Anderson were surprised and attacked.	14				
July 1	CAPE MAY, N.J. Rebel battery fired on HMS Camilla, Capt. Phipps, preventing it from taking a grounded schooner.					
July 2 or 3	MACHIAS, ME. Mass. militia was attacked by British force.	3				
July 3	NEAR FORT STANWIX (ROME), N.Y. Sixteen American soldiers were attacked by Indians.	1	2	7		
July 4	NORWALK ISLAND, CONN. HMS Halifax, Lt. Quarme, was fired on by rebel cannon while stuck on a rock.					
	BOONESBOROUGH, KY. With British encouragement, 200 Indians laid siege to the fort.					
July 4 –5	PHILLIPSBURG, N.Y. HMS Dependence, Lt. Clark, exchanged fire with rebel boats.					

| DATE | ENGAGEMENT | AMERICAN LOSSES | | | | |
		K	W	C	M	D
July 6	CASTLETON, VT. A British foraging party sent out by Gen. Fraser raided the town.	2	1	3		
July 7	HUBBARDTON, VT. Gen. St. Clair's rear guard under Col. Seth Warner was attacked by British Gen. Simon Fraser. The enemy lost about 200.	(30)	(96)	(228)		
	HUBBARDTON, VT. A skirmish in the town occurred in conjunction with the battle outside.	1		7		
	FORT ANNE, N.Y. A detachment of 220 men under Capt. James Gray retreating to Albany had a skirmish with the British, killing 3.	2	3			
	QUIBBLETOWN (NEW MARKET), N.J. Gen. William Maxwell's brigade attacked the rear of the British army and took several prisoners.					
	WEST OF NORWALK, CONN. Local militia prevented a British landing.					
	FAIRFIELD, CONN. Capt. Thomas Nash's company harassed a British raiding party that burned the town.	1				
July 10	NEWPORT, R.I. Lt. Col. William Barton led 40 men in a night raid against the British and captured Gen. Richard Prescott and 2 others.					
July 14	FORT STRADLER, W.VA. Indian attack was made on the garrison under Capt. John Minor.	2				
July 21	BOSTON NECK, R.I. A British raiding party from Conanicut Island seized some militia as prisoners.			(5)		
July 24 -25	PHILLIPSBURG, N.Y. HMS Dependence, Lt. Clark, exchanged fire with rebels on shore.					
July 26	PRUDENCE ISLAND, NARRAGANSETT BAY. Maj. Adams and party captured 3 men from HMS Lark, Capt. Smith.					
July 27	FORT EDWARD, N.Y. Four hundred British and Indians surprised a picket guard, seized Jane McCrea and scalped her.	(5)				
July 28	HUDSON RIVER, N.Y. HMS Dependence, Lt. Clark, exchanged fire with rebels on shore who were plundering some Loyalists.					
Aug. 1	LOGSTOWN, PA. Indians fired on 3 militia and 2 boys up the river.	1		1		
Aug. 2	DUTCH ISLAND, R.I. Col. Robert Elliot's artillery fired on HMS Renown, Capt. Banks, and forced it to move up the bay.					

DATE	ENGAGEMENT	AMERICAN LOSSES				
		K	W	C	M	D
Aug. 2 -5	SARATOGA, N.Y. Gen. John Glover's brigade skirmished with British-allied Indians for four days.	27		30		
Aug. 2 -8	FORT STANWIX, N.Y. Col. Peter Gansevoort's garrison was besieged by 1400 British and Indians under Col. Barry St. Leger before they withdrew.	3	9			
Aug. 5	BOSTON NECK, R.I. British landed 200 men whom the militia under Col. Charles Dyer resisted and finally drove off.		2	8		
	AQUIDNECK ISLAND, R.I. Capt. Charles Dyer took 60 men to the island and attacked 70 British soldiers who had been firing on fishing boats.		1			
	WESTERLY, R.I. British cruiser drove a sloop ashore and then was shelled by R.I. artillery.					
Aug. 6	ORISKANY, N.Y. Gen. Nicholas Herkimer, with about 800 N.Y. militia and Indians, was ambushed by Loyalists and Indians.	72	(75)			
	VERPLANCK'S POINT, N.Y. HMS Dependence, Lt. Clark, exchanged fire with rebel battery.					
c. Aug. 8	OFF LEWES, DEL. Capt. Murphy seized an enemy sloop, then had to defend it against a British attempt to recapture it.		1			
Aug. 10	ST. SIMON'S ISLAND, GA. British attacked Capt. Arthur Carney's company of 1st Ga. regiment.			6		
Aug. 11	SCHENECTADY, N.Y. Maj. Abraham Switz' N.Y. militia captured a dozen Loyalists.					
Aug. 13 -14	MACHIAS, ME. Four British ships landed marines who were repulsed by militia and Indians under Col. Jonathan Eddy. The ships were fired on. The enemy lost 3 K, 18 W.	1	1			
Aug. 14	SPUYTEN DUYVIL CREEK, N.Y. HMS Dependence, Lt. Clark, had to fire on rebels to cover retreat of its foraging party.					
	CAMBRIDGE, VT. About 50 of Gen. John Stark's brigade skirmished with 30 British and 50 Indians under Col. Friedrich Baum. Enemy casualties may have been 1 or 32.			5		
Aug. 16	NEAR BENNINGTON, VT. Actually 2 battles occurred, beginning with Gen. John Stark's attack on Col. Friedrich Baum's 550 Germans, Loyalists, and Canadians. After their defeat, about 640 reinforcements under Col. Heinrich von Breymann came up and were routed by Stark, who had been reinforced by 150 Continentals from Col. Seth Warner's regiment. Enemy lost 696 captured and perhaps 200 killed.	30	50			
Aug. 19	KITTANNING, PA. Some of American Capt. Samuel Morehead's Pa. independent company were attacked by Indians.	3				
	TARRYTOWN, N.Y. HMS Dependence, Lt. Clark, exchanged					

DATE	ENGAGEMENT	AMERICAN LOSSES				
		K	W	C	M	D
Aug. 19	TARRYTOWN, N.Y. (cont.) fire with a rebel battery.					
Aug. 20	CROSS ISLAND, ME. Detachment under Maj. Stillman happened on to a watering party from HMS Blonde, killed 2, wounded 3, captured 3.					
Aug. 21	STAMFORD HARBOR, CONN. Boats from HMS Halifax, Lt. Quarme, captured an American schooner even though fired on by rebel battery on shore.					
Aug. 22	SETAUKET, LONG ISLAND, N.Y. Gen. Samuel Parsons led a raid across the Sound to destroy a Loyalist stockade, but was unsuccessful beyond inflicting a few casualties.	(4)				
	STATEN ISLAND, N.Y. A raid by Gen. John Sullivan's division ended in confusion and disaster.	13		172		
Aug. 23	MILFORD FARMS, CONN. HMS Swan, Capt. Ayscough, landed 40 men, who were repulsed by the inhabitants.					
	SPESUTIE ISLAND, CHESAPEAKE BAY. Capt. Francis Holland on a foraging expedition met fire from two British ships, had to abandon his cattle and retreat down the island.					
Aug. 24	FORT STANWIX, N.Y. After the British siege was lifted, Col. Peter Gansevoort pursued the enemy and captured several prisoners and deserters.					
Aug. 28	ELKTON, MD. British troops who had landed 4 days earlier exchanged shots with troops under Col. Samuel Patterson.			3		
	MACHIAS, ME. British marines raided the port but were repulsed by militia.	1	1			
Aug. 30	PHILLIPSBURG, N.Y. A party of rebels was dispersed by fire from HMS Dependence, Lt. Clark.					
Aug. 31	FORT RANDOLPH, VA. Scouting party from American Capt. Mathew Arbuckle's garrison was attacked by Indians.	2				
	NEAR WILMINGTON, DEL. A skirmish occurred between a British advance and Continentals.	3				
	ELK FORGE, MD. Detachments of 23rd and 49th British regiments were attacked by a party of rebels. The enemy lost 1 K and 6 W.			(5)		
Sep. 1	FORT HENRY (WHEELING), W.VA. Indians numbering 350 led by Simon Girty attacked the garrison under Col. Sheppard. Indian losses amounted to 40 or 50.	23				
	NEAR WILMINGTON, DEL. Maj. William Darke led an assault		1		2	

| DATE | ENGAGEMENT | AMERICAN LOSSES | | | | |
		K	W	C	M	D
Sep. 1	NEAR WILMINGTON, DEL. (cont.) on an enemy picket and killed several.					
Sep. 2	WESTMORELAND CO., VA. British-inspired Indians attacked a small party of Va. militia on Connemaugh River.	1		5		
Sep. 3	COOCH'S BRIDGE, DEL. Gen. William Maxwell with about 700 men was attacked by a similar force of British and Germans under Gen. Cornwallis, who lost 3 K and 21 W.	(20)	(20)			
Sep. 4	PRUDENCE ISLAND, R.I. Gen. Ezekiel Cornell's R.I. militia ambushed a watering party from HMS Juno, killed 3, captured 16.					
	ISLAND OF R.I. American party from Seconnet landed and captured 3 British seamen.					
Sep. 7	OFF RED BANK, N.J. USS Delaware, Capt. Alexander, was fired on by British shore batteries until it surrendered.					
Sep. 10	TANGIER ISLAND, CHESAPEAKE BAY. HMS Perseus, Capt. Elphinstone, exchanged fire with rebels on shore.					
Sep. 11	BRANDYWINE CREEK, PA. Washington had 11,000 men to stop Howe's advance toward Philadelphia with 13,000. In an all day battle the British pushed the Americans aside after losing 90 K, 448 W, 6 M. American losses are only estimated.	(200)	(500)	(400)		
	OUTSIDE FORT GREENBRIER, W.VA. Shawnees attacked the family of rebel Col. James Graham.	2	1			
	CAPT. JOSEPH BOWMAN'S FARM, KY. A Va. militia company was attacked by Indians while shelling corn.	1	6			
	PHILLIPSBURG, N.Y. HMS Diligent, Lt. Farnham, exchanged fire with rebels on shore.					
Sep. 12	DOBBS FERRY, N.Y. HMS Dependence, Lt. Clark, fired on rebels ashore who were attacking a British foraging party.					
	SLOTTERDAM, N.J. British Gen. Sir Henry Clinton invaded N.J., sending Gen. John Vaughan as far as Passaic River, where he met American resistance and had to withdraw.					
Sep. 13	BEMIS HEIGHTS, N.Y. An American scout captured 3 British soldiers digging potatoes.					
Sep. 14	NEAR HACKENSACK, N.J. Col. Aaron Burr led a detachment of Americans at night against a British picket guard, killed 2, and captured 30.					
Sep. 15	NEAR BEMIS HEIGHTS, N.Y. An American scouting party was driven back by British-allied Indians.					
Sep. 16	CHESTER COUNTY, PA. Continentals and militia under Gen.	12		30		

| DATE | ENGAGEMENT | AMERICAN LOSSES | | | | |
		K	W	C	M	D
Sep. 16	CHESTER COUNTY, PA. (cont.) Anthony Wayne were attacked by advanced troops of Gen. Cornwallis.					
Sep. 18	LAKE GEORGE, N.Y. On way to Ticonderoga, Col. John Brown and 500 militia captured British seamen at the lake, seized Mt. Hope and Mt. Defiance, and took 3 companies of British, 293 altogether.	4	4			
	ROAD TO PHILADELPHIA, PA. As Gen. Cornwallis followed Gen. Washington toward the city, shots were exchanged and he took a few American prisoners.			(7)		
Sep. 19	ROAD TO PHILADELPHIA, PA. British Lt. Col. William Harcourt led a cavalry troop on a raid into the American lines.			9		
	BEMIS HEIGHTS, N.Y. Gen. John Burgoyne moved on Gen. Horatio Gates' fortified position and met hot resistance from Gen. Benedict Arnold. The British suffered 556 casualties. This engagement is also known as the first battle of Freeman's Farm.	80	200		36	
Sep. 21	PAOLI, PA. Gen. Anthony Wayne's division of 1500 men was surprised at night by Gen. Charles Grey leading 3 regiments using bayonets only. The British lost 6 K and 22 W.	(200)	(100)	71		
	CAPE COD, MASS. HMS Scarborough, Capt. Barkley, exchanged shots with rebels on shore protecting a U.S. ship.					
Sep. 22	GORDON'S FORD (PHOENIXVILLE), PA. Hessian grenadiers were attacked as they crossed the ford.	2				
Sep. 23	DIAMOND ISLAND, LAKE GEORGE, N.Y. Col. John Brown led 420 Americans against a British post, 25 miles south of Fort Ticonderoga, but after an exchange of fire could not land.					
	WOODBURY, N.J. Hessian troops had a skirmish with Americans and then returned toward Philadelphia.					
Sep. 23 -24	NORRINGTON, PA. British troops moving toward Philadelphia exchanged shots with Americans and took some mounted men.			4		
Sep. 25	GERMANTOWN, PA. British cavalry captured some stray Americans.			6		
	NEAR WILMINGTON, DEL. Three British ships fired on Americans to cover a landing of troops.					
	BEMIS HEIGHTS, N.Y. American scouting party clashed with British outpost, killing 6 and capturing 1.					
Sep. 26	PHILADELPHIA, PA. After Gen. Cornwallis entered the city, an American detachment attacked the Queen's Rangers and killed 2.	1				
Sep. 27	GRAVE CREEK, W.VA. A party of 46 Va. militia under Capt. William Foreman was ambushed by British-allied Indians.	21	4			

41

DATE	ENGAGEMENT	AMERICAN LOSSES				
		K	W	C	M	D
Sep. 27	BEMIS HEIGHTS, N.Y. An American detachment tried to surprise an advanced British post.	1	3			
	GRAY'S FERRY ROAD, BELOW PHILADELPHIA, PA. A party of 100 Continentals was attacked by the Queen's Rangers. The British lost 1 K and 3 W.					
	DELAWARE RIVER NEAR PHILADELPHIA, PA. Two U.S. frigates and 5 row gallies cannonaded the city, but British batteries disabled and captured one frigate and one galley and drove off the others.	5	12			
Oct. 2	BILLINGSPORT, N.J. After the British seized the American fort here, rebel ships fired on it till beaten off.					
Oct. 3	NEAR SANDY HOOK LIGHTHOUSE, N.J. Capt. John Dennis led some N.J. militia against a British detachment and wounded one soldier.		1	6		
Oct. 4	GERMANTOWN, PA. Gen. Washington sent 11,000 troops against the British, but the divided columns did not proceed uniformly, and the enemy resistance was stubborn. Panic among the Americans forced a general retreat. The British casualties were about 550.	(152)	(500)	438		
Oct. 5	PEEKSKILL, N.Y. HMS _Dependence_ and _Diligent_ fired on rebels on shore and covered a landing party to destroy some boats.					
Oct. 6	BILLINGSPORT, N.J. British burned an American fort they had captured. Commodore John Hazelwood drove British ships down the Delaware River.					
	FORTS CLINTON AND MONTGOMERY, N.Y. Gen. Israel Putnam commanded the Highlands of the Hudson River when Gen. Sir Henry Clinton assaulted the two forts, held by Gens. James and George Clinton. The British captured both and burned some ships, suffering about 200 casualties. The Americans lost about 250.	(50)	(100)	(100)		
Oct. 7	BEMIS HEIGHTS, N.Y. At the second battle of Freeman's Farm, Gen. John Burgoyne made his second attack on Gen. Horatio Gates' superior force and was defeated. The British suffered over 600 casualties, and many Germans deserted afterward. Gates never reported his casualty figures. Burgoyne retreated and ten days later surrendered at Saratoga.	(30)	(100)			
	BELOW PEEKSKILL, N.Y. Some British ships tried to break the chain across the Hudson, but were beaten off by American fire.					
Oct. 9	DELAWARE RIVER, PHILADELPHIA, PA. Commodore John Hazelwood exchanged fire with British on shore, inflicting some					

DATE	ENGAGEMENT	AMERICAN LOSSES				
		K	W	C	M	D
Oct. 9	DELAWARE RIVER, PHILADELPHIA, PA. (cont.) casualties.					
Oct. 11	CARPENTER'S ISLAND, NEAR PHILADELPHIA, PA. Americans seized British who were erecting a battery, but in turn were surprised by a second British detachment that recovered most of the British prisoners.	(3)	(5)			
Oct. 12	PROVINCE ISLAND, NEAR PHILADELPHIA, PA. Americans from Fort Mifflin attacked a British redoubt on the island, destroyed it, and took 54 prisoners.	2	5			
	NEAR POUGHKEEPSIE, N.Y. HMS Dependence, Lt. Clark, burned 2 American ships and some storehouses.					
	HUDSON RIVER HIGHLANDS, N.Y. HMS Diligent, Lt. Farnham, burned barns and mills on shore in spite of being fired on.					
Oct. 13	NEW WINDSOR, N.Y. American battery fired on HMS Dependence, Lt. Clark, and other ships as they passed by returning the fire.					
	FISHKILL, N.Y. HMS Diligent, Lt. Farnham, had 2 men wounded in exchange of fire with rebels on shore.					
	DELAWARE RIVER, NEAR CHESTER, PA. American ships launched fire rafts against British ships down stream, and both sides exchanged fire, but the British avoided the rafts.					
Oct. 14	NEW YORK. Some American cavalry crossed the Hudson from N.J., skirmished with British troops, and took some prisoners.					
Oct. 15	POUGHKEEPSIE, N.Y. HMS Diligent, Lt. Farnham, exchanged fire with rebels on shore.					
	BILLINGSPORT, N.J. Landing party from HMS Liverpool, Capt. Bellew, tried to destroy fort.					
	NEWCASTLE, DEL. A party of 60 Del. militia seized 3 or 4 British sailors ashore.					
Oct. 16	ESOPUS (KINGSTON), N.Y. British force under Gen. John Vaughan landed despite rebel cannonade and burned the town. Several British soldiers were wounded.					
Oct. 17	FORT MIFFLIN, MUD ISLAND, DELAWARE RIVER. British troops on Pa. shore cannonaded the island fort.	1	4			
Oct. 18	SLAPSHINE ISLAND, HUDSON RIVER. HMS Dependence and Diligent exchanged fire with rebels on shore, destroyed stores on island and again at Livingston Manor.					
Oct. 19	MIDDLETOWN, R.I. During an abortive attempt to land troops, Americans were fired on by British battery.	1	1			

DATE	ENGAGEMENT	AMERICAN LOSSES				
		K	W	C	M	D
Oct. 19	TERRY POINT, N.Y. Skirmish occurred between British and Americans.	1	1			
Oct. 20	LOGSTOWN, PA. Capt. John Lucas' company of Va. militia was attacked by Indians.	1	1			
Oct. 21	FORT MERCER, RED BANK, N.J. Col. Christopher Greene's R.I. troops defended the fort against an attack by about 1500 Germans under Col. Carl von Donop. The enemy suffered 153 killed and more than 200 wounded.	14	23	1		
Oct. 22	FORT MIFFLIN, MUD ISLAND, DELAWARE RIVER. British attack on the fort held by Col. Christopher Olney's R.I. militia was repulsed with heavy enemy losses.	(15)		1		
Oct. 23	FORT MIFFLIN, MUD ISLAND, DELAWARE RIVER. British ships began cannonading the fort, which replied and with aid of American gallies set 2 enemy ships on fire.		2			
	POUGHKEEPSIE, N.Y. Four British ships exchanged fire with Americans on shore.					
Oct. 24	BUTTER HILL, N.Y. HMS Dependence, Lt. Clark, which was fired on the day before, exchanged shots with Americans on shore farther along.					
Oct. 26	FRANKFORD, PA. Some of Lt. Col. John G. Simcoe's Rangers attacked a detachment of 21 American troops.		2	19		
Late Oct.	PALMER'S FORT, LIGONIER VALLEY, PA. Ens. Wood's militia was routed by a force of Indians and Canadians.	11				
Nov. 5	DELAWARE RIVER BELOW RED BANK, N.J. HMS Isis and Pearl exchanged fire with a rebel battery on the N.J. shore.					
	DELAWARE RIVER. HMS Somerset and Roebuck were fired on by American forces.					
c. Nov. 6	POINT JUDITH, R.I. HMS Syren, Capt. Furneaux, a transport and a schooner ran aground at the Point, were attacked by R.I. militia under Col. Charles Dyer, and 166 prisoners taken. Later another British ship set the Syren on fire.					
Nov. 8	NEAR PHILADELPHIA, PA. Two squads of American light horse were attacked by a British unit.			3		
Nov. 10 -15	FORT MIFFLIN, MUD ISLAND, DELAWARE RIVER. British ships and a land battery kept up a steady cannonade on the fort, commanded by Lt. Col. Samuel Smith. At night of the 15th, he set fire to his barracks and withdrew. The enemy had 7 K and 5 W.	(20)	(40)			

44

DATE	ENGAGEMENT	AMERICAN LOSSES				
		K	W	C	M	D
c. Nov. 11	NEAR WHITEMARSH, PA. A troop of 16 American dragoons under Capt. Leigh attacked a British detachment and captured 14.					
c. Nov. 12	NEAR WHITEMARSH, PA. American dragoons under Gen. Casimir Pulaski encountered a British detachment, killed 5, and took 2 prisoners.	1		2		
Nov. 18	DARBY, PA. When Gen. Cornwallis and the 33rd British regiment passed the Blue Bell tavern, they were fired on by Pa. militia. Cornwallis sent his men into the tavern, and they bayoneted 33.		33			
Nov. 19	UPSTATE NEW YORK. When the 1st Conn. regiment paraded, it was fired on by the British.	1	2			
Nov. 21	PHILADELPHIA, PA. A large troop of American cavalry attacked the British lines, but was driven off with loss.		(3)			
Nov. 22	PHILADELPHIA, PA. Americans attacked British pickets but were driven off.			9		
Nov. 25	GLOUCESTER, N.J. Gen. Jedidiah Huntington's brigade, 170 of Morgan's riflemen, and N.J. militia under Lafayette attacked German troops of Gen. Cornwallis' division.	1	5			
Nov. 27	NEAR NEW ROCHELLE, N.Y. Col. Samuel Webb's regiment skirmished with British troops.		2			
Dec. 5	NEAR BERGEN POINT, N.J. A small American force skirmished with some British under Col. Turnbull.	1		1		
	NEAR WHITEMARSH, PA. Some 600 troops under Gen. James Irvine skirmished with the British.	(8)		1		
Dec. 6	CHESTNUT HILL, PA. A force made up of Morgan's riflemen, Webb's Conn. regiment, Gist's Md. militia, and Potter's Pa. militia battled the British for two hours. Enemy casualties were as heavy.	30	40	15		
Dec. 10	SETAUKET, LONG ISLAND, N.Y. In transporting American troops from Norwalk, Conn., to Long Island, Col. Samuel Webb had 73 men aboard the Schuyler. It was chased by HMS Falcon, Capt. Harwood, ran aground, and most of the Americans were captured.			68		
Dec. 11	GULPH MILLS, PA. A brigade of Pa. militia under Gen. James Potter fought a British force.	6	20	20		
Dec. 12	POTOMAC RIVER, MD. A boat with 3 men from HMS Emerald landed and was captured by American sentries.					
Dec. 15	AUGUSTA COUNTY, VA. An Indian raiding party was pursued					

DATE	ENGAGEMENT	AMERICAN LOSSES				
		K	W	C	M	D
Dec. 15	AUGUSTA COUNTY, VA. (cont.) by Capt. Wilson and militia after 4 civilians had been killed.					
Dec. 22 -28	NEAR DARBY, PA. Gen. William Howe took 7000 British soldiers out of Philadelphia on an extensive foraging expedition. He was followed and harassed by an American force under Col. Daniel Morgan, who captured a few British.			39		
Dec. 29	NEAR WILMINGTON, DEL. Gen. William Smallwood sent a detachment of 100 men to capture a British transport that had run aground. They took 68 soldiers and a dozen seamen.					
	DELAWARE RIVER, NEAR PHILADELPHIA, PA. HMS Viper, Capt. Pakenham, exchanged shots with rebels on the N.J. side of the river.					
Dec. 30	GLOUCESTER POINT WHARF, PHILADELPHIA, PA. HMS Viper, Capt. Pakenham, prevented some rebels from attempting to burn 2 transports.					
	NEWCASTLE, DEL. Capt. Erskine captured a British sloop and ran it ashore, but was driven off by armed Tories.					
Late Dec.	FORT RANDOLPH, POINT PLEASANT, W.VA. Part of Capt. William McKee's Va. militia company fell into an Indian ambuscade.	2				
	NEAR WEEHAWKEN, N.J. A detachment of N.J. militia under Capt. Johnston had a skirmish with the enemy.		1			
	TOTALS for the year 1777:	1389	2253	2169	38	2

DATE	ENGAGEMENT	AMERICAN LOSSES				
		K	W	C	M	D
Jan. 2	BOMBAY HOOK, DEL. Lt. Silas Snow with about 30 Del. militia attempted to capture an enemy ship caught in the ice.					
Jan. 2 -3	PROVIDENCE PASSAGE, NARRAGANSETT BAY. HMS Diamond, Capt. Fielding, ran aground and was bombarded by rebels on shore until it was refloated.					
Jan. 3	DELAWARE RIVER ABOVE WILMINGTON. Col. William Smallwood led a boarding party on a British brig driven ashore. A few of the enemy got away, but he captured 50 to 60, 40 women, many muskets, uniforms, etc.					
Jan. 11	DELAWARE RIVER, N.J. SHORE. A boat from HMS Roebuck, Capt. Hamond, helped destroy a rebel breastwork and captured 2 galleys.			(10)		
Jan. 20	NEAR VALLEY FORGE, PA. British dragoons surprised a party of light horse under Capt. Elisha Lee, but suffered 2 K and 4 W.		1			
Jan. 25	SAWPITS, CONN. Two Conn. officers were attacked, apparently by Loyalists.	1				
	NEW PROVIDENCE, BAHAMA ISLANDS. Men from USS Providence, Capt. Rathburne, captured Fort Nassau and turned the cannon on the town.					
Jan. 28	NEW PROVIDENCE, BAHAMA ISLANDS. HMS Gayton, Capt. Chambers, was beaten off by Capt. Rathburne's men (above), who departed next day.					
Feb. 4	OUTSIDE PHILADELPHIA, PA. American pickets were captured and taken into the city.			30		
Feb. 8	LOWER BLUE LICKS, KY. Capt. Daniel Boone and 27 men from Boonesborough, who were making salt, were captured by a band of Shawnees under Chief Blackfish.			28		
Feb. 13	NEAR WHITEMARSH, PA. British cavalry in a night raid on Wright's Tavern captured Maj. Wright and some others, probably civilians.			1		
Feb. 14	NEAR SMITHFIELD, PA. British troops captured 7 civilians and about 30 militia.			30		
Feb. 18	NEWTOWN, PA. British cavalry surprised a detachment of the 13th Pa. regiment under Maj. Francis Murray.			29		
	NATCHEZ, MISS. Capt. James Willing led his Americans ashore from river boats and seized civilians, slaves, and property.					
Feb. 23	MANCHAC, LA. Lt. Thomas McIntyre with 18 men from Capt.					

DATE	ENGAGEMENT	AMERICAN LOSSES				
		K	W	C	M	D
Feb. 23	MANCHAC, LA.(cont.) Willing's force seized 2 ships and carried them to New Orleans.					
Feb. 25	SMITHTOWN, LONG ISLAND, N.Y. A detachment of 30 men from the 6th Conn. regiment under Maj. David Humphreys seized an armed British ship and 2 other boats.					
Feb. 29	NEAR COOPER'S FERRY, N.J. British foraging party under Lt. Col. John G. Simcoe was moving wagons across Delaware River when attacked by Americans under Gen. Pulaski. After inflicting some casualties, Pulaski retreated.					
Late Feb.	BELOW NEW ORLEANS, LA. Party of Capt. James Willing's troops and others under Capt. Joseph Calvert seized two English ships, Neptune and Dispatch, Capt. McCraight.					
Mar.	DUNKARD CREEK, VA. Enemy Indians raided outlying posts.	6	2	4		
	TREMLEY POINT, N.J. American guard post opposite Staten Island was raided by British.	1	1	8		
Early Mar.	MARCUS HOOK, PA. Capt. Enoch Anderson and 30 troops captured 8 British seamen and killed 4 who were ashore, despite firing from their ship.					
Mar. 6	NEAR CHESTNUT HILL, PA. British mounted troops surprised 300 Americans.			19		20
Mar. 9	LOWER DELAWARE RIVER. HMS Dispatch, Capt. Mason, exchanged fire with a rebel battery.					
Mar.12	SHELBURNE, VT. Col. Thomas Sawyer and 16 men were guarding Pierson house when it was attacked by 57 Loyalists and Indians. Two civilians, 1 Loyalist, and 1 Indian were killed.					
Mar.13	FORT BARRINGTON, GA. Lt. Col. Thomas Brown at the head of 100 E. Fla. Rangers and 10 Creeks captured and burned the fort, running off the cattle. The enemy suffered 1 K and 4 W.	2	4	23		
Mar.14	MANCHAC, LA. Loyalists retook the town after attacking Americans at the guardhouse.	(2)	(3)	13		
Mar.16 -17	DELAWARE RIVER. HMS Viper, Capt. Pakenham, exchanged fire with rebels on shore erecting a breastwork.					
Mar.18	QUINTON'S BRIDGE, N.J. About 200 militia under Col. Edward Hand crossed the bridge into an ambush set by Lt. Col. Charles Mawhood and Lt. Col. John G. Simcoe. One British soldier was killed, but most of the Americans fled.	1		(10)		
Mar.20	BLACK HORSE TAVERN, LANCASTER ROAD, NEAR PHILA-DELPHIA, PA. Forty German mounted riflemen fell on 60 Americans in the tavern.	2		11		

DATE	ENGAGEMENT	AMERICAN LOSSES				
		K	W	C	M	D
Mar. 21	HANCOCK'S BRIDGE, N.J. British infantry and Queen's Rangers surprised a gathering of rebels at Hancock's house.	(25)				
Mar. 22	NEAR PAULUS HOOK, N.J. Col. George Turnbull's N.Y. Volunteers (Tory) had a skirmish with half a dozen N.J. militia.					
Mar. 23	BEYOND ALLOWAY CREEK, N.J. A cavalry patrol under Lt. Col. John G. Simcoe was attacked by a small party of Americans.			1		
Mar. 24	GREENWICH, CONN. British marines landed from HMS Halifax and Raven and set fire to a rebel galley, but met such heavy fire they had to retreat.					
	OYSTER BAY, LONG ISLAND, N.Y. Marines landed from HMS Dependence and lost a man in a skirmish with Americans.					
Mar. 31	ALLENTOWN, N.J. Some American troops clashed with a body of Loyalists.			1		
Apr. 5	NEAR HADDONFIELD, N.J. A British detachment crossed the Delaware River and surprised an American picket of 50 officers and men.	8		37		
Apr. 7	SMITHFIELD, PHILADELPHIA CO., PA. Some Pa. Loyalist cavalry fell on some Continental troops and captured a few. British Capt. John Montresor also reported this battle and results of two other patrols by the British 17th dragoons.	38	1	(10)		
Apr. 8	SMITHFIELD, PHILADELPHIA CO., PA. Some Continentals under Capt. Humphrey were attacked by the enemy.	1	2	1		
	YORK ROAD, PA. Pa. militia unit was attacked near Dr. Benneville's house.	5	2			
Apr. 14	GROGTOWN (KENTON), DEL. Militia under Lt. Col. Charles Pope destroyed a fort the Loyalists were building and chased them away.			1		
Apr. 15	NATCHEZ, MISS. Party of Americans under Lt. Reuben Harrison was ambushed at the White Cliffs by Loyalists under Anthony Hutchins.	5	3	(10)		
	VERPLANCK'S POINT, N.Y. HMS Dependence, Lt. Clark, exchanged fire with a party of rebels.					
	OUTSIDE PHILADELPHIA, PA. Cathcart's cavalry had a skirmish with some rebels.	1	7			
	GERMANTOWN, PA. A detachment of British light infantry made one capture.			1		
Apr. 17	BRISTOL, PA. Loyalist cavalry fell on a detachment of Americans.	1	2	65		

49

DATE	ENGAGEMENT	AMERICAN LOSSES				
		K	W	C	M	D
Apr. 17	OUTSIDE PHILADELPHIA, PA. British patrol brought in one prisoner.			1		
	BILLINGSPORT, N.J. Men from HMS Experiment, Capt. Wallace, seized some rebels and stores.			(8)		
	JORDAN'S ISLAND, CHESTER RIVER, DEL. Lt. Col. Charles Pope attacked some Loyalists in a fort.					
Apr. 19	ST. SIMON'S ISLAND HARBOR, GA. Col. Samuel Elbert put 300 men on board 3 gallies and captured 3 British sloops. One British captain drowned.					
Apr. 24	BARREN HILL, PA. British light infantry had a skirmish with some Americans.	1	4	51		
Apr. 25	NORTH WALES, PA. British attacked the wagoners of the Northampton Co. militia.		(5)	6		
Apr. 28	WALLACE'S FORT, WESTMORELAND CO., PA. Indians raided western fort, garrisoned by militia.	9	1			
May	CAPT. ANDREW DONNALLY'S FORT (NORTH OF LEWISBURG), W. VA. Fort was attacked by 200 Indians, but was relieved by arrival of Col. Samuel Lewis and 66 militia, who reportedly killed 17 Indians.	4				
May 1	CROOKED BILLET, PA. British regulars and Pa. Loyalists attacked about 500 Pa. militia under Gen. John Lacey. The enemy had 9 casualties.	26	9	(30)		
	BORDENTOWN, N.J. British detachment crossed the Delaware River and attacked N.J. militia.	3				
May 5	HUNTINGTON BAY, LONG ISLAND, N.Y. HMS Raven, Capt. Stanhope, exchanged fire with rebels on shore.					
May 8	BORDENTOWN, N.J. British infantry under Maj. John Maitland crossed the Delaware river, burned ships, and chased some rebel militia and cavalry into Bordentown.	14				
May 9	BILES'S ISLAND, N.J. British troops in boats supported by 3 armed vessels landed and had skirmish with Americans.					
May 10	BURLINGTON, N.J. HMS Viper, Capt. Pakenham, exchanged fire with some rebel cavalry.					
May 16	POINT PLEASANT, W. VA. Two militia men shot at by Indians outside Fort Randolph.	1	1			
	JENKINTOWN, PA. Detachment of 400 British light infantry and Simcoe's Rangers converged on the market town and were attacked by rebels.	2		5		

DATE	ENGAGEMENT	AMERICAN LOSSES				
		K	W	C	M	D
May 20	BARREN HILL, PA. British detachment similar to those above marched out of Philadelphia night before to cut off Gen. Lafayette's division, but failed to do more than skirmish.	6		12		
May 22	NORWALK, CONN. HMS Dependence, Lt. Clark, exchanged fire with a rebel battery.					
May 25	FALL RIVER, MASS. A British raiding party under Maj. Ayers was repulsed by 30 local militia under Maj. J. Durfee. Four British were killed.[1]					
	BRISTOL, R.I. British 22nd regiment under Lt. Col. John Campbell landed at Warren and proceeded to Bristol, where it was harassed by 200 militia under Col. William Barton. Numerous civilians were taken prisoner by the British.		1			
May 27	MIDDLETOWN POINT, N.J. A party of Loyalists or Germans lost 3 K in a clash, probably with militia.			(8)		
May 30	COBLESKILL, N.Y. A large party of Loyalists and Indians raided the town and burned several houses before being repulsed by a company from Col. Ichabod Alden's regiment and some Tryon County militia under Maj. Thomas Cheson.	17				
June 2	NEAR CHERRY VALLEY, N.Y. Two militia officers were killed by British-allied Indians.	2				
June 3	JENKS' MILL, NEAR NEWTOWN, PA. British dragoons and infantry captured a guard of Continental troops.			(16)		
	NEWTOWN, PA. Same British troops were met by Pa. militia and Continentals under Maj. Francis Murray.	5	4	16		
	CHESTNUT HILL, PA. A detachment from 3 British regiments had a skirmish with some Pa. militia.			4		
June 6	CHESTNUT HILL, PA. Simcoe's Queen's Rangers and 2 battalions of British light infantry suffered 3 wounded in skirmish with Americans.	3		4		
June 8	CHESTER, PA. HMS Greyhound, Capt. Dickson, exchanged fire with rebels on shore.					
June 11	WILMINGTON, DEL. HMS Camilla, Capt. Collins, exchanged fire with rebels while taking some Loyalists aboard.					
	GLOUCESTER POINT, N.J. Some American cavalry apparently skirmished with N.J. Loyalists and captured them.					
	FORT SCHUYLER (UTICA), N.Y. Timber cutting party was ambushed by some British-allied Indians.	1	1			
June 12	DELAWARE RIVER. Party from HMS Viper, Capt. Pakenham,					

1. Reported only in Orin Fowler, An Historical Sketch of Fall River (Fall River: Benjamin Earl, 1841), pp. 22-23.

DATE	ENGAGEMENT	AMERICAN LOSSES				
		K	W	C	M	D
June 12	DELAWARE RIVER (cont.) chasing 2 deserters was fired on by rebels and had 1 killed.					
	AMBOY, N.J. A British ship was fired on by N.J. militia.					
June 13	CHESTER, PA. HMS Greyhound, Capt. Dickson, sent an armed boat to assist a grounded sloop which was under rebel attack.					
June 18	PHILADELPHIA, PA. While British were evacuating the city, Capt. Allen McLane's company came upon a British patrol, opened fire, and captured 32.					
	GERMAN FLATS, N.Y. Militia responding to call from settlements suffering Indian raid were ambushed en route.	1		2		
June 19	EVESHAM, N.J. Part of Gen. Alexander Leslie's division skirmished with some rebels under Capt. Beasley.	1	1			
June 20	MOUNT HOLLY, N.J. Another skirmish occurred between the marching British and some American units.	5		2		
June 23	CROSSWICKS, N.J. British dragoons under Capt. Stevenson had a brush with a large detachment of Americans. Stevenson was wounded.	3		7		
	NEAR DOBBS FERRY, N.Y. HMS Dependence, Lt. Clark, chased a rebel sloop ashore and exchanged fire with rebel cavalry.					
June 27	PHILLIPSBURG, N.Y. HMS Dependence, Lt. Clark, fired on a party of rebels who were harassing a wood gathering crew from the ship.					
June 28	MONMOUTH, N.J. Moving in pursuit of Gen. Sir Henry Clinton's 10,000 British troops, Gen. Washington's advance division of 5400 troops under Gen. Charles Lee caught up with the enemy. Lee bungled the battle, and his retreating troops were reformed by Washington, who forced Clinton to break away. The extra 37 dead were among the missing who were found dead of sunstroke. Clinton reported British losses at 147 K, 170 W, and 64 M, but evidently did not count the Germans, as American burial parties buried 251 British and Germans.	69 37	161		95	
June 29	CABBAGE SWAMP, ST. MARY'S RIVER, FLA. With 900 troops, American Gen. James Screven forced Lt. Col. Thomas Brown's E. Fla. Rangers into a swamp where they stood off Screven.					
July	STRAWBERRY HILL (WOODBRIDGE), N.J. A British foraging party was routed by Capt. Marsh's militia company, and 42 Germans were captured.					
July 3	WYOMING VALLEY, PA. Cols. Zebulon Butler and Nathan Denison led 360 regulars and militia out of Forty Fort to attack	227		61		

DATE	ENGAGEMENT	AMERICAN LOSSES				
		K	W	C	M	D
July 3	WYOMING VALLEY, PA. (cont.) an invading force of about 1000 Loyalists, Senecas, and Cayugas under Maj. John Butler. The Americans were severely defeated; Col. Denison escaped back to the fort with 60, who surrendered next day. The enemy lost 3 K and 8 W.					
c. July 6	ALLIGATOR CREEK BRIDGE, NORTH FLA. Gen. Robert Howe, having occupied the abandoned Fort Tonyn on the St. Mary's River, sent 300 Ga. militia to test the strength of the enemy under Maj. J. M. Prevost encamped 14 miles southward. A detachment under Ga. Col. Elijah Clarke killed 1 and wounded 7 before being driven off.	3	9			
July 9	FALLARD'S POINT, HUDSON RIVER. HMS Dependence, Lt. Clark, chased some rebel boats ashore, firing on them and taking them.					
July 12	TARRYTOWN, N.Y. HMS Tartar, Capt. Howorth, and Dependence, Lt. Clark, exchanged fire with a rebel battery.					
July 13	SPUYTEN DUYVIL CREEK, N.Y. HMS Tartar, Dependence, and Crane were cannonaded by a rebel battery and forced to move.					
July 21	CRANBERRY ISLAND, ME. A British foraging party burned 7 barns and carried off some cattle, despite being fired on by Americans, who said they killed 1 and wounded 3.					
c. July 24	PENN VALLEY, PA. Capt. John Finley's company of the 8th Pa. regiment had a skirmish with some Indians.	2				
Late July	NEAR FORT HAND, WESTMORELAND CO., PA. Capt. Samuel Miller of the 8th Pa. regiment was leading a reinforcement to the fort when attacked by Indians.	8				
Aug.	NEAR WOODBRIDGE, N.J. An enemy force from Amboy was attacked by Col. Samuel Potter and 300 N.J. militia.					
	CHERRY VALLEY, N.Y. Capt. Boland's company of N.Y. militia captured some Loyalists and cattle.					
	SCHOHARIE, N.Y. Pa. riflemen under Capt. Long captured some Loyalists.		1			
Aug. 10	COCHECTON, SULLIVAN CO., N.Y. Militia detachment under Capt. Tyler attacked a party of Indians and Loyalists.	3	2	3		
Aug. 18	NEWPORT, R.I. British cannonaded the American lines.	1	1			
Aug. 19	MIDDLETOWN, R.I. Maj. Samuel Ward and a detachment attacked a British battery and inflicted several casualties.	1	2			
Aug. 24	MIDDLETOWN, R.I. British cannonaded the American lines.	1	2			
Aug. 26	MIDDLETOWN, R.I. Col. Israel Angell reported on a raid by the British on the American lines.		15			

DATE	ENGAGEMENT	AMERICAN LOSSES				
		K	W	C	M	D
Aug. 27	MIDDLETOWN, R.I. Gen. James M. Varnum assaulted British picket but was driven off.	4				
	NEWPORT, R.I. British raided a line of American sentries.		8			
Aug. 29	NEWPORT, R.I. Gen. John Sullivan with over 7500 regulars and militia had laid siege to the British Gen. Robert Pigot and 6700 troops in Newport, but gave up when the French fleet left him and 3000 militia marched off. Pigot then stormed the American position at Butt's Hill, but was repulsed with heavy losses.	30	137		44	
Aug. 29 -30	OFF BRISTOL, R.I. HMS Vigilant, Capt. Christian, and Sphynx, Capt. Graeme, assisted the British land attack by firing on Americans, and next day exchanged fire with them.					
Aug. 30	NEWPORT, R.I. The British fired a few guns at the retreating Americans.	1				
Aug. 31	MILE SQUARE ROAD, WESTCHESTER CO., N.Y. A detachment of Americans and Indians under Capt. Daniel Williams and Chief Ninham was ambushed by British cavalry under Lt. Cols. John G. Simcoe and Banastre Tarleton.	37	(8)	10		
End of Aug.	SOUTHERN GEORGIA. Loyalist Rangers from E. Fla. raided into Georgia, and 3 were killed by Ga. scouts.					
Sep. 5	HOEBUCK, N.J. British boat from King's Bridge, N.Y., was fired on from N.J. shore, forced to land, and burned.					
Sep. 6	NEW BEDFORD, MASS. Four British warships and some transports landed a large force under Gen. Charles Grey and burned most of the port. The British lost 1 K and 4 W.	1				
Sep. 9 -18	BOONESBOROUGH, KY. The fort was besieged by 350 Shawnees under Chief Blackfish and 8 British-allied Frenchmen from Detroit, until they withdrew.	1	3			
Sep. 16	WESTCHESTER, N.Y. A minor skirmish occurred.					
	NEAR HEAD OF UNADILLA RIVER, N.Y. A scouting party of militia sent out by Col. Peter Bellinger was attacked by Indians.	2		5		
Sep. 17	GERMAN FLATS, N.Y. A large party of Loyalists and Indians attacked Forts Dayton and Herkimer and burned houses, barns, and mills on the German Flats. Militia under Col. Peter Bellinger resisted.	2	1			
Sep. 22	LIBERTY POLE (ENGLEWOOD), N.J. Capt. Elias Romeyn's N.J. militia company was attacked by a regiment of British cavalry.	(6)		27		
Sep. 27	ACQUACKANONK BRIDGE, N.J. A skirmish occurred between N.J. militia and the enemy.		1			

DATE	ENGAGEMENT	AMERICAN LOSSES				
		K	W	C	M	D
Sep. 28	OFF ELIZABETHTOWN, N.J. Some British ships exchanged fire with Americans on shore.					
	OLD TAPPAN, N.Y. Col. George Baylor's 3rd Continental Light Horse was surprised by a large British force under Gen. Charles Grey.	16	16	38		
Sep. 30	BERGEN COUNTY, N.J. A minor skirmish occurred between N.J. militia and the enemy.	1				
Oct. 6	CHESTNUT CREEK, LITTLE EGG HARBOR, N.J. British landing party under Capt. Patrick Ferguson had a brush with a small body of N.J. militia and suffered one man wounded.					
Oct. 15	MINCOCK ISLAND, N.J. Gen. Casimir Pulaski's Legion was attacked by a force of 200 British under Capt. Patrick Ferguson. Pulaski reported total casualties at 25 to 30; the British thought they killed 50.	(5)	(20)	5		
Late Oct.	AMBOY, N.J. British raiding party from New York landed at Amboy, marched to Brunswick and pillaged, and on returning to Amboy was engaged by local militia and lost 4 K and 6 C.					
Nov.	KAKIAT (NEW HEMPSTEAD), N.Y. Six N.Y. Loyalists disarmed a guard and captured 2 officers.			2		
Nov. 6	WESTERN VA. American Gen. Lachlan McIntosh's expedition was harassed by Indians.	1				
Nov. 8	TRURO, MASS. Crew of HMS Somerset was captured by local militia after it ran aground.					
Nov. 11	CHERRY VALLEY, N.Y. Large force of Loyalists under Capt. Walter Butler and Indians under Chief Joseph Brant attacked the settlement, which was protected only by 7th Mass. regiment of 250. At least 32 civilians were killed, and some of the captured may have been civilians.	(7)		71		
Nov. 24	BULLTOWN SWAMP, GA. Mounted Ga. militia under Col. John Baker encountered enemy troops, probably marching north from Fla.		3			
	MIDWAY, GA. Continental troops and Ga. militia under Col. John White skirmished with a large force of British regulars, Fla. Rangers, and Indians under Maj. J. M. Prevost.	1				
Nov. 25	SUNBURY, GA. A second British force from St. Augustine under Lt. Col. Lewis V. Fuser raided the town, but failed to take Fort Morris, commanded by Col. John McIntosh. Fuser was not joined by Prevost (see above).					

DATE	ENGAGEMENT	AMERICAN LOSSES				
		K	W	C	M	D
Dec. 17	VINCENNES, IND. Setting out from Detroit with 162 British regulars and French militia, and 70 Indians, Lt. Gov. Henry Hamilton picked up more Indians as he approached Vincennes, where only Capt. Leonard Helm and 3 Virginians represented an American garrison. They surrendered.			4		
Dec. 20	POINT JUDITH, R.I. When a British transport ran aground, local militia captured 41 seamen and troops.					
Dec. 25	FOUR CORNERS, WESTCHESTER CO., N.Y. Joseph Youngs' house, containing several rebel soldiers, was raided by a Loyalist party under Maj. Baremore.			(5)		
Dec. 29	GLOUCESTER POINT, N.J. Three British ships on a foraging expedition were caught in the ice and burned by the rebels.					
	SAVANNAH, GA. British expeditionary force under Lt. Col. Archibald Campbell attacked and captured the town from Gen. Robert Howe's smaller force of regulars and Ga. militia. The British lost 7 K and 19 W.	83	11	453		
	TOTALS for the year 1778:	753	443	1212	139	20

DATE	ENGAGEMENT	AMERICAN LOSSES				
		K	W	C	M	D
Jan. 6 -10	SUNBURY, GA. Gen. Augustine Prevost led a new expedition of 900 British regulars and E. Fla. Rangers into Ga. and laid siege to Fort Morris, garrisoned by 223 men under Maj. Joseph Lane. After the British brought up their cannon, Lane surrendered.	4	7	212		
Jan. 13	BERGEN POINT, N.J. A detachment from the British 26th regiment captured 3 N.J. militia.			3		
Jan. 23	COSHOCTON, O. Delawares killed a soldier of the 13th Va. regiment.	1				
Jan. 26	MONMOUTH COUNTY, N.J. N.J. militia under Capt. Benjamin Dennis routed some of the enemy, probably Loyalists, and killed 3.					
Jan. 30	SPIRIT CREEK, NEAR AUGUSTA, GA. On his way up the Savannah River to capture Augusta, Lt. Col. Archibald Campbell was attacked by militia under Gen. Samuel Elbert, Col. John Twiggs, and Cols. William and Benjamin Few. The British suffered about 20 casualties, but occupied Augusta next day without further resistance.					
Late Jan.	FORT LAURENS (NEAR BOLIVAR), O. American Capt. John Clark with 15 men was attacked 3 miles from the fort by Mingoes under Simon Girty.	2	4	1		
Feb.	EDGEFIELD, S.C. Militia under Col. LeRoy Hammond defeated a party of Loyalists.					
	NEAR BROWNSBURG, GA. Capt. John Cooper with a dozen men captured some British troops.					
Feb. 2	WOODBRIDGE, N.J. Capt. Fitz-Randolph and 15 men were surprised in a house by Capt. Samuel Ryerson and Loyalist troops.	2		14		
Feb. 3	BEAUFORT, S.C. About 300 Charleston militia under Gen. William Moultrie were attacked by some 200 British light infantry under Maj. Gardiner. The British loss was heavy.	7	25			
Feb. 10 -11	CARR'S FORT, GA. Cols. Andrew Pickens and John Dooly with 350 men laid siege to a Loyalist force under Lt. Col. John Hamilton in the fort. The Loyalists lost 9 K and 3 W. Pickens broke off the siege to pursue Col. Boyd; see below.	5	7			
Feb. 12	CHEROKEE FORD, SAVANNAH RIVER, GA. Capt. Robert Anderson with about 80 S.C. Rangers tried to stop the advance of a large force of Loyalists under Col. Boyd.	(6)	(10)	16		
Feb. 14	KETTLE CREEK (NEAR WASHINGTON), GA. Cols. Andrew Pickens and John Dooly, joined by Col. Elijah Clarke, with their Ga. and S.C. militia caught up with the Loyalist force under Col. Boyd and surprised his camp. The enemy lost 75 K, including	9	20			

DATE	ENGAGEMENT	AMERICAN LOSSES				
		K	W	C	M	D
Feb. 14	KETTLE CREEK (NEAR WASHINGTON), GA. (cont.) Boyd, and 75 C.					
c. Feb. 15	HERBERT, GA. With some Ga. militia, Col. John Twiggs attacked a British detachment of about 70.					
Feb. 23	FORT LAURENS (NEAR BOLIVAR), O. A detachment of 19 men from the 13th Va. regiment under Col. John Gibson was attacked outside the fort.	17		2		
Feb. 23 -24	VINCENNES, IND. With some Va. militia and French volunteers, 170 altogether, Col. George Rogers Clark retook the town from Lt. Gov. Henry Hamilton and his garrison. The enemy had 7 W and all 80 captured; his Indian allies lost 2 K, 3 W, and 6 C.		1			
Feb. 24	ELIZABETHTOWN, N.J. Gen. William Maxwell was attacked by a British force of 2500 under Lt. Col. Thomas Stirling.	3	4	23		
Feb. 25	EAST CHESTER, N.Y. Capt. Titus Watson led about 30 Continental cavalry to reconnoitre a British position and was attacked.	1				
Feb. 26	HORSENECK (WEST GREENWICH), N.Y. Militia under Gen. Israel Putnam were driven out of town by a British and German force under Gen. William Tryon. The enemy lost about 38 C.		2	10		
End of Feb.	OUIATENON (NEAR LAFAYETTE), IND. Col. George Rogers Clark sent Capt. Leonard Helm and 50 men up the Wabash River to intercept British supplies from Detroit destined for Vincennes. Helm captured 40 British and French.					
Early Mar.	MUSKINGUM RIVER, O. Maj. Richard Taylor's detachment carrying provisions to Fort Laurens was fired on by Indians.	2				
Mar. 3	BRIAR CREEK AT SAVANNAH RIVER, GA. A large force of N.C. militia, perhaps 1600, and 100 Ga. Continentals, all under Gen. John Ashe, were surprised in camp by about 900 British regulars and Loyalists under Lt. Col. J.M. Prevost. The enemy suffered 6 K and 2 W in scattering the Americans.	150		227		
Mar. 8	OFF CAPE HENRY, VA. Three British ships ran a rebel sloop ashore and were fired on by Americans on land. HMS Richmond, Capt. Gudoin, returned the fire.					
Mar.28	CLOSTER, N.J. Lt. John Huyler led a militia detachment in a skirmish with a Loyalist company under Capt. David Peek. The enemy had 1 K and 2 W.					
	FORT LAURENS (NEAR BOLIVAR), O. Maj. Frederick Vernon lost an officer and soldier to Indians outside the fort.	2				

DATE	ENGAGEMENT	AMERICAN LOSSES				
		K	W	C	M	D
Apr. 2	BERGEN NECK, N.J. A detachment of the British 64th regiment at Paulus Hook encountered a dozen men from Col. Israel Shreve's 2nd N.J. regiment under Lt. James Paul.			13		
Apr. 3	FALMOUTH, MASS. Ten British ships fired on the town, but militia under Gen. James Otis prevented the enemy from landing.					
After Apr. 4	LOWER TANGIER ISLANDS, CHESAPEAKE BAY. Capt. Smoot's Md. militia routed out some Loyalists.					
Apr. 10	CHICKAMAUGA, TENN. Col. Evan Shelby led an expedition of several hundred American troops against the Cherokees and burned this main village.					
Apr. 12	LITTLE FERRY, BERGEN CO., N.J. A detachment of Loyalists under Capt. William Van Allen seized an American outpost.			11		
Before Apr. 15	NORTHEAST GA. American militia fought some Loyalists and Indians, killed several, and took prisoners.		3			
Apr. 17	WEEHAWKEN, N.J. An American militia patrol scattered a party of Loyalists, killing one.					
Apr. 19	WYOMING VALLEY, PA. An American detachment under Capt. Davis was ambushed by Indians.	7				
Apr. 20	HACKENSACK VALLEY, N.J. Capt. Samuel Ryerson with 44 N.J. Loyalists skirmished with a guard of Continentals and had 2 W.					
Apr. 21	ONONDAGA, N.Y. Col. Goose Van Schaick, commanding more than 500 troops, destroyed the Onondaga town of 50 houses, killed 17 warriors, and took 32 prisoners.					
	WAGARAW, N.J. A Loyalist raiding party killed a militia officer.	1				
Apr. 22	DE GROOT'S, ENGLISH NEIGHBORHOOD, N.J. Capt. Joshua Bowman of the N.C. brigade clashed with some British or Loyalist troops.		3			
Apr. 23	YAMASEE BLUFF, GA. Some S.C. militia under Lt. Col. John Henderson were surprised by a party of Loyalists and Indians, but ran them off.					
Apr. 25	OSWEGATCHIE (OGDENSBURG), N.Y. Col. Goose Van Schaick (see above) sent Lt. Thomas McClennan and 34 men to Oswegatchie, which they attempted to take but were driven off after killing 2 of the enemy.					
Apr. 26	FORT HAND, WESTMORELAND CO., PA. Capt. Samuel Morehead's garrison of 17 men was attacked by Indians.	1	2			
	SHREWSBURY, N.J. N.J. militia under Col. Asher Holmes were attacked by a British force under Capt. Patrick Ferguson which pursued them to Middletown.		2	20		

DATE	ENGAGEMENT	AMERICAN LOSSES				
		K	W	C	M	D
May	BASIN HARBOR, VT. A scouting party from Fort Mott in Pittsford under Lt. Ephraim Stevens was attacked by Indians.[1]	1		3		
May 3	COOSAWHATCHIE RIVER, S.C. Two S.C. regiments under Gen. William Moultrie and Lt. Col. John Laurens fought a British force under Gen. Augustine Prevost, and were forced to retreat.	3	8			
May 9	FORT NELSON, NORFOLK, VA. British ships landed troops who took Portsmouth while their cannon bombarded Fort Nelson, garrisoned by Va. militia under Maj. Thomas Matthews, into submission. The garrison fled.					
	CLOSTER, N.J. Capt. John Huyler's militia company retook some cattle from a Loyalist foraging expedition.	2	(5)	4		
May 11 -13	CHARLESTON NECK, S.C. Gen. Augustine Prevost (see above) marched on to Charleston, where he was finally checked by American Continentals and militia under Gens. William Moultrie and Casimir Pulaski. American losses were believed to total 42.	(13)	(17)	(12)		
May 12	SUFFOLK, VA. Col. Edward Riddick sent out a party of militia to spy on a British advance. The party was attacked.[2]	1		3		
May 15	MIDDLETOWN, N.J. Militia had a skirmish with some British troops.					
May 20	JOHN'S ISLAND, S.C. A detachment of Gen. Augustine Prevost's British force attacked some of Gen. William Moultrie's troops.	(5)				
May 21	SOUTH KINGSTON, R.I. A British landing party burned a house, plundered, and carried off 15 soldiers and inhabitants.			(5)		
May 23	PORTSMOUTH, VA. Seamen from HMS Rainbow, Capt. Collier, set fire to several American vessels on the stocks in the shipyard.					
Before May 26	MIDDLESEX, CONN. A Loyalist Capt. Glover led a raid on a house and was repulsed by militia who wounded most of his men.					
June	CHILLICOTHE, O. Col. John Bowman led 296 Ky. militia against a Shawnee town and killed Chiefs Blackfish and Red Hawk.					
June 1	FORT LAFAYETTE, VERPLANCK'S POINT, N.Y. A British squadron escorted transports up the Hudson and landed troops on both sides of the river. Gen. John Vaughan subdued Fort Lafayette and captured it, while across the river Stony Point was abandoned to Gen. Sir Henry Clinton's troops.			75		
June 4	MIDWAY, GA. Rebel Capt. Spencer surprised a group of enemy officers.					
June 8	BYRAM RIVER, N.Y.-CONN. Loyalists under Maj. Baremore attacked militia under Capt. David Leavenworth.	3	(5)	4		

1. Reported only in H. P. Smith and W. S. Rann, History of Rutland County, Vermont (Syracuse: Mason & Co., 1886), p. 734.

2. Reported only in R. D. Whichard, The History of Lower Tidewater Virginia (N.Y.: Lewis Historical Publishing Co., 1959), II, 161.

DATE	ENGAGEMENT	AMERICAN LOSSES				
		K	W	C	M	D
June 9	TINTON FALLS, N.J. A detachment of 50 Loyalists fell on a party of 30 militia and suffered 3 W.	2	10	(8)		
June 11	SHREWSBURY, N.J. Possibly the same Loyalists as above struck at a militia troop.	3	14	7		
c. June 15	BELOW FORT HAND, WESTMORELAND CO., PA. A band of 9 enemy Indians killed a soldier.	1				
June 17	BYRAM RIVER, N.Y.-CONN. A detachment of 32 Loyalists under Capt. Bonnel were foraging for cattle when they surprised the river guard, who made their escape but fired on the enemy for 2 hours.					
	PRIOR'S MILLS, NEAR PAULUS HOOK, N.J. This British post repulsed an attack by rebels.					
June 20	STONO FERRY, S.C. British 71st regiment and a German regiment under Lt. Col. John Maitland were attacked by Gen. Benjamin Lincoln at the head of 1200 troops. Gen. William Moultrie failed to support the attack, and the Americans had to withdraw. The enemy lost 26 K and 103 W. Maitland retreated southward.	34	113		18	
June 24	CROMPOND, N.Y. Some British regulars under Lt. Col. Banastre Tarleton attacked a detachment of militia under Col. Samuel Drake.	(5)	11	34		
June 26	NEAR OGEECHEE RIVER, GA. Col. John Twiggs and some Ga. militia attacked a larger number of British troops under Capt. Miller, killed 8, wounded 9, and captured 28.		2			
June 27	MIDWAY, GA. Ga. militia under Col. John Twiggs and Maj. John Baker defeated a party of British troops, killing several.					
June 28	WOODBRIDGE AND RAHWAY, N.J. A detachment of about 80 Loyalists and regulars of the 37th regiment raided these towns and fought militia and civilians. The enemy had 1 K.	1		2		
June 29	BYRAM RIVER AND SHERARD'S BRIDGE, CONN. About 30 German dragoons under Lt. Col. Andreas Emmerich and 30 Loyalists under Maj. Baremore attacked two groups of pickets.	5	(7)	12		
July	FORT LAURENS (NEAR BOLIVAR), O. Indians picked off 2 of the American garrison.	2				
	FORT McINTOSH (BEAVER), PA. Indians fired on the American garrison.	1	1			
July 2	BEDFORD AND POUND RIDGE, N.Y. Lt. Col. Banastre Tarleton led an expedition into Westchester Co. that attacked Col. Elisha Sheldon's dragoons and N.Y. militia. Tarleton said he inflicted 41 casualties.	(6)	(15)	(20)		

61

DATE	ENGAGEMENT	AMERICAN LOSSES				
		K	W	C	M	D
July 5 -6	NEW HAVEN, CONN. Gen. William Tryon and 2600 troops were transported to Conn. coast for raids on ports. Here he was repulsed by 4 regiments of Conn. militia under Gen. Andrew Ward. The British lost 12 K, 43 W, and 25 M.	23	15	12		
July 7	FAIRFIELD, CONN. Gen. William Tryon's task force was landed here, burned the town, and took a fort at Grover's Hill commanded by Lt. Isaac Jarvis. Col. Samuel Whiting commanded the defending militia.	9				
July 10	CLOSTER, N.J. A party of Loyalists under Lt. Walker had 2 men captured in a skirmish with militia under Capt. Haring.					
July 11	NORWALK, CONN. Gen. William Tryon's force was landed in 3 divisions and spread out from the town, which they burned. After hours of skirmishing against regulars and militia under Gen. Samuel H. Parsons, the British re-embarked.	4	7			
July 13	NEAR TIVERTON, R.I. A squad under Sgt. Simon Griffin tried to burn a Loyalist house, but was driven off by British sentinels on shore.					
July 16	LITTLE COMPTON, R.I. A Loyalist raid was aimed at some militia officers.	1		4		
	STONY POINT, N.Y. Gen. Anthony Wayne and 1200 troops using bayonets took the fort, garrisoned by about 600 British, who lost 63 K, 71 W, and 442 C.	15	85			
Before July 19	NEAR PURRYSBURG, S.C. A militia company under Capt. Smith was attacked by the enemy.			2		
July 19	MIRAMICHI BAY, N.B. Seamen from HMS Viper, Capt. Hervey, captured some Indians allied with the Americans.			15		
July 21	SAKONNET POINT, R.I. Some British landed here and seized a guard squad.	1		17		
July 22	MINISINK (GREENVILLE), N.Y. Indians and Loyalists under Chief Joseph Brant caught 150 militia under Col. John Hathorn in an ambush.	44				
July 23	BERGEN, N.J. A company of Loyalists under Capt. William Van Allen chased 3 Americans.			2		
July 26	PENOBSCOT BAY, ME. Mass. expedition of 2000 men under Gens. Solomon Lovell and Peleg Wadsworth was carried by ships under Cdre. Dudley Saltonstall to wipe out the British base under Col. Francis MacLean for cutting ship timbers. On this day the Americans landed under fire on Nautilus Island.	3				
July 28	PENOBSCOT BAY, ME. The American force landed on Bagaduce peninsula and stormed a British redoubt.	(20)	(30)			
July 29 -31	PENOBSCOT BAY, ME. Commodore Saltonstall's ships exchanged fire with the British fort and ships.		2			

DATE	ENGAGEMENT	AMERICAN LOSSES				
		K	W	C	M	D
Aug. 1	PENOBSCOT BAY, ME. American detachment under Gen. Peleg Wadsworth assaulted a British battery on the Bagaduce peninsula.	10		4		
	TIVERTON, R.I. The British ambushed a militia patrol.	1		4		
Aug. 2 -13	PENOBSCOT BAY, ME. The American force continued to bombard the British fort and ships, which replied. Some damage was done, but casualties on either side were few.	1	1	1		
Aug. 3	BUCKHEAD CREEK, GA. Col. John Twiggs and 150 Ga. militia had a skirmish with the British.					
Aug. 5	MORRISANIA, N.Y. American cavalry and infantry under Cols. Elisha Sheldon and Stephen Moylan were returning with prisoners from a raid on Loyalist quarters when they were engaged in a running fight by cavalry under Lt. Cols. John G. Simcoe and Andreas Emmerich.	2	2			
c. Aug. 9	AROUND TOMS RIVER, N.J. A party of Loyalists ambushed 2 militia officers.	2				
Aug. 13	SAVANNAH RIVER, S.C. A party of Loyalists and Indians crossed the river near Black Swamp and fell on Capt. Stafford's guard post, but most of the guards were out on patrol.	1	2			
	CHEMUNG, N.Y. Gen. John Sullivan's advance troops under Gen. Edward Hand first engaged the Indians they had set out to fight. Hand returned to Tioga (Athens), Pa.	7	11			
Aug. 14	PENOBSCOT BAY, ME. The British post was reinforced by a squadron under Capt. George Collier. Commodore Dudley Saltonstall re-embarked Gen. Solomon Lovell's troops, sailed up the Penobscot River, and landed the men, who ran into the wilderness. The U.S. ships were set on fire.					
	BRIAR CREEK, GA. Some Ga. militia under Col. John Twiggs and Va. cavalry under Lt. Col. John Jameson attacked 25 British troops under Maj. McGirt, killing 5 and capturing 9.		1			
Aug. 15	UPPER ALLEGHENY RIVER, PA. Advance detachment of 23 Americans under Lt. John Hardin attacked a superior force of Senecas and killed 5. This was the only resistance met by Col. Daniel Brodhead's expedition of 605 men against the Senecas, Aug. 11 to Sept. 14.		3			
Aug. 17	TIOGA (ATHENS), PA. Six soldiers of 11th Pa. regiment in search of horses were attacked by Indians.	1	1			
Aug. 19	PAULUS HOOK, N.J. Major Henry Lee with about 400 Va. and Md. troops surprised the enemy post under Maj. William Sutherland and Capt. Heinrich von Schaller, killing perhaps 50 and capturing 158.	4	3	7		
	LIBERTY POLE (ENGLEWOOD), N.J. Maj. Henry Lee's troops returning from Paulus Hook were held up briefly by 30 of Lt. Col. Abraham Van Buskirk's Loyalists. They were also harassed by			3		

| DATE | ENGAGEMENT | AMERICAN LOSSES | | | | |
		K	W	C	M	D
Aug. 19	LIBERTY POLE (ENGLEWOOD), N.J. (cont.) some British regulars under Col. Cosmo Gordon. PEEKSKILL, N.Y. British gunboats fired on a foraging party under Lt. Col. Rufus Putnam.					
Aug. 28	FOX ISLAND, PENOBSCOT BAY, ME. British marines landed from HMS Albany, Capt. Mowat, in search of Americans.			1		
Aug. 29	NEWTOWN, N.Y. Gen. John Sullivan's expedition was challenged here by 800 Indians and 200 Loyalists under Chief Joseph Brant and Maj. John Butler. At least 11 Indians were killed, and others wounded.	4	35			
Aug. 30	TARRYTOWN, N.Y. Lt. Col. Andreas Emmerich's German dragoons surprised an American guard.[1] ASH'S POINT, PORT ROYAL RIVER, S.C. Lt. John Hamilton surprised a British picket, killing 1 and capturing 4.	4		10		
Sep. 2	FORT GEORGE, LAKE GEORGE, N.Y. Col. Seth Warner's American garrison was attacked by Indians.			2		
Sep. 5	LLOYD'S NECK, LONG ISLAND, N.Y. Maj. Benjamin Tallmadge crossed the Sound with 130 cavalry and destroyed a fortified Loyalist post, capturing many of the garrison.					
Sep. 7	FORT BUTE, MANCHAC, LA. Spanish troops, Indians, and American militia under Gov. Bernardo de Gálvez captured the British post, killing 1 and capturing 20.					
Sep. 12	BAGADUCE RIVER, ME. A boat's crew from HMS Albany, Capt. Mowat, was captured by rebel scouts.					
Sep. 13	GENESEO, N.Y. Lt. Thomas Boyd and 23 men, detached from Gen. John Sullivan's expedition, were captured by Indians and killed.	24				
Sep. 14	SAVANNAH, GA. Gen. Casimir Pulaski and his cavalry on way to join Gen. Benjamin Lincoln's siege of Savannah cut off an advanced British picket. He killed and wounded 5, and captured 6.					
Sep. 21	BATON ROUGE, LA. British post under Col. Dickson surrendered after being shelled by combined Spanish, Indian, and American militia under Gov. Bernardo de Gálvez. Of the enemy, 4 were killed and 2 wounded.					
Sep. 22	SAVANNAH, GA. A French fleet and army of 4450 under Adm. Comte d'Estaing had arrived off Savannah on Sept. 1 and was joined by Gens. Lincoln and Pulaski with over 2100 men. They laid siege to the 2500 British regulars and Loyalists in the town under Gen. Augustine Prevost. On this day a French detachment					

1. Reported only in Robert Bolton, History of the County of Westchester (N.Y.: Alexander S. Gould, 1848), I, 230.

DATE	ENGAGEMENT	AMERICAN LOSSES				
		K	W	C	M	D
Sep. 22	SAVANNAH, GA. (cont.) of 50 under Col. Vicomte de Noailles attacked a British outpost and lost 6 K and several W.					
Sep. 24	SAVANNAH, GA. A British sortie against the French trenches cost the enemy 4 K and 15 W, but the French lost 70 K and W.					
Late Sep.	FALMOUTH, MASS. Local militia captured HMS Leslie, killed 1 sailor and captured 26.					
Oct. 4	SAVANNAH, GA. Bombardment of the town began from French artillery in siege lines.					
	OHIO RIVER AT MOUTH OF LITTLE MIAMI, O. Col. David Rogers commanding boats destined for New Orleans and a guard of about 50 men was ambushed by Indians under Simon Girty. Some civilians were along.	(35)		14		
Oct. 9	SAVANNAH, GA. Franco-American besieging forces launched an attack on the British fortification and were beaten off, with heavy losses. Gen. Pulaski was killed, and D'Estaing wounded. Ten days later the French withdrew and sailed away; Gen. Lincoln retreated to Charleston. Altogether during the siege the British lost 40 K, 62 W, and 48 D. Numerous French seamen died of scurvy, and others deserted; whether they are included in the French casualty count is uncertain. The most reliable figures seem to be 183 K and 454 W among the French. There is also great variation in the American count, but a total of 457 K and W seems authentic.	(125)	(332)			
Oct. 10	SANDY POINT, PENOBSCOT RIVER, ME. Local militia repulsed a party of British troops and Loyalists. The British lost 3 K and 7 W.					
Oct. 12	PENOBSCOT RIVER, ME. A canoe of 2 militia officers and 4 Indians was captured by a party of French Canadians and Indians.			6		
	AMBOY, N.J. A detachment under Capt. Davis from a state regiment had a skirmish with the British.					
Oct. 16	FORT MONTGOMERY, N.Y. British gunboats exchanged fire with Americans on the Hudson River bank.					
Oct. 24	NEAR BRUNSWICK, N.J. Lt. Col. John G. Simcoe and 100 Queen's Rangers on a raid were met by state militia under Capt. Peter Van Vorhees. The British lost 3 K, 6 C including Simcoe, and several wounded. Van Vorhees was killed after he was captured.	1		3		
Oct. 26	BRUNSWICK, N.J. About 70 of the Queen's Rangers under Capt. John Saunders skirmished with a party of militia under Capt. Isaac Morrison. The enemy had one killed. Saunders rejoined Maj. Richard Armstrong at Old Bridge; Armstrong had taken several prisoners.	2	1	(5)		

DATE	ENGAGEMENT	AMERICAN LOSSES				
		K	W	C	M	D
Oct. 27	FOX ISLAND, PENOBSCOT BAY, ME. Some crew members of HMS _Albany_, Capt. Mowat, were ashore when fired on by militia and 2 were killed.					
Nov 7	SOUTH OYSTER BAY, LONG ISLAND, N.Y. A raid by cavalry under Capt. Hawley aroused a troop of British cavalry in opposition.			6		
c. Dec.	MIDDLE MISSISSIPPI RIVER. Lt. Isaac Bowman set off from Kaskaskia with 7 or 8 men; his boat was taken by Chickasaws and most of the men were killed.	7				
Dec. 21	PAULUS HOOK, N.J. Shots were exchanged between a detachment from Gen. Anthony Wayne's brigade and the British garrison at the Hook.					
	TOTALS for the year 1779:	659	829	859	18	

DATE	ENGAGEMENT	AMERICAN LOSSES				
		K	W	C	M	D
Jan.	NEAR MT. VERNON, N.Y. Three militia who tried to recover stolen cattle were pursued by a body of enemy troops.			1		
Jan. 12	SANDY HOOK, N.J. A dozen of Maj. Henry Lee's light horse were caught in a house by the British.			7		
Jan. 15	NEAR SANDY HOOK, N.J. A company of Maj. Henry Lee's light horse under Capt. Patten captured the crews of 3 British ships.					
Jan. 18	NEW ROCHELLE, N.Y. After capturing 13 Loyalists, Capt. Daniel Lockwood and a detachment of 131 Conn. militia were pursued by Maj. Huggersford and engaged in a second battle.	23		40		
Jan. 21	WILLIAMS BRIDGE (NEAR WEST GREENWICH), N.Y. A detachment under Gen. Samuel H. Parsons was attacked by Loyalists under Lt. Col. James De Lancey, who lost 16 K, 32 W, and 17 C. No report was made on American casualties.					
Jan. 25	ELIZABETHTOWN, N.J. Lt. Col. Abraham Van Buskirk and his 4th N.J. Loyalists surprised an American garrison with little gun fire.			52		
	NEWARK, N.J. Maj. Charles Lumm with companies of the British 44th regiment and some German units surprised the American post, but lost 5 C.	8		15		
Jan. 30	NEAR ELIZABETHTOWN, N.J. Lt. Wynantz and 8 privates of the N.J. militia were taken in a skirmish with 30 mounted Loyalists.			9		
Late Jan.	HENRY'S POINT, VA. Col. John Cropper and Va. militia fired on a British barge which was on a plundering expedition.[1]					
c. Feb. 1	NEAR WOODBRIDGE, N.J. Lt. Col. John G. Simcoe and 200 Queen's Rangers were checked by American patrols and lost a trooper; they turned back toward the ferry to Staten Island where they were fired on by the Americans and suffered a few wounded.		(6)			
Feb. 3	FOUR CORNERS, WESTCHESTER CO., N.Y. Lt. Col. Joseph Thompson and 250 of the 10th Mass. regiment were attacked by 600 British, Germans, and Loyalists under Col. Norton.	13	18	96		
Feb. 22	STONO, S.C. Some militia cavalry under Maj. Hezekiah Maham seized a Lt. McDonald and 8 privates without loss.					
Feb. 26	JAMES ISLAND, S.C. USS _Ranger_ and _Providence_ fired on British troops who had entered the ruined Fort Johnson.					
Feb. 28	JAMES ISLAND, S.C. USS _Ranger_ and _Boston_ exchanged fire with the British who were digging trenches at Fort Johnson.					

1. Reported only in R. A. Stewart, The History of Virginia's Navy of the Revolution (Richmond: Mitchell and Hotchkiss, 1934), pp. 64-67.

DATE	ENGAGEMENT	AMERICAN LOSSES				
		K	W	C	M	D
Feb. 29	MOBILE BAY, ALA. The British garrison in Fort Charlotte held off an attack by Spanish, Indians, and Americans under Gov. Bernardo de Gálvez.					
Mar. 2	FORT JOHNSON, JAMES ISLAND, S.C. U.S. galleys fired on the British in the fort.					
Mar. 8	BOONESBOROUGH, KY. Indians attacked two officers outside the fort.	2				
Mar.10	FORT CHARLOTTE, MOBILE, ALA. Gov. Bernardo de Gálvez led a mixed troop of 300 in erecting a battery near the British fort and was fired on.	6	5			
Mar.11	MOUTH OF WAPPOO CREEK, S.C. USS Notre Dame exchanged fire with the British on land.					
Mar.12	FORT CHARLOTTE, MOBILE, ALA. Gov. Bernardo de Gálvez, reinforced by more militia and free Negroes and the USS West Florida, Capt. Pickles, fired all day on the fort, killing 3 and wounding 9. Lt. Gov. Elias Durnford surrendered his garrison of 300 next day.	8	12			
c. Mar.17	TENSA REGION, ALA. Some of Gov. Bernardo de Gálvez' force surprised and captured a company of West Fla. Royal Foresters under Capt. Patrick Strachan.					
Mar.18	SALKEHATCHIE BRIDGE, S.C. Lt. Col. Banastre Tarleton's Legion surprised a detachment of 80 militia.	17	4	29		
Mar.20	NEAR CHARLESTON, S.C. Some militia cavalry under Capt. William Sanders surprised a party of Loyalists, killed 2, and captured 1.					
	OGEECHEE RIVER, GA. Col. Andrew Pickens with 300 men had a skirmish with Loyalists under Col. Daniel McGirth.					
Mar.21	FORT JOHNSON, JAMES ISLAND, S.C. USS Ranger, Capt. Simpson, exchanged fire with the British fort as he sailed up to Charleston.					
c. Mar.22	SKENESBOROUGH, N.Y. A party of 100 Indians and 3 Loyalists attacked some militia and civilians.	2		10		
Mar.23	PARAMUS, N.J. British detachments of 600 men under Lt. Cols. John Howard and Duncan McPherson attacked about 250 of the 5th Pa. regiment under Maj. Christopher Stuart. The enemy lost 10 K, 30 M, and over 18 W.		2	65		
	PONPON, S.C. Lt. Col. Banastre Tarleton's Legion fell on a party of mounted militia.	3	1	4		
Mar.26	NEAR RANTOWLE'S BRIDGE, STONO RIVER, S.C. Col. William					

| DATE | ENGAGEMENT | AMERICAN LOSSES | | | | |
		K	W	C	M	D
Mar. 26	NEAR RANTOWLE'S BRIDGE, STONO RIVER, S.C. (cont.) Washington's cavalry repulsed Lt. Col. Banastre Tarleton's Legion, taking 8 prisoners.					
Mar. 28	LIBERTY COUNTY, GA. A party of militia routed some Loyalists and Indians, killing 10.					
Mar. 30	SHREWSBURY, N.J. A Loyalist plundering party had 1 killed in a raid on the town.			9		
Apr. 4	CHARLESTON, S.C. USS Ranger, Capt. Simpson, ran up Town Creek and fired on the British camp outside the city. Enemy guns forced her back.					
	OGEECHEE RIVER FERRY, GA. Col. Andrew Pickens' militia had a skirmish with a British detachment under Capt. Conklin, killing 3 and wounding 5.					
Apr. 7	HARPERSFIELD, N.Y. Party of 19 Indians and Loyalists under Chief Joseph Brant struck a settlement guarded by Capt. Harper's company.	3		10		
	SACANDAGA BLOCKHOUSE, N.Y. After 7 Indians had approached the rebel-held blockhouse, they were pursued and 5 of of them killed.					
Apr. 8	SULLIVAN'S ISLAND, CHARLESTON HARBOR, S.C. A squadron of 11 British ships in passing the island exchanged fire with Fort Moultrie, 27 seamen being killed or wounded.					
Apr. 12	SULLIVAN'S ISLAND, CHARLESTON HARBOR, S.C. Three British sloops exchanged fire with Fort Moultrie as they passed up the Ashley River.					
Apr. 13	CHARLESTON, S.C. The British opened their siege by cannonading the city.					
Apr. 14	MONCK'S CORNER, S.C. Gen. Isaac Huger's camp of cavalry and militia was surprised before dawn by a British striking force under Lt. Col. Banastre Tarleton and Capt. Patrick Ferguson. The British had only 3 wounded.	14	19	64		
Apr. 16	NEW BRIDGE, N.J. An enemy force of 300 German infantrymen and over 100 cavalry under Col. Johann Du Puy struck an American outpost held by a captain and 30 men and killed or took most of them.	(5)		(20)		
	HOPPERTOWN, N.J. The same enemy force under Col. Johann Du Puy marched on and attacked about 270 of the 3rd Pa. regiment under Maj. Thomas L. Byles.	4	6	40		
Apr. 20	CHARLESTON, S.C. American batteries fired on 4 British ships that moved to Fort Johnson.					

69

DATE	ENGAGEMENT	AMERICAN LOSSES				
		K	W	C	M	D
Apr. 23	CHARLESTON, S.C. American battery on Mt. Pleasant exchanged fire with HMS Sandwich.					
Apr. 24	CHARLESTON, S.C. Lt. Col. William Henderson led a sortie of 320 men against a British trench, killed several of the enemy and brought in 12 prisoners.	1	3			
	SHREWSBURY, N.J. Loyalists attacked some militia and withdrew.	2				
Apr. 25	SULLIVAN'S ISLAND, CHARLESTON HARBOR, S.C. HMS Germain exchanged fire with Fort Moultrie as she passed.					
Apr. 28	HADDREL'S POINT, CHARLESTON HARBOR, S.C. Col. F. M. de Malmedy and a party were surprised and taken prisoner.			(10)		
Apr. 30	SHREWSBURY, N.J. A party of Loyalists and Negroes attacked both civilians and militia.			2		
May 6	LENUD'S FERRY, SANTEE RIVER, S.C. Lt. Col. Banastre Tarleton and 150 cavalry surprised a body of cavalry under Col. Anthony White. Tarleton lost only 2 men.	11	30	67		
May 12	CHARLESTON, S.C. Gen. Benjamin Lincoln surrendered the town and forts to Gen. Sir Henry Clinton after a siege of one month. British losses were 76 K and 189 W. The Americans captured were 2571 Continentals, including the wounded, and about 800 militia and armed citizens.	89	138	3371		20
May 14	TOMS RIVER, N.J. Militia Maj. John Van Emburgh and 8 or 9 men were captured by some Loyalists, but escaped next day.					
May 15	SANDY HOOK, N.J. HMS Swift, Capt. Aplin, sent armed boats to shore, but they were fired on by the Americans.					
May 22	CAUGHNAWAGA, N.Y. Sir John Johnson led a force of 400 Loyalists and British regulars plus 200 Indians on a sweep through the area burning and stealing and capturing various civilians.	(5)	2	(5)		
May 26	NEWARK, N.J. A detachment from the British 57th regiment raided the neighborhood and captured 20 civilians.		2			
	CAHOKIA, ILL. British Lt. Gov. Patrick Sinclair of Fort Michilimackinac conducted a raid on the Spanish and French of St. Louis. When he turned on Cahokia, Col. George Rogers Clark repulsed him.	4	5			
May 28	NEAR BULL'S FERRY, N.J. Fifty militia under Capts. John Huyler and Thomas Blanch failed to attack strong Loyalist post, but later fell on 6 Loyalists, killing 2 and taking 2.		1			
May 29	WAXHAWS, S.C. Col. Abraham Buford with 380 Continental	113	150	53		

DATE	ENGAGEMENT	AMERICAN LOSSES				
		K	W	C	M	D
May 29	WAXHAWS, S.C. (cont.) infantry and a troop of horse were attacked by Lt. Col. Banastre Tarleton's Legion of 270, which showed astonishing cruelty. The British had 5 K and 12 W. MOBLEY'S MEETING HOUSE, NEAR WINNSBORO, S.C. A party of Loyalists was dispersed by militia under Col. William Bratton.					
June 7	CONNECTICUT FARMS (UNION), N.J. When Gen. Wilhelm von Knyphausen took 5000 men from Staten Island to Elizabethtown Point, his expedition advanced toward Springfield as far as Connecticut Farms, where it met solid resistance from N.J. regulars and militia under Col. Elias Dayton and Continentals under Gen. Lafayette. The Germans were stopped and dug in for 2 days. They burned 30 buildings before retiring to their landing place. GERMAN FLATS, N.Y. Militia from Fort Herkimer drove off a party of Indian raiders.	15	40			
June 8	CLOSTER, N.J. Local militia under Capts. John Huyler and Thomas Blanch drove off a raiding party of Loyalists, killing 1 and wounding several.					
June 9	COLT'S NECK, N.J. A party of black and white Loyalists under Ty, a Negro, was driven off by militia under Capt. Joshua Huddy which killed 6 and wounded several.		1			
June 10	CLOSTER, N.J. A raiding party of 30 British, landed from HMS Vulture, Capt. Sutherland, was pursued by militia under Capt. Thomas Blanch who captured 12.					
June 15	NEAR DELAWARE RIVER, N.Y. Lt. Ephraim Vroman and a militia unit pursued some Indians who had a white captive and caught up with them near the upper river. NEAR ELIZABETHTOWN, N.J. A small detachment from Gen. Knyphausen's force (see above) was caught outside the lines, with 1 K and 5 C.		1			
June 16	BASIC CREEK, N.Y. The Albany Guards attacked some enemy Indians and killed 6. NEAR SCOTCH PLAINS, N.J. An enemy foraging party was attacked by militia under Lt. Joseph Catterline, who killed 1 and captured 3.					
June 19	GREENWICH, CONN. A Loyalist foraging party was chased off by some cavalry under Nathan Frink.			2		
June 20	RAMSOUR'S MILL (NEAR LINCOLNTON), N.C. Col. Francis Locke with 350 N.C. militia attacked 700 N.C. Loyalists under Lt. Col. John Moore. The losses on both sides were about equal.	(70)	(100)			

DATE	ENGAGEMENT	AMERICAN LOSSES				
		K	W	C	M	D
June 21	CONASCUNG, N.J. About 60 black and white Loyalists and 36 Queen's Rangers clashed with the militia. The enemy lost 3 W and several C.					
	PENOBSCOT RIVER, ME. Capt. John Blunt with 45 men in 5 whale boats captured a British schooner and a privateer. The enemy had 1 K and 1 W.					
June 22	RUDDLE'S STATION, BOURBON CO., KY. Capt. Henry Bird of Detroit took 150 regulars and militia and about 1000 Indians to invade Kentucky. After they fired their cannon at the fort, Capt. Ruddle surrendered on promise of protection to prisoners. Bird moved on 5 miles to take Martin's Station June 28 without resistance. The enemy lost one officer killed and one Indian wounded. At least 350 prisoners were taken, but most were women and children.	1		(75)		
June 23	SPRINGFIELD, N.J. Gen. Wilhelm von Knyphausen (see June 7) advanced to Springfield bridge, but could not get around Gen. Nathanael Greene's Continentals and N.J. militia, so after burning 46 houses he withdrew.	15	49		9	
July 1	GEORGETOWN, S.C. British Capt. John B. Ardesoif sailed into harbor and captured the town and ships there.					
	NEAR GREENWICH, CONN. Some Conn. militia under Lt. Col. Bezaleel Beebe engaged about 200 mounted Loyalists and drove them off with casualties.	1	2			
July 12	CAMP, FIVE MILES FROM UNION COURT HOUSE, S.C. Capt. Thomas Brandon and about 70 S.C. militia were attacked in camp by Loyalists and routed.					
	LOWER NORTH CAROLINA. Capt. Thomas Neal led 80 to 90 militia in a surprise attack on 130 Loyalists under Col. Ferguson, killing 14 and capturing 30.		1			
	WILLIAMSON'S PLANTATION, YORK CO., S.C. Col. William Bratton led about 250 militia against Capt. Christian Huck's camp of 115 British Legion and Loyalists, killing Huck and 35 others, and capturing 29.	1	1			
July 13	CEDAR SPRINGS, SPARTANBURG CO., S.C. Col. Elijah Clarke led 168 Ga. militia against about 200 mounted Loyalists and British cavalry and killed possibly 35.	4	23			
July 14	GOWEN'S OLD FORT, GREENVILLE CO., S.C. With about 35 Ga. militia, Col. John Jones led an attack on a party of 40 Loyalists, killing 1, wounding 3, and capturing most of the remainder.					
July 15	McDOWELL'S CAMP, PACOLET RIVER, S.C. Loyalist Col. Ambrose Mills of N.C. with about 300 men surprised the militia	(10)	(20)			

DATE	ENGAGEMENT	AMERICAN LOSSES				
		K	W	C	M	D
July 15	McDOWELL'S CAMP, PACOLET RIVER, S.C. (cont.) force of Cols. Charles McDowell and John Jones. As he withdrew he was pursued by 52 men under Capt. Edward Hampton, who killed 8 of the Loyalists.					
July 16	TANGIER ISLAND, CHESAPEAKE BAY. Capt. William Thompson and a Loyalist crew boarded a Del. ship, but were repulsed by Capt. Allen McLane's militia, with 2 K, 4 W, and 4 C.					
July 17	NEWARK, N.J. A small party of Loyalists under Lt. Ebenezer Ward seized 4 Americans.			4		
July 20	FLAT ROCK, KERSHAW CO., S.C. Col. William Davie with N.C. and S.C. militia and some Catawbas defeated some Loyalists under Maj. John Carden.	1	3			
July 21	COLSON'S MILL (3 MILES EAST OF NORWOOD), N.C. Lt. Col. William L. Davidson led about 160 militia against a larger force of Loyalists under Col. Samuel Bryan and inflicted about 45 casualties.		3			
	BULL'S FERRY (NORTH OF HOBOKEN), N.J. Gen. Anthony Wayne led a large force against a British blockhouse in a reckless manner and after inflicting 21 casualties failed to take it.	15	49			
July 22	COMPO (NEAR WESTPORT), CONN. Some Loyalists from Long Island on a foraging expedition also captured a guard of 7 men.			7		
July 27	FORT SCHUYLER (UTICA), N.Y. British, Germans, Loyalists and Indians to the number of 800 approached the fort but were driven off by cannon fired by the garrison under Lt. Col. John Graham.					
July 30	THICKETTY FORT, SPARTANBURG CO., S.C. Ga. and S.C. militia under Col. Charles McDowell captured the Loyalist garrison of 93 under Col. Patrick Moore.					
Summer	OUTSIDE BOONE'S STATION, FAYETTE CO., KY. American Capt. James Welch's scouting party was surprised by Indians on its return.	1				
Aug. 1	ROCKY MOUNT (NEAR GREAT FALLS), S.C. Gen. Thomas Sumter led militia against the Loyalist fort under Lt. Col. George Turnbull, who repulsed them with similar losses to Sumter.	6	8			
	HUNT'S BLUFF, DARLINGTON CO., S.C. Some militia under Gillespie attacked a force of Loyalists under Col. Ambrose Mills and captured many of them.[1]					

1. Reported only in Edward McCrady, History of South Carolina in the Revolution (N. Y.: Macmillan, 1901-2), I, 646.

DATE	ENGAGEMENT	AMERICAN LOSSES				
		K	W	C	M	D
c. Aug. 5	ENGLISH NEIGHBORHOOD, N.J. A party of militia engaged some British cavalry and killed 1 rider and captured 4.					
Aug. 6	HANGING ROCK (NEAR HEATH SPRINGS), S.C. Gen. Thomas Sumter led 800 N.C. and S.C. militia against 500 Loyalists in camp under Maj. John Carden. The stubborn four-hour battle resulted in 200 enemy casualties and dispersal of the rest.	12	41			
c. Aug. 6	OHIO RIVER, OPPOSITE MOUTH OF KENTUCKY RIVER. American Capt. Hugh McGary's company was looking for Clark's expedition (see below) when attacked by Shawnees.	(3)	(6)			
Aug. 8	PIQUA, O. Gen. George Rogers Clark led an expedition of 1000 against the Shawnee town, 5 miles west of modern Springfield, and destroyed it, inflicting probably 70 casualties.	14	13			
	CEDAR SPRINGS, ON PACOLET RIVER, SPARTANBURG CO., S.C. S.C. and Ga. militia under Cols. Isaac Shelby and Elijah Clarke attacked a body of Loyalists under Col. Ferguson at Wofford's Iron Works.	4	23			
Aug. 15	WATEREE RIVER FERRY, BELOW CAMDEN, S.C. Gen. Thomas Sumter sent a detachment under Col. Thomas Taylor to take a redoubt being erected by Col. Matthew Carey. Taylor killed 7 and captured 30 along with supplies.					
Aug. 16	CAMDEN, S.C. Gen. Horatio Gates moved his 3050 troops toward Camden and met Gen. Lord Cornwallis' 2100 British and Loyalists north of town. The British suffered 324 casualties but routed Gates' force so thoroughly that only 700 reached N.C. in flight. American casualties totaled about 1050, amid conflicting reports; the wounded were captured. Gen. Johann Kalb was mortally wounded.	(250)	(800)			
Aug. 18	FISHING CREEK (5 MILES NORTH OF GREAT FALLS), S.C. Loaded with booty and 100 prisoners, Gen. Thomas Sumter's force of 700 was surprised in camp by Lt. Col. Banastre Tarleton's 160 cavalry and infantry and put to rout.	(50)	(100)	310		
	MUSGROVE'S MILL (NEAR CROSS ANCHOR), S.C. Cols. Elijah Clarke, Isaac Shelby, and James Williams led about 200 Ga. and S.C. militia against 500 Loyalists and British regulars under Col. Alexander Innes and severely defeated them, killing and wounding 150 and capturing 70.	4	7			
Aug. 20	GREAT SAVANNAH (ABOVE NELSON'S FERRY, SANTEE RIVER), S.C. Col. Francis Marion captured a British escort of about 25 under Capt. Jonathan Roberts and released 150 American prisoners.	1	1			
Aug. 27	KINGSTREE, S.C. Maj. John James tried to stop a British force under Maj. James Wemyss and inflicted as many casualties as he received: 30.	(5)	(15)	(10)		
Aug. 29	MIDDLESEX, CONN. Loyalists from Long Island were opposed by a militia guard.	1	2			

DATE	ENGAGEMENT	AMERICAN LOSSES				
		K	W	C	M	D
Aug. 31	CHESAPEAKE BAY. Some Md. militia under Col. William Haddaway seized 2 Loyalists in a boat who were part of a raiding party.					
Sep. 4	LITTLE PEE DEE RIVER, S.C. Col. Francis Marion with 52 men surprised a camp of Loyalists under Maj. Micajah Ganey. He first met an advance of 45 men and inflicted 30 casualties; then he hit the main body of about 200 and put them to flight in a swamp.		4			
c. Sep. 9	ANSON CO., N.C. Col. Abel Kolb led 80 to 100 S.C. militia against some Loyalists in two locations, killing 3, and wounding more than 5.		2			
Sep. 10	MASK'S FERRY, PEE DEE RIVER, N.C. Capt. Herrick led some light horse against a party of Loyalists, killed some of them, and took 11 prisoners.					
Sep. 11	NEAR GNADENHUTTEN (NEAR NAZARETH), PA. Lt. Moyer's militia party of 41 was attacked by Indians and Loyalists.	4	19			
Sep. 14 -18	AUGUSTA, GA. Col. Elijah Clarke with 350 Ga. militia and Lt. Col. James McCall with 80 S.C. militia forced the Loyalists under Col. Thomas Brown to withdraw from Augusta to a nearby trading post called the White House. Clarke kept Loyalists and Indians bottled up under fire until a relief column forced him to withdraw. Of the 29 captured, 13 were hanged in the house. Twenty Indians were killed.	(30)		29		
Sep. 21	WAHAB'S PLANTATION, CATAWBA RIVER, N.C. Col. William Davie with less than 100 riflemen attacked Lt. Col. Banastre Tarleton's camp and inflicted about 60 casualties: 12 K, 47 W, and 1 C.		1			
Sep. 26	CHARLOTTE, N.C. Col. William Davie was in the town when Gen. Lord Cornwallis approached. He held off the advance troops, but finally had to withdraw, after inflicting 22 casualties.	(8)	(10)	(12)		
Sep. 28	SHEPHERD'S FERRY, BLACK MINGO CREEK, S.C. Col. Francis Marion surprised Col. John C. Ball's Loyalist camp of 46 men, killing 3, wounding 1, and capturing 13.	2	8			
Oct. 3	NEAR CHARLOTTE, N.C. Capt. William Thompson and a small force of militia drove off from Bradley's plantation a British foraging party, inflicting 20 casualties.					
Oct. 6	BROWN'S FERRY, PASSAIC RIVER, N.J. Some Continental troops in boats were attacked by Loyalists under Capt. Frederick Hauser.	1	2	4		

DATE	ENGAGEMENT	AMERICAN LOSSES				
		K	W	C	M	D
Oct. 7	KING'S MOUNTAIN, S.C. About 1550 militia from N.C. and Tenn. under 7 colonels--Sevier, Shelby, Campbell, Cleveland, Williams, Graham, McDowell--swarmed up the mountain to annihilate more than 1000 Loyalists under Maj. Patrick Ferguson. The latter was killed along with about 150 others, about 160 were wounded and taken, and another 700 were captured.	28	62			
	CHARLOTTE, N.C. A militia detachment under Capts. Rutledge and Joseph Dickson attacked and captured some Loyalists around the town.	1	1			
	BERGEN POINT, N.J. Capt. Thomas Ward's Loyalist post was attacked by militia and about 30 of the enemy were captured.					
c. Oct. 8	NEAR FORT SCHUYLER (UTICA), N.Y. Col. William Malcolm with troops on their way to relieve Fort Schuyler charged and routed a party of enemy Indians, killing 2.					
Oct. 10	FORT ANNE, N.Y. Capt. Seth Sherwood surrendered his garrison after being surrounded by 778 British, Loyalist, and Indian troops under Maj. Christopher Carleton.			75		
Oct. 11	FORT GEORGE, LAKE GEORGE, N.Y. Capt. John Chipman surrendered his garrison after being attacked by Maj. Christopher Carleton's force (see above).			(40)		
Oct. 14	SHALLOW FORD, YADKIN RIVER, N.C. Loyalists moving toward the Moravian settlement were attacked by Maj. Joseph Cloyd's Va. and N.C. militia, who killed 15 and wounded 4.		5			
Oct. 16	MIDDLE FORT, MIDDLEBURG, N.Y. Sir John Johnson's large force of British, Loyalists, and German troops burned the town, but after firing on the fort, garrisoned by 200 militia under Maj. Melancthon Woolsey, finally withdrew. Many civilians were killed.	2	1			
	BALLSTON, N.Y. A detachment of British, Loyalists, and Indians under Maj. John Munro attacked some militia.	1	1	22		
Oct. 17	LOWER FORT, SCHOHARIE, N.Y. Although Sir John Johnson (see above) burned the settlement, the fort held out against him. The enemy lost 5 K and 2 C.					
	RANDOLPH, VT. Col. John House and N.H. militia failed to stop a raiding party of 300 Indians and 20 Loyalists who had burned Royalton the day before and were retreating with civilian prisoners.					
Oct. 19	STONE ARABIA, N.Y. On orders from Gen. Robert Van Rensselaer, Col. John Brown with about 130 men advanced to meet Sir John Johnson's superior force and was defeated.	40		2		
	KLOCK'S FIELD (NEAR ST. JOHNSVILLE), N.Y. Gen. Robert Van Rensselaer with nearly 1500 militia caught up with Sir John Johnson's force of British, Loyalists, and Indians and defeated them. Casualties were not reported.					

| DATE | ENGAGEMENT | AMERICAN LOSSES | | | | |
		K	W	C	M	D
Oct. 22	KANADESAGA (GENEVA), N.Y. A detachment of 60 militia under Capt. Walter Vrooman, from Gen. Van Rensselaer's force, was attacked and surrounded by Sir John Johnson's invaders.	4		56		
Oct. 25	TEARCOAT SWAMP, BLACK RIVER, S.C. With 150 men Col. Francis Marion routed some Loyalists under Col. Samuel Tynes, killed 3, wounded 14, and captured 23.					
Early Nov.	MOBILE, ALA. The Spanish post was attacked by Indians and Loyalists, and at least 4 Spaniards were killed before the enemy was driven off.					
Nov. 3	GREAT SWAMP, BLADEN CO., N.C. Col. John Senf dispatched about 90 men to skirmish with some enemy, probably Loyalists. Two were killed and several wounded.		1			
Nov. 5	NEAR MIAMITOWN (FORT WAYNE), IND. Col. Augustin de la Balme leading over 100 French militia from Illinois allied with the Americans was defeated by Miami Indians under Chief Little Turtle and others.	(15)		1		
Nov. 8	BENONI'S POINT, CHOPTANK RIVER, MD. Militia under Maj. Jeremiah Banning fought off the landing of a Loyalist raiding party.					
Nov. 9	FISHDAM FORD, CHESTER CO., S.C. Gen. Thomas Sumter and over 500 militia were attacked by half that number of British under Maj. James Wemyss, but drove them off after killing 4 and wounding 20.	4	10			
Nov. 15	ALSTON'S PLANTATION, NEAR GEORGETOWN, S.C. Col. Francis Marion's camp was attacked by Loyalists but drove them off, killing 3 and capturing 12.	2	3			
Nov. 20	BLACKSTOCK'S PLANTATION, UNION CO., S.C. Gen. Thomas Sumter's force of over 400 militia was attacked by Lt. Col. Banastre Tarleton's 300 cavalry and mounted infantry. The Americans inflicted heavy losses: possibly 92 K and 75 W.	3	4			
Nov. 21	NEAR NEWARK, N.J. About 100 Loyalists under Capt. Thomas Ward clashed with a militia force under Col. Philip Van Cortlandt. The enemy had 7 casualties.	3	7			
Nov. 23	FORT ST. GEORGE, LONG ISLAND, N.Y. Maj. Benjamin Tallmadge led 60 men across the Sound, dismantled the fort, burned forage, and captured 46.		1			
Dec. 4	RUGELEY'S MILLS, CLERMONT, S.C. Lt. Col. William Washington with his dragoons fired on about 110 Loyalists gathered in a fortified barn under Col. Henry Rugeley. He					

DATE	ENGAGEMENT	AMERICAN LOSSES				
		K	W	C	M	D
Dec. 4	RUGELEY'S MILLS, CLERMONT, S.C. (cont.) tricked them into surrendering. No casualties apparently.					
Dec. 5	LE PETIT FORT (NEAR TREMONT), IND. After raiding Fort St. Joseph for furs, a band from Illinois under halfbreed Jean B. Hamelin was pursued by some British-allied Indians under Lt. Du Quindre who defeated the invaders.	4	2	7		
Dec. 9	COMPO HARBOR, CONN. A landing party from HMS Beaver was driven back by local militia.					
	HORSENECK, CONN. A detachment of British cavalry surprised Col. Levi Wells' militia guard and captured most of them.		3	26		
Dec. 11	LONG CANE CREEK, ABBEVILLE CO., S.C. Col. Elijah Clarke with Ga. and S.C. militia clashed with Loyalists under Col. Allen.	14	7			
Dec. 12 -13	SANTEE RIVER AND SINGLETON'S MILLS, S.C. Col. Francis Marion with 700 men forced Maj. Robert McLeroth's force of 200 into a swamp, then pursued the enemy to the mills, inflicting only 6 casualties.		(6)			
c. Dec. 15	NEAR NINETY-SIX, S.C. Col. William Few and his Ga. militia clashed with the enemy and suffered some casualties.		(10)			
Dec. 16	BOYD'S CREEK, TENN. Col. John Sevier led 300 militia against the Cherokees and killed 28. He was joined on Dec. 22 by Col. Arthur Campbell with Va. and N.C. militia.		3			
Dec. 25	CHILHOWEE, TENN. In the continuing campaign against the Cherokees, Capt. Crabtree with 60 militia burned this town, was attacked by a superior force of Cherokees, and retreated safely.					
Dec. 28	NEAR GEORGETOWN, S.C. Col. Peter Horry led 32 cavalry against some Queen's Rangers, who retreated into town; Maj. Micajah Ganey's mounted Loyalists rode out to meet Horry, but were routed and Ganey wounded.					
	TELLICO RIVER, TENN. Maj. Martin's militia patrol attacked a party of Indians and killed 3.	1				
	HAMMOND'S STORE, ABBEVILLE CO., S.C. Lt. Col. William Washington with his own cavalry and mounted militia, amounting to 275, attacked about 250 Loyalists and dispersed them after inflicting heavy casualties and capturing 40.					
Dec. 30	WILLIAMSON'S PLANTATION, NEWBERRY CO., S.C. Cornet James Simons leading 35 men had a skirmish with a much larger Loyalist force under Gen. Robert Cunningham and drove them off.					
	TOTALS for the year 1780:	984	1886	4661	9	20

DATE	ENGAGEMENT	AMERICAN LOSSES				
		K	W	C	M	D
Jan. 5	RICHMOND HILL, VA. Gen. Benedict Arnold sent Simcoe's Queen's Rangers to the capital, where they drove off 200 Va. militia and burned part of the town.					
	JAMES RIVER, VA. Shots were exchanged between HMS Swift, Capt. Graves, and militia on Hood's farm. A landing party spiked the American cannon.					
Jan. 7	MOBILE, ALA. British, Germans, and Loyalists under Col. von Hanxleden suffered 38 casualties in an unsuccessful attack on the Spanish post. Of the defenders, 14 were killed and 23 wounded.					
Jan. 8	CHARLES CITY COURT HOUSE, VA. Gen. Benedict Arnold sent Simcoe's Queen's Rangers into the town that was guarded only by 150 militia under Col. Dudley. The British had 1 K and 3 W.	2	3	(8)		
Jan. 10	BLAND'S MILLS, VA. The Queen's Rangers, with British troops, attacked a force of Va. militia in a wooded camp and lost about 20 K and W.					
c. Jan. 11	AMBOY, N.J. A small party of militia under Ens. Fitz-Randolph was surprised by a British detachment.			(10)		
Jan. 12	FREELAND'S STATION (NASHVILLE), TENN. A war party of Chickasaws attacked the American post, defended by 11 men under Col. James Robertson. One Indian was killed.	2				
c. Jan. 13	WACCAMAW NECK (ABOVE GEORGETOWN), S.C. On a foraging expedition with 40 horsemen, Col. Peter Horry was surprised by Lt. Col. George Campbell with 65 Queen's Rangers, who lost 3 K and 2 C.		1			
Jan. 15	PAGAN CREEK (NEAR SMITHFIELD), VA. The Queen's Rangers under Lt. Col. John G. Simcoe surprised two parties of Va. militia.			25		
Jan. 17	COWPENS, CHEROKEE CO., S.C. Gen. Daniel Morgan with 800 regulars and militia was attacked by Lt. Col. Banastre Tarleton and about 1100 cavalry and infantry. Tarleton's losses were about 110 K, 200 W, and another 527 C.	12	60			
Jan. 19	KEITHFIELD, BERKELEY CO., S.C. Capt. James De Peyster and 29 Loyalists were sent to seize Capt. John Postell's foraging troop. At the encounter, all the Loyalists were captured.					
Jan. 22	MORRISANIA, N.Y. Lt. Col. William Hull with a detachment from Gen. Samuel H. Parson's division broke up a Loyalist camp and captured about 50.	5	13			
Jan. 24	GEORGETOWN, S.C. After being joined by Lt. Col. Henry Lee's Legion, Gen. Francis Marion attacked the British garrison in town, taking the commandant and 4 others, but could not defeat the garrison in a brick redoubt.					
Jan. 25	PORTSMOUTH–GREAT BRIDGE ROAD, VA. Militia attacked a British artillery detachment and killed one officer.					

DATE	ENGAGEMENT	AMERICAN LOSSES				
		K	W	C	M	D
Feb. 1	COWAN'S FORD, CATAWBA RIVER, N.C. When Gen. Lord Cornwallis tried to cross the ford he was opposed by Gen. William L. Davidson and a small body of militia. Davidson was killed, as was a British officer.	4		3		
	TORRENCE'S TAVERN (ON ROAD TO SALISBURY), N.C. After Cornwallis crossed the Catawba River in pursuit of Gen. Greene, Lt. Col. Banastre Tarleton's Legion rode on ahead and dispersed a body of N.C. militia, after the militia had killed and wounded 7 British.	10				
c. Feb. 2	SARVIS' MILL, ROWAN COUNTY, N.C. Capt. William Armstrong with 9 mounted militia exchanged fire with a British foraging party, which withdrew.					
Feb. 3	TRADING FORD, YADKIN RIVER, N.C. Gen. Daniel Morgan's force of regulars and militia was pursued by British Gen. Charles O'Hara.			(10)		
Feb. 5	NEAR GREAT BRIDGE, VA. Some Queen's Rangers under Col. Thomas Dundas had a skirmish with Va. militia.			1		
Feb. 6	GRANT'S CREEK, ROWAN COUNTY, N.C. Col. Francis Locke at the head of a militia unit repulsed a reconnaissance party under Lt. Col. Banastre Tarleton and partially destroyed a bridge.		1			
Feb. 7	SHALLOW FORD, YADKIN RIVER, N.C. Some 40 militia under Capt. Joseph Graham skirmished with the rear of Gen. Lord Cornwallis' army, killed 1 man and took 5 prisoners.	1				
Feb. 8	NEAR PLEASANT VALLEY, N.J. Capt. John Schenk and a party of militia skirmished with some Loyalists under Lt. Stevenson, wounded 3, and took 12 prisoners.	1	1			
Feb. 10	NEAR SALEM, N.C. Col. Otho Williams held up Gen. Lord Cornwallis' pursuit in a delaying action.					
Feb. 12	FORT ST. JOSEPH (NILES), MICH. Capt. Don Eugenio Pouré led 65 Spaniards and French militia from St. Louis and Cahokia, plus 60 Potawatomies, in capture of the British post and its fur traders.					
Feb. 13	NEAR DIX'S FERRY, N.C.-VA. LINE. Lt. Col. Henry Lee turned on Cornwallis' advance troops under Lt. Col. Banastre Tarleton, killed 18, and captured several.	1				
Feb. 17	THOMASTON, ME. A British patrol from Major-Biguyduce had 3 men wounded in an attack on the headquarters of Gen. Peleg Wadsworth.	1		4		

DATE	ENGAGEMENT	AMERICAN LOSSES				
		K	W	C	M	D
Feb. 19 -20	FORT GRANBY, S.C. Gen. Thomas Sumter laid siege to the fort under Maj. Andrew Maxwell, but had to lift it as British reinforcements approached.					
Feb. 20	HART'S MILL, NEAR HILLSBORO, N.C. Capt. Joseph Graham and about 40 militia fell on a British foraging party of 28, killed 9, and captured 19.					
Feb. 23	BELLEVILLE, ORANGEBURG CO., S.C. Gen. Thomas Sumter's militia captured a wagon train from an escort of 50 British soldiers, killing 7 and wounding 7.					
	HAW RIVER (NEAR ALAMANCE), N.C. Lt. Col. Henry Lee's Legion and Gen. Andrew Pickens' militia surprised 400 Loyalists under Col. John Pyle, killed 90, wounded others, and dispersed the rest.	1				
Feb. 28	FORT WATSON, S.C. Gen. Thomas Sumter rashly attacked the fort and lost a number of men before giving up.	18		38		
	COMPO (NEAR WESTPORT), CONN. A British landing party burned 2 houses before being driven off by local militia.					
Mar.	TUCKASEGEE, N.C. Col. John Sevier and about 130 militia surprised a Cherokee town and killed about 50.	1	1			
	DUTCHMAN'S CREEK, FAIRFIELD CO., S.C. A body of militia was attacked by a regiment of N.Y. Loyalists under Capt. Grey.	18		18		
Mar. 2	MUD LICK, NEAR FORT WILLIAMS, S.C. Lt. Col. James Roebuck and 150 militia had a skirmish with British regulars and Loyalists from Fort Williams. The latter were routed with losses.	1	2			
	CLAPP'S MILL ON ALAMANCE CREEK, N.C. Lt. Col. Banastre Tarleton's Legion charged Lt. Col. Henry Lee's cavalry and N.C. militia. The British had 21 casualties.	9				
	FORT SCHUYLER (UTICA), N.Y. A regiment under Col. Pierre Van Cortlandt was attacked by 140 Indians and Loyalists under Chief Joseph Brant.	1		17		
Mar. 5	NEAR LOUISVILLE, KY. Some militia under Col. William Linn and Capts. Abraham Tipton and John Chapman were ambushed by Shawnees.	3				
Mar. 6	LYNCHES RIVER, KERSHAW CO., S.C. Gen. Thomas Sumter and his militia had a skirmish with S.C. Loyalists under Maj. Thomas Fraser, who had about 20 casualties.	10	40			
	WIBOO SWAMP, CLARENDON CO., S.C. Gen. Francis Marion's militia clashed with Lt. Col. John Watson's regulars and Loyalists, but had to withdraw. The British lost at least 3	(6)	(12)			

DATE	ENGAGEMENT	AMERICAN LOSSES				
		K	W	C	M	D
Mar. 6	WIBOO SWAMP, CLARENDON CO., S.C. (cont.) and probably more.					
	WETZELL'S MILL, REEDY FORK CREEK, N.C. Lt. Cols. Banastre Tarleton and James Webster led British regulars in attack on militia and Continental cavalry under Col. Otho Williams, who had to retreat. The British had 30 casualties plus numerous desertions.	(8)	(12)			
Mar. 8	TOMPKINS' BRIDGE, NEAR HAMPTON, VA. Col. Francis Mallory led about 40 militia against a much larger British foraging party under Col. Thomas Dundas. The enemy suffered several casualties.	7	(7)			
Mar.10	SANTA ROSA ISLAND, PENSACOLA, FLA. Spanish infantry captured 9 British seamen despite firing from HMS Port Royal and Mentor.					
Mar.11	GREAT BRIDGE, VA. Some of the Queen's Rangers under Capt. McCrea attacked a party of militia under Capt. Weeks.	1		2		
Mar.12	CLOSTER, N.J. A plundering party of 200 Loyalists under Thomas Ward was driven off by local militia.					
c. Mar.12	WORCESTER CO., MD. Some local militia under Col. Joseph Dashiel prevented the landing of a British naval party.					
Mar.14 -15	LOWER BRIDGE, BLACK RIVER, S.C. Gen. Francis Marion again fought Lt. Col. John Watson for 2 days until the British withdrew. They probably suffered 15 to 20 casualties.	(5)	(8)			
Mar.15	GUILFORD COURT HOUSE, N.C. Gen. Nathanael Greene placed his 4400 Continentals and militia and waited for the attack by Gen. Lord Cornwallis and his 1950 troops. Cornwallis held the battlefield, but lost a third of his army.	78	183		(1000)	
Mar.17	GUILFORD, CONN. In a brief skirmish between local militia and Loyalists, one man was hurt.		1			
Mar.19	NEAR PENSACOLA, FLA. A party of Indians under British Capt. Stevens attacked a Spanish boat, killing 10 and capturing 1.					
	NEAR PORTSMOUTH, VA. Capt. Johann von Ewald's Hessian detachment attacked Gen. Peter Muhlenberg's brigade of 700 and lost 2 K, 3 W, and 5 C. Ewald reported the American loss, which seems exaggerated.	31				
c. Mar.20	SOUTH OF GUILFORD COURT HOUSE, N.C. Capt. John Taylor and a detachment were trailing Gen. Lord Cornwallis when they met a British patrol of 8, killed 1, and captured 3.					
Mar.22 -23	PENSACOLA BAY, FLA. The British fired on Spanish ships bringing reinforcements.					
Mar.24	BEATTIE'S MILL, ABBEVILLE CO., S.C. Gen. Andrew					

DATE	ENGAGEMENT	AMERICAN LOSSES				
		K	W	C	M	D
Mar. 24	BEATTIE'S MILL, S.C. (cont.) Pickens sent a detachment of militia to attack Maj. James Dunlap's 75 Loyalists. The latter lost 35 K and the rest surrendered.					
Mar. 25	PENSACOLA, FLA. British-allied Indians killed 2 Spaniards outside their lines.					
Mar. 27	ELIZABETHTOWN, N.J. Some Loyalists and regulars under Maj. George Beckwith from Staten Island raided the area and had 1 K and 1 C.			6		
Mar. 28	SAMPIT BRIDGE, NEAR GEORGETOWN, S.C. As Col. John Watson retreated toward Georgetown, Gen. Francis Marion's troops caught up with him and killed 20.		1			
	PENSACOLA, FLA. British and Indians under Capt. Byrd twice attacked the Spanish camp with little effect. Four Indians were wounded.					
Mar. 30	PENSACOLA, FLA. Another attack by Loyalists and Indians on the Spanish camp was beaten off after several Spaniards were killed and wounded.					
c. Mar. 31	CHESAPEAKE BAY, VA. SHORE. A detachment under Capt. Allen McLane captured a notorious Loyalist.					
Mar. 31	CHALK POINT, NEAR ANNAPOLIS, MD. Local militia failed to stop a landing party from 2 British ships.					
End of Mar.	SNOW'S ISLAND, MARION CO., S.C. Col. Welbore Doyle with a Loyalist regiment captured Gen. Francis Marion's favorite rendezvous from the defenders under Col. Hugh Ervin.	7	15			
Apr.	WIGGINS HILL, COLLETON CO., S.C. Col. William Harden attacked Col. Thomas Brown's camp of over 500 regulars, Loyalists, and Indians, but was repulsed. Enemy losses were about the same as Harden's, but many of the Loyalists deserted to join Harden.[1]	7	11	12		
	HORN'S CREEK, EDGEFIELD CO., S.C. Capt. Thomas Kee surprised Loyalist Capt. Clarke at his residence, killed him, and captured others.[1]					
	MATHEWS' BLUFF, GA. Capt. McKoy and 30 militia attacked a similar sized party of Loyalists under Lt. Kemp and killed half of them.[1]					
	(BETWEEN SHELBYVILLE AND LOUISVILLE), KY. While moving his settlers to Fort Nelson, Louisville, Capt. Squire Boone was attacked by Indians. Col. John Floyd led 30 militia in pursuit and was ambushed.[2]	(15)				
	SALT MARSHES SOUTH OF HACKENSACK, N.J. Capt. John		1			

1. Reported in Edward McCrady, History of South Carolina in the Revolution (N.Y.: Macmillan, 1901-2), II, 259-62.

2. Reported in Robert Cotterill, History of Pioneer Kentucky (Cincinnati: Johnson and Hardin, 1917), p. 174.

DATE	ENGAGEMENT	AMERICAN LOSSES				
		K	W	C	M	D
Apr.	SALT MARSHES SOUTH OF HACKENSACK, N.J. (cont.) Outwater led some militia against a British landing party, killing 7 and taking 1 prisoner.					
Apr. 2	FORT NASHBOROUGH, TENN. Lt. James Robertson and 20 mounted militia were ambushed by Indians but got back to the fort.		(4)			
Apr. 7	FOUR HOLES, S.C. Col. William Harden with a militia force captured a Loyalist officer and 25 men.					
Apr. 8	POCOTALIGO ROAD, COLLETON CO., S.C. Col. William Harden moved on and skirmished with Col. Edward Fenwick's cavalry, killing 1, wounding 7, and capturing 2.		2	1		
Apr. 11	FORT BALFOUR, BEAUFORT CO., S.C. Col. William Harden laid siege to the fort and took Col. Fletcher Kellsal and garrison of 90.					
Apr. 12	PENSACOLA, FLA. British Lt. George Pinhorn led a sortie against the Spanish lines and was killed, but the Spaniards lost 1 K and 9 W.					
Apr. 14	THROGG'S NECK, N.Y. Capt. Jabez Fitch with 112 men had a skirmish with a British detachment for 2 hours, killing 6 and wounding 1.	1	3			
Apr. 15	NEAR CAMDEN, S.C. A scouting party from Gen. Francis Marion's brigade attacked a Loyalist house and killed several soldiers.		1			
c. Apr. 15	PORT TOBACCO, MD. Nine Md. militia under Col. Harris repulsed a British landing party.					
Apr. 17	BURWELL'S LANDING, JAMES RIVER, VA. Simcoe's Queen's Rangers captured a few militia.			(6)		
Apr. 19	EAST HAVEN, CONN. Loyalists from Long Island captured the guard house and released prisoners.	1		11		
	LICHTENAU (NEAR COSHOCTON), O. Col. Daniel Brodhead with 300 Continentals and militia attacked Indians at old Moravian town, killed 15 and captured 15.					
Apr. 20	BURWELL'S LANDING, JAMES RIVER, VA. Col. James Inness sent 200 militia to skirmish with a larger enemy force and drove them off.					
Apr. 21	NEAR ELIZABETHTOWN, N.J. A dozen militia under Capt. Hendricks had a skirmish with 70 British from Staten Island and killed 1 and wounded 1.					
Apr. 22	PENSACOLA, FLA. A Spanish reconnaissance party was fired on by British guns and had 1 W.					
	FORT PANMURE, NATCHEZ, MISS. About 200 Loyalists and					

| DATE | ENGAGEMENT | AMERICAN LOSSES | | | | |
		K	W	C	M	D
Apr. 22	FORT PANMURE, NATCHEZ, MISS. (cont.) Indians under John Blommart forced the surrender of the Spanish garrison of 77 after 1 was killed.					
Apr. 23	FORT WATSON, CLARENDON CO., S.C. Gen. Francis Marion and Lt. Col. Henry Lee forced the surrender of the garrison of 120 under Lt. James McKay.	2	6			
Apr. 24 -30	PENSACOLA, FLA. British and Indians tried repeatedly to stop the besieging Spanish troops from entrenching, killing 13 and wounding 28.					
Apr. 25	HOBKIRK'S HILL, NEAR CAMDEN, S.C. With about 1550 Continentals and militia, Gen. Nathanael Greene battled about 900 British under Lt. Col. Lord Francis Rawdon, inflicting 258 casualties.	18	108		138	
	NEAR PETERSBURG, VA. Gen. Benedict Arnold's British and German troops, about 2500 in all, attacked and drove back Gen. Peter Muhlenberg's militia.	10				
Apr. 27	OSBORNE'S, JAMES RIVER, VA. Gen. Benedict Arnold moved down river from Petersburg (above) to confront some militia on the opposite bank, trying to guard some 20 naval and cargo ships. Arnold drove off the militia and captured all the vessels not sunk. Casualties are incomplete.			3		
Apr. 29	POTOMAC RIVER. HMS Swift, Capt. Graves, exchanged fire with Americans on shore.					
Early May	NEAR MARTHA'S VINEYARD, MASS. Col. Bassett and a party of militia commandeered a ship and captured 3 or 4 British privateers.					
May 1	FRIDAY'S FERRY, RICHLAND CO., S.C. Col. Henry Hampton, with a detachment from Gen. Thomas Sumter's force, cleared away the ferry guard, killing perhaps 13.					
c. May 2	BUSH'S RIVER, NEWBERRY CO., S.C. Col. John Thomas, with a detachment from Gen. Thomas Sumter's force, attacked a Loyalist party, killing 3 and capturing 12.					
May 3	PENSACOLA, FLA. Loyalists and German troops under Lt. Col. DeHorn made a bayonet attack on the Spanish entrenchments, losing 1 K and 1 W, but causing the Spaniards to lose 21 K, 15 W, and 4 C.					
May 4	McAFEE STATION (MERCER CO.), KY. Garrison was attacked by Indians, who were driven off by Capt. Hugh McGary's troops. They killed 2 Indians.	2	1			
May 8	NEAR HERKIMER, N.Y. A party of 40 militia under Lt. Woodworth was ambushed by Indians.	25				

85

DATE	ENGAGEMENT	AMERICAN LOSSES				
		K	W	C	M	D
May 9	FORT GEORGE, PENSACOLA, FLA. British Gen. John Campbell surrendered the garrison of 1600 after Spanish attack under Gov. Bernardo de Gálvez's 5000 troops blew up the fort's powder magazine. The Spaniards lost 96 K and 202 W; the British had 90 K and 54 W.					
May 11	ORANGEBURG, S.C. Gen. Thomas Sumter captured the enemy post garrisoned by 15 British regulars and 70 Loyalists, without losses.					
May 12	FORT MOTTE, CALHOUN CO., S.C. Gen. Francis Marion and Lt. Col. Henry Lee laid siege to a fortified house garrisoned by 150 British under Lt. Charles McPherson, who surrendered.					
May 13	RANDOLPH CO., N.C. Loyalist Col. David Fanning caught up with a detachment from Gen. Greene's army and engaged in a running battle.	5	3	3		
May 14	NEAR CROTON RIVER, WESTCHESTER CO., N.Y. A detachment under Col. Christopher Greene was surprised by 260 Loyalists under Col. James DeLancey.	14	(10)	30		
May 15	FORT GRANBY, LEXINGTON CO., S.C. Lt. Col. Henry Lee attacked the garrison of 350 under Loyalist Maj. Andrew Maxwell, who surrendered.					
	FORT LEE, N.J. About 100 Loyalists from N.Y. seized a blockhouse and held off 2 companies of N.J. militia under Col. Richard Dey.					
	BEECH ISLAND, SAVANNAH RIVER, S.C. Some militia under Col. Elijah Clarke defeated some Loyalists under Lt. Col. Thomas Brown.	6				
May 18	FORT LEE, N.J. Col. Richard Dey with a larger force of militia dislodged the Loyalists from N.Y., with casualties on both sides.		(8)			
May 21	FORT GALPHIN, SAVANNAH RIVER, S.C. Lt. Col. Henry Lee's Legion and some militia captured this stockaded farm house, garrisoned by about 125 Loyalists, who suffered 3 or 4 K.	1	8			
May 23	CARY'S MILLS, CHESTERFIELD CO., VA. On his way north to join Gen. Lord Cornwallis, Lt. Col. Banastre Tarleton's Legion skirmished with some local militia.	6		40		
May 30	COMPO (NEAR WESTPORT), CONN. A militia company under Capt. Daniel Bouton fought off a landing party of Loyalists who burned the guard house.		1			
June 5	AUGUSTA, GA. Two forts here, Grierson and Cornwallis, were besieged by Gen. Andrew Pickens' militia and Lt. Col. Henry					

DATE	ENGAGEMENT	AMERICAN LOSSES				
		K	W	C	M	D
June 5	AUGUSTA, GA. (cont.) Lee's Legion. Fort Grierson surrendered May 22, and Col. Thomas Brown capitulated this day. The British had numerous casualties.					
June 6	HORSE SHOE, COLLETON CO., S.C. Col. Isaac Hayne's militia unit, which had captured Loyalist Gen. Andrew Williamson the day before, was defeated by 90 cavalry under Loyalist Maj. Thomas Fraser. Hayne was later hanged as a spy.	14	1	1		
June 8	STAMFORD, CONN. About 60 horsemen from Col. James DeLancey's Loyalist regiment attacked a picket guard.			5		
June 18	LEETE'S ISLAND, NEAR GUILFORD, CONN. A British landing party was repulsed by local militia under Lt. Timothy Field, who inflicted 6 or 7 casualties.	2	3			
	ROAD TO NINETY-SIX, S.C. Col. Charles Myddelton's detachment of 150 militia caught up with Lt. Col. Lord Francis Rawdon's rear guard and was routed by a strong British attack. Casualties are not known.					
June 19	NINETY-SIX, S.C. After a four-weeks' siege of the fort, Gen. Nathanael Greene with about 1000 Continentals tried to storm the garrison of 550 Loyalists under Lt. Col. John H. Cruger before Lord Rawdon's reinforcements arrived. Greene was repulsed, although the Loyalists suffered 27 K and 58 W.	59	72	1	20	
June 21	MONMOUTH CO., N.J. A large body of British and German troops under Gen. Cortlandt Skinner clashed with N.J. militia and suffered some casualties.	1	3			
June 22	BOSTON HARBOR, MASS. British prisoners on board a guard ship overpowered their guards and escaped.	5				
June 26	SPENCER'S ORDINARY, NEAR WILLIAMSBURG, VA. Gen. Lafayette detached Col. Richard Butler with his Pa. regiment and some Va. militia to intercept Lt. Col. John G. Simcoe's Queen's Rangers. After a hot clash, Simcoe broke off the action, having had 33 casualties.	9	14	32		
July 1	SAWMILL RIVER, N.Y. A German patrol under Capt. Carl von Rau was ambushed by militia and the captain mortally wounded.					
July 3	KINGSBRIDGE, N.Y. Lt. Col. Ernst von Prueschenck with 230 Germans attacked some Continentals, who had landed nearby, and drove them back to Gen. Benjamin Lincoln's main body of 900 troops.	6	52			
July 6	GREEN SPRING (NEAR JAMESTOWN), VA. Gens. Lafayette and Anthony Wayne with 900 Continentals were surprised by an attack from Gen. Lord Cornwallis' army of 7000. By also attacking, Wayne extricated his troops and pulled back. The British loss was 75 K and W.	28	99		12	

DATE	ENGAGEMENT	AMERICAN LOSSES				
		K	W	C	M	D
July 8	LEXINGTON CO., S.C. Capt. Joseph Egleston's company of Lee's Legion captured most of a British cavalry unit of 50.					
c. July 8	NEAR NEW BERN, N.C. Gen. Richard Caswell ordered some militia to resist British raids, but they retreated after this clash, having killed 1 and wounded several of the enemy.					
July 10	NANTUCKET SOUND, MASS. Col. Bassett and a party of militia captured 2 British privateers, killing 1 seaman and wounding 3.		1			
	SHARON SPRINGS SWAMP, N.Y. Col. Marinus Willett led 150 militia from Canajoharie and attacked 300 Loyalists and Indians under Col. John Doxtader, defeating him and killing 40.	6	8			
July 11	OHIO RIVER, 75 MILES UPSTREAM FROM LOUISVILLE. Capt. Coulson with some Va. militia in a boat was attacked by Indians.	4				
July 15	TARRYTOWN, N.Y. American and French troops exchanged fire with British ships in the river.	1	1			
	QUARTER HOUSE, CHARLESTON NECK, S.C. Col. Wade Hampton with a detachment from Gen. Thomas Sumter's force skirmished with some British troops.	1				
July 16	WADBOO CREEK BRIDGE, BERKELEY CO., S.C. Maj. Hezekiah Maham with a detachment from Gen. Thomas Sumter's force destroyed the bridge and set 2 ships on fire.					
	BIGGIN CREEK BRIDGE, BERKELEY CO., S.C. Lt. Col. John Coates' British dragoons surprised Col. Peter Horry's camp but were driven off. Coates then began a retreat to Charleston.					
July 17	QUINBY CREEK BRIDGE, BERKELEY CO., S.C. Gen. Thomas Sumter's force caught up with Lt. Col. John Coates' retreating 19th regiment and attacked imprudently until ammunition gave out. Marion and Lee left Sumter in disgust. The British suffered about 7 K, 39 W, and some C.	(30)	(30)			
	BEDFORD, N.Y. A patrol from Gen. Duc de Lauzun's Legion was attacked by cavalry from Col. James DeLancey's Loyalist regiment.	1				
July 19	DOBBS FERRY, N.Y. American batteries fired on British ships in the Hudson River.					
July 22	KINGSBRIDGE, N.Y. French and American troops exchanged fire with British ships in the Hudson River, causing some casualties. On the march the allies killed 3 or 4 British and captured 8 or 10.	(2)	1	(5)		
July 26	SOUTHEASTERN N.C. Col. Archibald Murphy and his militia kept up a running attack on Col. Hector McNeil's Loyalists retreating to Wilmington.					
July 27	PUNGOTEAGUE, VA. Capt. Robinson with 100 men in 4 barges plundered the inhabitants until driven off by local militia, who					

DATE	ENGAGEMENT	AMERICAN LOSSES				
		K	W	C	M	D
July 27	PUNGOTEAGUE, VA. (cont.) killed one invader.					
July 29	DEEP RIVER, CUMBERLAND CO., N.C. Capt. David Fanning's Loyalists surrounded Col. John Alston's house and forced his party of militia to surrender.	4	7	14		
Late July	NEAR ORANGEBURG, S.C. Capt. Watts with 20 of Lt. Col. William Washington's dragoons charged a similar sized detachment of British dragoons, killed 2, wounded some, and captured 6.					
Aug.	FORT JEFFERSON (WICKLIFFE), KY. British-allied Chickasaws and Choctaws under Loyalist Capt. James Colbert besieged Capt. Robert George's garrison of 30 for 6 days before withdrawing after Colbert was wounded.					
Aug. 1	LAURENS CO., S.C. Gen. Robert Cunningham's Loyalists skirmished with local militia.	8				
Aug. 2	ROCKFISH CREEK, DUPLIN CO., N.C. Col. James Kenan's 330 militia were scattered by an attack from the British out of Wilmington.			20		
Aug. 4	DROWNING CREEK, BETWEEN MONTGOMERY AND MOORE COS., N.C. Local militia attacked a bridge held by the enemy and drove them off, killing 7 and wounding others.		4			
Aug. 13	PARKER'S FERRY, COLLETON CO., S.C. Loyalist Thomas Fraser took 200 cavalry to support an uprising of 450 Loyalists. Gen. Francis Marion reinforced Col. William Harden, and with about 400 men they set an ambush that killed or wounded about 100 of Fraser's troops.					
Before Aug. 17	NEAR KINSTON, N.C. Some of Gen. Richard Caswell's militia retreated before a charge by Loyalist cavalry and infantry under Maj. James Craig.					
Before Aug. 19	WEBBER'S BRIDGE, TRENT RIVER, N.C. Some of Gen. Alexander Lillington's militia held the bridge against Maj. James Craig's attack, killing 3 and wounding 5 of the enemy.					
Aug. 21	BRYANT'S MILL, NEAR NEW BERN, N.C. Col. William Graham and 150 militia were surprised by a party of Loyalists, who suffered 12 casualties.	1				
Aug. 22	NEAR WILLIAMSBURG, VA. A picket guard of Col. Thomas Mathews' militia was surprised by the British and suffered about 15 casualties.	(5)	(10)			
	WAWARSING, N.Y. A force of 300 Indians and 90 Loyalists under Capt. William Caldwell attacked area settlements until militia under Col. Albert Pawling drove them off, killing 3 and wounding 4.					

DATE	ENGAGEMENT	AMERICAN LOSSES				
		K	W	C	M	D
c. Aug. 23	MORSE'S RIVER, N.J. A party of 15 Loyalists attacked a boat load of militia and suffered 4 K, 4 W, and 7 C.		1			
Aug. 24	BELOW MOUTH OF LAUGHERY CREEK ON OHIO RIVER (NEAR AURORA), IND. Col. Archibald Lochry was leading about 105 Pa. reinforcements to Gen. George Rogers Clark when his camp was attacked by Canadians and Indians under Chief Joseph Brant. Lochry and other prisoners were killed later.	41		60		
Late Aug.	ELIZABETHTOWN, N.C. Some militia under Col. Thomas Brown made a night attack on Col. Slingsby's Loyalist camp, killing Slingsby and wounding several others.		4			
Aug. 31	NEAR CHARLESTON, S.C. Maj. Samuel Cooper with a mounted detachment from Gen. Francis Marion's force captured several Loyalists in a sweep toward the capital.					
Sep.	GREENSBORO, VT. Capt. Nehemiah Lovewell at Peacham sent out a scouting party of 4 Vermont militiamen toward the Greensboro blockhouse, and they were attacked by Indians.	2		2		
Sep. 4	NEAR DROWNING CREEK, BETWEEN MONTGOMERY AND MOORE COS., N.C. Col. Thomas Wade with over 400 militia marched to attack Loyalist Col. Hector McNeil, but he was reinforced by Col. David Fanning's Loyalists. Wade's detachment was defeated.	23		50		
Sep. 6	NEW LONDON, CONN. Gen. Benedict Arnold with British regulars, Loyalists, and Germans burned the town and overran Forts Trumbull and Griswold, under Capt. Adam Shapley and Col. William Ledyard. Most of the casualties occurred after the forts surrendered.	85	60	70		
	TURKEY CREEK, EDGEFIELD CO., S.C. Loyalists under Capt. Williams attacked and scattered a party of militia.	(4)	(6)			
Sep. 7	NEAR FORT PLAIN, N.Y. A party of 40 militia under Lt. Solomon Woodworth was ambushed presumably by Indians.	26	4			
Sep. 8	EUTAW SPRINGS, S.C. Gen. Nathanael Greene at the head of about 2200 Continentals and militia attacked Lt. Col. Alexander Stewart's camp of about 2000 British regulars and Loyalists. They fought stubbornly to a draw, the enemy losing 85 K, 351 W, and 257 M.	138	375		41	
Sep. 12	HILLSBORO, N.C. Cols. David Fanning and Hector McNeil with a large force of Loyalists marched from Wilmington, raided the rebel capital, and captured the governor among others.	15	20	200		
Sep. 13	LINDLEY'S MILL, ALAMANCE CO., N.C. The Loyalist force under Cols. David Fanning and Hector McNeil (see above) was attacked by militia under Gen. John Butler and Col. Thomas Wade. The enemy had 27 K, 90 W, and 10 C, but did not lose					

| DATE | ENGAGEMENT | AMERICAN LOSSES | | | | |
		K	W	C	M	D
Sep. 13	LINDLEY'S MILL, ALAMANCE CO., N.C. (cont.) their prisoners.					
Sep. 23	SARATOGA, N.Y. Gen. John Stark sent out a scouting party that clashed with a Canadian party and killed one.					
Sep. 25	SARATOGA, N.Y. Capt. Dunham captured a British scouting party of 5 that had been sent out from St. Johns, Canada.					
Sep. 30	YORKTOWN, VA. Col. Alexander Scammell with a reconnoitering party was captured by some of Lt. Col. Banastre Tarleton's Legion and then mortally wounded.	1				
Oct.	NEAR SCHRAALENBURGH, N.J. When a party of militia under Lt. Campbell failed to attack some Loyalists, 2 soldiers advanced anyway and captured 2 Loyalists and 7 horses.					
	PASSAMAQUODDY BAY, ME. A party of militia under Low was attacked.			2		
Oct. 3	FORT SLONGO, LONG ISLAND, N.Y. Maj. Lemuel Trescott led over 100 cavalry and infantry in a assault on a British post, killing 4 and taking 21 prisoners.		1			
	NEAR GLOUCESTER, VA. The Duc de Lauzun's cavalry and Lt. Col. John Mercer's infantry attacked Lt. Col. Banastre Tarleton's Legion, which was protecting a foraging party. Tarleton lost 13 troopers.	2	11			
Oct. 5	OFF SANDY HOOK, N.J. Capt. Adam Huyler with some militia in 3 boats exchanged fire with 5 British vessels.					
	STEVENS CREEK, EDGEFIELD CO., S.C. A militia detachment under Lt. Col. Hugh Middleton had a skirmish with some Loyalists.	8	17			
Oct. 7	NEAR LINDLEY'S MILL, ALAMANCE CO., N.C. Col. David Fanning, who had been severely wounded on Sep. 13 (see above) and secreted near Brush Creek, was discovered and attacked by local militia. After a skirmish, Fanning and his men retreated without loss.	1	(4)			
Oct. 10	YORKTOWN, VA. American shore batteries set fire to 3 British ships.					
Oct. 14	YORKTOWN, VA. Col. William Deux-Ponts led 400 French troops in capture of Redoubt 9 from 120 British and Germans under Lt. Col. Duncan McPherson. The French suffered 15 K and 77 W; the enemy had 18 K and 50 C.					
	YORKTOWN, VA. At the same time as the above action, Lt. Col. Alexander Hamilton led 400 Continentals in the capture of Redoubt 10 from 45 British, half of whom were taken prisoner.	9	25			

DATE	ENGAGEMENT	AMERICAN LOSSES				
		K	W	C	M	D
Oct. 16	WINOOSKI RIVER, VT. A group of Loyalists attacked a militia scouting party.	1	2	4		
	YORKTOWN, VA. Lt. Col. Robert Abercromby led 350 British troops in a sortie against the French trenches. The British lost 8 K and 12 C while inflicting 20 casualties on the French.	1				
Oct. 17	CROTON RIVER, N.Y. A detachment of Col. James DeLancey's Loyalists surprised a party of militia.			19		
	YORKTOWN, VA. Gen. Lord Cornwallis proposed a cessation of arms and surrendered 2 days later. Total British casualties were 596 K and W, 8081 C. The French suffered 60 K and 192 W during the siege. The Americans had a total of 24 K (10 accounted for above) and 65 W (25 accounted for above).	14	40			
Oct. 25	JOHNSTOWN, N.Y. Maj. John Ross, who had led about 570 British regulars and Loyalists and 130 Indians towards Schenectady, was pursued in retreat by Col. Marinus Willett and 400 militia. They clashed just before dark, and Willett was stopped. He inflicted casualties of 7 K, about 40 W, and 50 C.	13	23		5	
Oct. 30	JERSEYFIELD, N.Y. Col. Marinus Willett (see above) caught up with Maj. John Ross again at West Canada Creek. The enemy lost Maj. Walter Butler and a dozen others.	1	7			
Nov. 2	NEAR OGEECHEE RIVER FERRY, BURKE CO., GA. Col. James Jackson with 390 militia and Continentals had 2 skirmishes with a militia party and a British force under Lt. Col. Archibald Campbell, inflicting over 50 casualties.	6	7	6		
	NEAR LAKE GEORGE, N.Y. A scouting party of Vt. militia was attacked by the enemy.	1		(5)		
c. Nov. 3	GOWEN'S FORT, GREENVILLE CO., S.C. A force of Cherokees and Loyalists under "Bloody" Bates forced surrender of the stronghold, then massacred the garrison and civilians, only a few escaping.	(10)				
Nov. 6	WILKES CO., GA. Col. Elijah Clarke led some militia against a band of British-allied Indians, killing 40 and capturing 40.					
Nov. 11	STONY BROOK, LONG ISLAND, N.Y. Maj. Benjamin Tallmadge sent a score of men to capture a British vessel. The enemy lost 6 to 8 K and W, and 1 C.					
c. Nov. 12	ORANGEBURG CO., S.C. Gen. Thomas Sumter sent Maj. James Moore with some state troops to bring in a Loyalist leader. They ran into 500 Loyalists under Maj. William Cunningham and were routed.	(4)	(8)			
Nov. 13	EAST CHESTER BAY, N.Y. A party of regulars and Conn. militia under Capt. Lockwood on an unarmed ship boarded and		4			

DATE	ENGAGEMENT	AMERICAN LOSSES				
		K	W	C	M	D
Nov. 13	EAST CHESTER BAY, N.Y. (cont.) captured a British warship and 40 prisoners, 5 of whom were wounded.					
c. Nov. 14	ORANGEBURG, S.C. Col. Richard Hampton's militia force was surprised by Maj. William Cunningham's Loyalists.	11				
Nov. 17	CLOUD'S CREEK, EDGEFIELD CO., S.C. Capt. Sterling Turner and 23 militia were overwhelmed by Maj. William Cunningham and 300 Loyalists.	23				
Nov. 19	HAYES' STATION, LAURENS CO., S.C. Col. Joseph Hayes and a militia party of 35 were assaulted by Maj. William Cunningham and about 150 Loyalists.	19				
Dec. 1	DORCHESTER, S.C. Gen. Nathanael Greene and 400 of his troops struck the British outpost and forced the garrison of 850 to retreat to Charleston after they suffered over 50 casualties.					
	NEAR LYME, CONN. Ens. Andrew Griswold and 5 men raided a house containing 10 Loyalists under Capt. Thomas Smith and captured 9 of them.					
	HALSTEAD'S POINT, N.J. Capt. Dayton routed 10 Loyalists, capturing 6, killing 1, and wounding 1.					
Dec. 2	WESTCHESTER CO., N.Y. Lt. Mosher's militia party of 27 was attacked by 45 mounted Loyalists under Lt. Col. Holmes, who suffered 2 K and 7 W.			1		
Dec. 6	BERGEN NECK, N.J. Capt. Baker Hendricks with a small party of men captured 5 Loyalist seamen.					
Dec. 15	OFF SANDY HOOK, N.J. Capt. Adam Huyler with some militia in whale boats captured 2 Loyalist mercantile ships.					
Dec. 23	MORRISANIA, N.Y. Capt. Daniel Williams with 25 mounted militia attacked a small body of Loyalists and captured 9.					
Dec. 30	DORCHESTER, S.C. Capt. James Armstrong and a mounted reconnoitering party clashed with a cavalry troop under British Maj. Coffin.			7		
Late 1781	BLACK RIVER SWAMP, S.C. Lt. Col. John Baxter pursued some Loyalists who had taken a loaded ship and exchanged fire.		1			
	NORTH CAROLINA. Loyalist Col. Edmond Fanning captured Capt. Kennedy and his party of militia.			9		
	TOTALS for the year 1781:	1003	1454	761	1216	

DATE	ENGAGEMENT	AMERICAN LOSSES				
		K	W	C	M	D
Jan. 2	NEW BRUNSWICK, N.J. Lt. Col. John Taylor's Middlesex militia skirmished with a force of 300 British regulars and Loyalists, killing 4.		5			
Jan. 3	VIDEAU'S BRIDGE, BERKELEY CO., S.C. Some mounted militia under Capt. Richard Richardson was routed by a Loyalist force of 350 under Maj. John Coffin, which suffered only 1 K and 1 W.[1]	57		20		
Jan. 11	NEAR FISHKILL, N.Y. Capt. Israel Honeywell led a troop of regulars and militia against the Loyalist pickets guarding DeLancey's Bridge, capturing 4.					
Feb. 24	WAMBAW CREEK BRIDGE, BERKELEY CO., S.C. Maj. John James, commanding some of Gen. Francis Marion's brigade, tried to stop a sortie of 700 British infantry and cavalry under Col. Benjamin Thompson, but was defeated.[1]	40		7		
	BEAUFORT, S.C. Some of Gen. Anthony Wayne's force under Capt. Robert Barnwell attacked an enemy detachment under Lt. Col. Andrew De Veaux, Jr.	5		5		
Feb. 25	TYDIMAN'S PLANTATION, BERKELEY CO., S.C. Gen. Francis Marion rallied his forces to oppose Col. Benjamin Thompson, but they broke before a charge.[1]	20		12		
Early Mar.	CHEROKEE TOWNS, S.C. Gen. Andrew Pickens and Col. Elijah Clarke led 300 militia westward to stop Indian raids. They burned 13 towns and killed 40 Cherokees.					
Mar. 1 -2	STRODE'S STATION (NEAR WINCHESTER), KY. A band of 25 Hurons besieged the American fort unsuccessfully.	2				
Mar. 4	MORRISANIA, N.Y. Capt. Israel Honeywell led 160 men against Col. James DeLancey's Loyalists.	2	4			
Mar. 7	GNADENHUTTEN, MUSKINGUM RIVER, O. Pa. militia under Col. David Williamson massacred 96 Christian Delawares.					
c. Mar.10	BATTLE RUN, BELOW BLUE LICKS, KY. Capt. John Holder with 63 militia was defeated in a skirmish with Indians.	1	3			
Mar.15	MIDDLETON PLANTATION, ASHLEY RIVER, S.C. Gen. Francis Marion reported a militia raid in the vicinity that killed 3 Loyalists and captured 1.					
Mar.19	ASHLEY RIVER, S.C. Capt. John Rudolph with 12 troopers from Lt. Col. Henry Lee's Legion captured HMS _Alligator_ after killing 4 and taking 28.					

1. Reported only in Edward McCrady, _History of South Carolina in the Revolution_ (N. Y.: Macmillan, 1901-2), II, 591, 603-4, 605. His casualty count was taken from a Loyalist newspaper and is probably exaggerated.

DATE	ENGAGEMENT	AMERICAN LOSSES				
		K	W	C	M	D
Mar. 22	NEAR MT. STERLING, KY. A band of 25 Hurons attacked a party of about 25 militia under Capt. James Estill. About 17 Indians were killed.	7				
Mar. 24	TOMS RIVER, N.J. Capt. Joshua Huddy and 25 militia were attacked by about 40 Loyalists and 80 seamen under Capt. Evan Thomas. Huddy was taken and hanged later. The enemy suffered 2 K and 6 W.	7	4	13		
Apr. 2	OCONEE RIVER, GA. Cols. Robert Anderson of S.C. and Elijah Clarke of Ga. with 400 militia attacked a party of Loyalists and Indians under Col. Black, killing about a dozen.	1				
Apr. 24	DORCHESTER, S.C. Capt. Ferdinand O'Neal with a company of Lt. Col. Henry Lee's Legion had a skirmish with some British cavalry under Capt. Dawkins which lost 1 K and 1 C.			9		
May	NEAR LORICK'S FERRY, SALUDA RIVER, S.C. The camp of Maj. William Cunningham and 20 Loyalists was surprised by Capt. William Butler with 30 cavalry of Gen. Andrew Pickens' brigade. The enemy was dispersed and 2 K.					
	NEAR SALLEY, S.C. A camp of Loyalists was attacked by a body of militia under Capts. Michael Watson and William Butler of Gen. Andrew Pickens' brigade. Despite laying an ambush, the Loyalists fled into Dean Swamp.	2	(8)			
May 15	MATTITUCK, LONG ISLAND, N.Y. Maj. Ayres with 8 men in a whaleboat was attacked by Capt. Marks and a party of Col. James DeLancey's Loyalists.	1	1			
May 19	NEAR GUILFORD, CONN. A party of the enemy landed and was fired on by local militia.	1				
May 22	OGEECHEE ROAD, NEAR SAVANNAH, GA. A detachment of militia under Lt. Col. James Jackson routed a party of British, inflicting several casualties.	5	2			
May 24	SHARON, GA. Gen. Anthony Wayne's camp of Pa. Continentals was attacked at night by Cherokees under a British officer. The enemy had at least 20 K.	6	(8)			
May 25	OFF SANDY HOOK, N.J. Capt. Adam Huyler and some militia attacked 25 British under Capt. Schaak in boats, inflicting 13 casualties.					
May 29	NEWARK BAY, N.J. A British force under Capt. McMichael was attacked by state troops under Capt. Peter Sanford, who killed 1 and captured 3.		1			

DATE	ENGAGEMENT	AMERICAN LOSSES				
		K	W	C	M	D
June 3	MARION CO., S.C. Gen. Francis Marion at the head of N.C. and S.C. militia attacked Maj. Micajah Ganey's Loyalists, who sued for peace and disbanded.		1			
June 4 -5	SANDUSKY, O. Col. William Crawford and 480 Va. militia were defeated by 340 Indians and over 100 Rangers under Capt. William Caldwell. The first day's battle caused Crawford to retreat, but the enemy caught up with him the next day. Crawford was taken and burned at the stake, in retaliation for Gnadenhutten (see Mar. 7).	(15)	(35)	3		
June 13	BERGEN POINT, N.J. Capt. Baker Hendricks captured 5 Loyalists.					
June 24	OGEECHEE ROAD, NEAR SAVANNAH, GA. Gen. Anthony Wayne's camp was attacked by 300 Creeks under Chief Emistisiguo, who with 30 others was killed.	5	8			
	BLACK ROCK, CONN. Capt. Parks and a score of militia fired on a boat of Loyalists and killed several.					
Late June	NEAR SCHRAALENBURGH, N.J. Three militiamen on patrol encountered some Loyalists.	1				
July 2	OFF SANDY HOOK, N.J. Capt. Adam Huyler and a militia party boarded HMS Skip Jack and burned it.					
Mid July	GEORGIA FRONTIER. As some Cherokees and Loyalists moved east to obtain supplies from the British, they were met by Col. Elijah Clarke and his militia, who defeated them, killing several.					
Aug. 14	NEAR FAYETTE, KY. Capt. John Holder took 20 militiamen in pursuit of some Hurons who had captured 2 boys. When he caught up with them he was repulsed.	4				
Aug. 15	BRYAN'S STATION, FAYETTE CO., KY. About 200 British-allied Indians under Capt. William Caldwell attacked the fort until a reinforcement under Col. Levi Todd brought relief. The Indians lost 5 K and 2 W.	5	2			
Aug. 19	LOWER BLUE LICKS (NEAR BLUE LICKS SPRINGS), KY. Va. militia amounting to 180 men under Cols. Todd, Trigg, and Boone gave battle to the Indians under Capt. William Caldwell and were defeated. The enemy lost only 7 K and 10 W.	77	12	8		
Aug. 27	COMBAHEE FERRY, COLLETON CO., S.C. When a large body of British troops tried to land from their ships, Col. John Laurens led a smashing attack of Continentals, but lost his life.	2	19	3		

DATE	ENGAGEMENT	AMERICAN LOSSES				
		K	W	C	M	D
Aug. 29	FAIR LAWN, BERKELEY CO., S.C. Gen. Francis Marion broke up a charge by Maj. Charles Fraser and his Loyalists, killing 9 and wounding 11.					
End of Aug.	BERKELEY CO., S.C. A scouting party of 12 of Gen. Francis Marion's force under Capt. G. S. Capers cut to pieces a troop of 26 British dragoons.	2				
Sep. 1	PORT ROYAL FERRY, S.C. When 2 British galleys tried to land, some of Gen. Mordecai Gist's infantry drove them off and captured one.					
Early Sep.	EGG HARBOR, N.J. Capt. Douglas with local militia fired on a boat containing 18 Loyalists, of which only 4 escaped.					
Sep. 11 -13	FORT HENRY (WHEELING), W. VA. The garrison and inhabitants were besieged by 250 Indians and 40 Loyalists.					
Sep. 12	BOTTLE HILL, N.J. Capt. Carter and a dozen militia killed one Loyalist and captured another.					
c. Sep. 15	FORT RICE, AUGUSTA CO., VA. A band of 100 Indians on their way home from Fort Henry (above) tried to surprise this post, held by only 6 men. The Indians had 3 K and 1 W.					
	BIG SANDY RIVER, W. VA.-KY. Va. militia in pursuit of marauding Indians recovered 2 captives and wounded several of the Indians.					
Oct. 3	PENOBSCOT BAY, ME. George Little and some local militia captured a ship from the British.					
Oct. 5	CAPE PORPOISE, ME. A party of 40 militia stopped a British raiding party from landing and inflicted severe casualties.	1				
Nov. 10	CHILLICOTHE, O. Col. John Floyd with 300 of Gen. George Rogers Clark's force destroyed this Shawnee town, killing 10 and capturing 10.					
Nov. 11	MIAMITOWN (FORT WAYNE), IND. Gen. Clark's 150 mounted troops under Col. Benjamin Logan destroyed the British trading post.	1	1			
Nov. 14	JAMES ISLAND, S.C. A party of mounted Md. Continentals under Col. Tadeusz Kosciuszko and Capt. William Wilmot attacked a party of woodcutters protected by British regulars.	5	(5)			

DATE	ENGAGEMENT	AMERICAN LOSSES				
		K	W	C	M	D
Dec.	OFF FAIRFIELD, CONN. Capt. Caleb Brewster with militia in 3 whaleboats battled 3 British boats.	1	4			
Dec. 5	BELL'S CREEK, GA. A rebel galley shelled a British camp.					
Dec. 27	CEDAR CREEK BRIDGE, N.J. Local militia under Capts. Richard Shreve and Edward Thomas attacked some Loyalists under John Bacon, killing 1, wounding 4, and capturing 7.	1	1			
	TOTALS for the year 1782:	277	124	80		

DATE	ENGAGEMENT	AMERICAN LOSSES				
		K	W	C	M	D
Feb. 20	OFF STRATFORD POINT, CONN. Learning that a British privateer was nearby, Maj. Benjamin Tallmadge put troops on board a vessel under Capt. Caleb Brewster which engaged the privateer. The British lost 9 K and 5 W.					
Mar.	ENGLISH NEIGHBORHOOD, N.J. Capt. John M. Hogenkamp with 30 to 40 militia skirmished with a party of British and Loyalists.		1	1		
Mar. 17	DUCK CREEK, KENT CO., DEL. Capt. Allen McLane and 5 militia attacked Loyalist Capt. Brooks, took his boats, and scattered his crew in Cedar Swamp.					
Apr. 3	EGG HARBOR, N.J. After news of the signing of the peace treaty had been received on March 23, a detachment of Capt. Richard Shreve's militia light horse under Cornet Cook surprised Loyalist John Bacon and killed him.					
Apr. 17 -24	FORT CARLOS III (ARKANSAS POST), ARK. With 100 Loyalists and 40 Indians, Capt. James Colbert captured 11 of the garrison, then laid siege to the remaining 40 under Capt. Raymondo DuBreuil, but they held out until Colbert withdrew on hearing of reinforcements coming. He released his prisoners as soon as he heard of the peace treaty. The fort was on the Arkansas River a few miles above its juncture with the Mississippi.[1]					
	TOTALS for the year 1783:		1	1		

1. Reported only in John Walton Caughey, <u>Bernardo de Gálvez in Louisiana, 1776–1783</u> (Berkeley: University of California Press, 1934), p. 240.

NAVAL ENGAGEMENTS
AND CASUALTIES

NAVAL ENGAGEMENTS
AND CASUALTIES

☆

The problem of defining what constitutes a naval action during the American Revolution proved to be rather complex. At first thought it might be considered to include any engagement involving a ship. However, we have already classified actions between British ships and rebel land batteries or muskets as military engagements. Further, just as we have not counted civilians who became casualties in land operations, we should not count civilian casualties at sea—that is, the crews of merchant ships carrying commercial cargoes which were attacked by naval warships. We were also faced by the problem of classifying other actions which took place on water but did not involve United States naval personnel. Militia might seize a few boats or a merchant ship to chase and engage a British ship. These were not, literally, "land actions," yet neither could they be credited to the navy. We have arbitrarily listed this type of action by soldiers with the preceding military engagements.

So far, so clear. There existed in Revolutionary naval warfare, however, a peculiar comrade-in-arms not found ashore: the privateer. This was a heavily armed ship which was commissioned by government to attack the enemy whenever a favorable opportunity might present itself. In addition, certain cargo carrying ships were armed with cannon and might attack enemy merchantmen. Both types of ship escaped the label of pirate by virtue of having a letter of marque and reprisal authorizing them to become belligerents. The Continental Congress, as well as the state governments, was generous in handing out letters of marque to all ship captains who applied for them. Their preying on British cargo ships was more lucrative than dangerous and made it difficult to recruit crews for naval ships. Hundreds of sea fights occurred between our privateers and British merchantmen, between United States and British privateers, and between our privateers and British naval vessels, but all such actions we have omitted. Privateers were not part of our navy; they were not under any higher orders; they reported to no official; and they were after prize money, not defeat of the enemy's warships.

Our view of a naval action is that a ship of the Continental Navy or of a state navy must be involved. Admittedly, it is difficult to draw a sharp line between privateers and state naval ships. Frequently the latter were private vessels leased for a year or a season, and when not under state control, they were given letters of marque to act as privateers. In either capacity they sank enemy ships, but we do not recognize their activity in a private capacity. The concept of state navies was incomprehensible to the British, and frequently they called all such opponents privateers, or even pirates. A single Continental Navy they could understand, even though they were a long time in respecting it; but as for six or eight state navies, they found it difficult to take seriously such ventures of a people they regarded as primarily fishermen or smugglers. The colonies had no naval tradition.

The sorting out of naval actions from private shipping engagements was not made easier by the number of ships which carried the same name or by the switching of naval captains from ship to ship.

In the list which follows, British naval ships are preceded by the initials HMS, for His Majesty's Ship, and followed by the full name of the captain when known. We did not add the names of captains to British merchantmen or privateers, nor have we mentioned the number or size of cannon on warships. United States or Continental Navy ships are preceded by the initials USS, or by the name of the state if the ship was part of a state navy, followed by the captain's name.

We have not recorded engagements between French or Spanish vessels on one side and British on the other, since no United States ships were involved and the battles did not occur on territory that became our country. Consequently, many actions in the West Indies, in the Atlantic, and in European waters between our allies and our enemy are not listed here.

Our list of naval engagements has some less than adequate predecessors. In his *History of the Navy of the United States of America,* 2 vols. (Philadelphia: Lea and Blanchard, 1839), James Fenimore Cooper devoted ten chapters of the first volume to actions of the Revolution. He listed the ships of the Continental Navy and recounted the more important battles. George F. Emmons, in *The Navy of the United States* (Washington: Printed by Gideon and Co., 1853), gave eight pages to a list of naval captures in the Revolution. Robert W. Neeser's *Statistical and Chronological History of the United States Navy* (New York: Macmillan, 1909) likewise gave a few pages in the second volume to

Revolutionary ships and actions. Marion and Jack Kaminkow included a list of captures based on British records in an appendix to their *Mariners of the American Revolution* (Baltimore: Magna Carta Book Co., 1967).

British naval records were much better kept than American. Each British warship filed a log or journal of its encounters with the enemy, whereas the logs of United States warships were captured when the vessels were taken or were often lost for want of an official depository. Occasionally American newspapers published accounts of naval clashes, but by and large we have had to depend on those British records gathered by the United States Naval History Division in conjunction with its admirable project of publishing the *Naval Documents of the American Revolution*, 7 vols. to date (Washington, D. C.: Government Printing Office, 1961 —). Since that office is proceeding chronologically, we found to our dismay that the logs of British ships after 1779 are by no means completely collected. The full naval history of the Revolution, with details on all engagements, has not yet been written, and it will not be written until the Navy Department finishes publishing its indispensable volumes. Vice Admiral Edwin B. Hooper and Dr. William Morgan were more than obliging in helping our researchers find the data we needed.

Again we must say that the engagements and casualties listed are the ascertainable minimum number, and the errors are likely to be those of omission. It became apparent that naval ship captains felt no obligation to report their casualties; the important news was whether the enemy ship had been sunk or captured, and whether their own ship was damaged. Rarely is even the size of the crew mentioned. Although some ships were much larger than others, no guesses could be made about the crew, since often a ship might be sailing short-handed. Consequently, when a United States naval ship was captured or sunk, the figures for captured or killed American sailors are woefully incomplete. The reader must allow also for the fact that in naval defeats the captured crew included both the wounded and the well.

A mere list of official naval engagements, with casualties insufficiently recorded, cannot indicate the impact of United States naval action. If old salts like Admirals Richard Howe, Samuel Graves, Sir Peter Parker, Sir Samuel Hood, and Marriot Arbuthnot underestimated the fledgling United States Navy, it is not surprising that the English public was shocked to the bone by the raids of Captain John

Paul Jones on English coasts. Tradition or not, a new naval power was rising from the waves Britain thought she ruled.

Not all British officers remained smug or imperceptive. George Brydges Rodney could and did learn new naval strategies, in the process violating his country's most sacred tactic by breaking the "line of battle" and shattering the French fleet in the West Indies in 1782. Similarly, there was a young captain of HMS *Hinchinbrook* cruising in American waters and learning the rudiments of amphibious warfare. His name was Horatio Nelson, and he was hardly a dozen years from international fame and national adulation.

The British Navy was probably stronger than the British Army, yet it did not try very hard to blockade the American coast. It was obliged to transport troops and do convoy duty to keep them provisioned from home. It too had captains who preferred to take commercial prizes rather than fight warships. The primary effect of the British Navy was to inflict hardship on the Americans by interrupting their trade, reducing supplies of needed war material from France, and indirectly raising prices throughout the colonies.

The rebels could not hope to challenge the strongest navy in the world. They never were able to put together a fleet, only occasional squadrons, and more frequently they put single warships into action. With the limited means available, however, the Americans did surprisingly well. They fought fiercely in individual battles. They captured British goods in partial replacement of lost imports. They drove up British insurance rates. It has been estimated that the American navies captured or sank nearly 200 enemy vessels of all kinds, and American privateers accounted for perhaps 600 others. Not a glorious record, but respectable.

DATE	ENGAGEMENT	AMERICAN LOSSES				
		K	W	C	M	D
June 12	OFF MAINE. HMS Margaretta, Capt. James Moore, was captured by Mass. Diligent, Capt. Jeremiah O'Brien, and Machias Liberty, Capt. Benjamin Foster. The enemy had 8 K and 5 W.	3	3			
Aug.	OFF ST. AUGUSTINE, FLA. S.C. Commerce, Capt. Clement Lempriere, captured HMS Betsy, Capt. Alvara Lofthouse.					
Oct.	OFF MAINE. Mass. Machias Liberty, Capt. Jeremiah O'Brien, captured an armed cutter.	1	2			
	OFF BOSTON. USS Hannah, Capt. Nicholson Broughton, in a running battle with HMS Nautilus, Capt. John Collins, ran aground. The British had 1 K and 1 W.					
c. Nov. 5	OFF NOVA SCOTIA. USS Harrison, Capt. William Coit, captured 2 British provision ships.					
Nov. 7	OFF MAINE. USS Lee, Capt. John Manley, recaptured Ranger, which had been taken by HMS Cerberus, Capt. John Symons.					
Nov. 11	CHARLESTON, S.C., HARBOR. S.C. Defence, Capt. Simon Tufts, exchanged shots with HMS Tamar and Cherokee as latter put out to sea.					
Nov. 24	BOSTON HARBOR. USS Harrison, Capt. William Coit, tried to capture 2 British transports.					
Nov. 25	PLYMOUTH, MASS. HARBOR. USS Washington, Capt. Sion Martindale, seized British provision ship Britannia.					
Nov. 27	OFF NEW ENGLAND. USS Lee, Capt. John Manley, captured British merchant ships Polly and Nancy.					
Dec. 1	OFF BOSTON. USS Lee, Capt. John Manley, captured British provision ship Concord.					
Dec. 5	OFF CAPE ANN, MASS. USS Washington, Capt. Sion Martindale, was captured by HMS Fowey, Capt. G. Montagu.			74		
c. Dec. 7	OFF MASSACHUSETTS. USS Lee, Capt. John Manley, captured British Jenny and Little Hannah.					
c.	OFF MASSACHUSETTS. USS Lee, Capt. John Manley, captured					

DATE	ENGAGEMENT	AMERICAN LOSSES				
		K	W	C	M	D
c. Dec. 16	OFF MASSACHUSETTS (cont.) British provision ship Betsey.					
	TOTALS for the year 1775:	4	5	74		

DATE	ENGAGEMENT	AMERICAN LOSSES				
		K	W	C	M	D
Jan. 12	WEST INDIES. Conn. Polly and Betsey was captured by HMS Pomona, Capt. William Young.					
Jan. 22	OFF NEW JERSEY. Four boats from Elizabethtown captured British transport Blue Mountain Valley.					
Jan. 25	OFF BOSTON. USS Hancock, Capt. John Manley, captured British Happy Return and Norfolk and fought off HMS General Gage.		1			
Jan. 29	OFF CAPE ANN, MASS. USS Franklin, Capt. Samuel Tucker, and Lee, Capt. Daniel Waters, captured British Henry and Esther and fought off HMS Fowey, Capt. G. Montagu.					
Mar. 5	OFF CAPE ANN, MASS. HMS Hope, Capt. George Dawson, was in a running fight with USS Hancock, Lee, Franklin, and Lynch, and had 1 seaman wounded.					
c. Mar. 6	OFF MASSACHUSETTS. USS Hancock, Capt. John Manley, and Franklin, Capt. Samuel Tucker, captured HMS Susannah, Capt. John Frazer.					
Mar. 10	OFF MASSACHUSETTS. USS Hancock, Capt. John Manley, captured HMS Stakesby, Capt. James Watts.					
Mar. 15	OFF CAROLINA. A U.S. transport carrying Capt. Francis Proctor's artillery company was captured by HMS Syren, Capt. Tobias Furneaux.			80		
Mar. 21	OFF MASSACHUSETTS. USS Hancock, Franklin, Lee, and Lynch captured a British ship, but lost it in a fight with HMS Savage, Capt. Hugh Bromedge, and Diligence.					
Apr. 2	OFF CAPE ANN, MASS. USS Franklin, Capt. Samuel Tucker, exchanged fire with HMS Milford, Capt. John Burr.					
Apr. 5	OFF BLOCK ISLAND, R.I. USS Alfred, Capt. Esek Hopkins, captured HMS Bolton, Lt. Edward Sneyd.					
Apr. 6	OFF BLOCK ISLAND, R.I. USS Alfred, Capt. Esek Hopkins, Cabot, Capt. J. B. Hopkins, and Columbus, Capt. Abraham Whipple, fought HMS Glasgow, Capt. Tyringham Howe.	10	14			
	OFF VIRGINIA CAPES. USS Lexington, Capt. James Barry, engaged the tender of HMS Liverpool, which had 1 K and 1 W.	2	2			
c. Apr. 8	OFF MASSACHUSETTS. USS Franklin, Capt. Samuel Tucker, captured British Lately.					

DATE	ENGAGEMENT	AMERICAN LOSSES				
		K	W	C	M	D
Apr. 12	OFF RHODE ISLAND. USS Andrew Doria, Capt. Nicholas Biddle, recaptured John and Joseph from the British.					
May 7	OFF SALEM, MASS. USS Hancock, Capt. Samuel Tucker, captured British Jane and William.					
May 9	DELAWARE RIVER. A dozen U.S. galleys engaged HMS Roebuck, Capt. Andrew S. Hamond, and Liverpool, Capt. Henry Bellew.	1	12			
	DELAWARE RIVER NEAR WILMINGTON. USS Wasp, Capt. Charles Alexander, recaptured a prize from HMS Liverpool, Capt. Henry Bellew.					
May 17	POINT SHIRLEY, MASS. USS Franklin, Capt. James Mugford, ran aground and was attacked by boats from an English warship, but they were beaten off with losses.	1				
May 21	OFF NEWPORT, R.I. USS Andrew Doria, Capt. Nicholas Biddle, captured British Two Friends.					
	OFF CHARLESTON, S.C. S.C. Comet, Capt. Joseph Turpin, and Defence, Capt. Simon Tufts, captured HMS St. James, Capt. Wilson.					
May 26	OFF NEW ENGLAND. USS Cabot, Capt. Elisha Hinman, captured British True Blue.					
May 29	OFF NEW ENGLAND. USS Andrew Doria, Capt. Nicholas Biddle, captured HMS Oxford and Crawford.					
c. June 1	ATLANTIC. Mass. Machias Liberty, Capt. Jeremiah O'Brien captured Two Friends and Polly from West Indies.					
June 8	OFF NEW ENGLAND. USS Warren, Capt. William Burke, Lee, Capt. Daniel Waters, and Lynch, Capt. John Ayres, captured HMS Anne, Capt. John Dennison, carrying troops.					
June 10	OFF CAPE ANN, MASS. USS Hancock, Capt. John Manley, engaged HMS Mermaid, Capt. Ewart Yoward, and wounded 5.					
June 16	BOSTON HARBOR. USS Lee, Franklin, Lynch, Warren, and Conn. Defence, Capt. Seth Harding, captured HMS Annabella, Capt. Hugh Walker, and George, Capt. Archibald Bog, after inflicting 12 K and 13 W.		9			
June 18	NEAR MARBLEHEAD, MASS. Mass. Tyrannicide, Capt. John Fisk, captured HMS Lord Howe, Capt. Robert Park.					
	OFF NEWPORT, R.I. USS Columbus, Capt. Abraham Whipple,		1			

DATE	ENGAGEMENT	AMERICAN LOSSES				
		K	W	C	M	D
June 18	OFF NEWPORT, R.I. (cont.) engaged HMS Cerberus, Capt. John Symons.					
June 19	OFF LONG ISLAND, N.Y. N.Y. General Schuyler, Lt. Charles Pond, retook HMS Crawford, Capt. Maclean.					
c. June 25	ATLANTIC. N.Y. Montgomery, Capt. William Rogers, and General Schuyler, Lt. Joseph Davidson, retook 4 prizes from HMS Greyhound, Capt. Archibald Dickson.					
June 28	CAPE MAY, N.J. USS Lexington, Capt. James Barry, and Wasp, Capt. John Baldwin, fought HMS Kingsfisher, Capt. Alexander Graeme.	1	1			
July 5	OFF EGG HARBOR, N.J. N.Y. General Putnam, Capt. Thomas Cregier, was attacked by 4 British ships.					
July 11	NORTH ATLANTIC. USS Andrew Doria, Capt. Nicholas Biddle, captured British merchantman Nathaniel and Elizabeth.					
July 12	OFF ST. GEORGE'S BANK. Mass. Tyrannicide, Capt. John Fisk, captured HMS Dispatch, Lt. John Goodridge, after the British had 2 K and 11 W.	1	2			
July 13	OFF NEW JERSEY. USS Reprisal, Capt. Lambert Wickes, captured HMS Friendship, Capt. Charles MacKay, and Peter, Capt. John Muckelno.					
c. July 25	NORTH ATLANTIC. USS Warren, Capt. William Burke, had to break off a battle with 2 British transports after powder blew up on his ship.	3	7			
July 27	OFF CAPE ANN, MASS. USS Hancock, Capt. Samuel Tucker, and Franklin, Capt. John Skimmer, captured Peggy, filled with Loyalists.					
	OFF MARTINIQUE. USS Reprisal, Capt. Lambert Wickes, was attacked by HMS Shark, Capt. John Chapman, but beat her off.					
Aug.	NORTH ATLANTIC. USS Andrew Doria, Capt. Nicholas Biddle, captured wheat ship Molly.					
	NORTH ATLANTIC. USS Columbus, Capt. Abraham Whipple, captured Royal Exchange.					
Aug. 4	NORTH ATLANTIC. MASS. Tyrannicide, Capt. John Fisk, captured Betsey and Three Brothers.					
Aug. 7	ST. MARY'S RIVER, FLA. Three U.S. vessels captured Pompey, but its commander, Capt. Graham, blew it up.					

DATE	ENGAGEMENT	AMERICAN LOSSES				
		K	W	C	M	D
Aug. 18	OFF MAINE. USS Nancy, Capt. R. Adams, was captured by HMS Viper, Capt. Samuel Graves.					
Aug. 26	OFF MASSACHUSETTS. USS Warren, Capt. William Burke, was taken by HMS Liverpool, Capt. Henry Bellew.			43		
Sep.	NORTH ATLANTIC. Mass. Massachusetts, Capt. Daniel Souther, captured HMS Henry and Ann, Capt. John Farrah.					
	NORTH ATLANTIC. USS Providence, Capt. John Paul Jones, during the month captured 18 ships and battled HMS Solebay, Capt. Thomas Symonds.					
Before Sep. 7	NORTH ATLANTIC. In rapid succession USS Andrew Doria, Capt. Nicholas Biddle, captured Elizabeth, Lawrence, and Peggy.					
Sep. 27	ATLANTIC. USS Lynch, Capt. John Ayres, escaped from fire of HMS Daphne, Capt. St. John Chinnery.					
	OFF NEW ENGLAND. USS Cabot, Capt. Elisha Hinman, captured 4 British ships.					
Sep. 30	DELAWARE RIVER. U.S. galleys exchanged fire with 4 British warships after a fire raft failed.					
Oct. 2	OFF NEW ENGLAND. USS Cabot, Capt. Elisha Hinman, captured merchantman Clarendon.					
Oct. 3	OFF RHODE ISLAND. Conn. Defence, Capt. Seth Harding, battled 2 British ships.					
Oct. 4	OFF NEW ENGLAND. USS Wasp, Capt. John Baldwin, captured a British ship.					
Oct. 5	OFF NEW ENGLAND. USS Cabot, Capt. Elisha Hinman, captured Georgiana.					
Nov.	BAY OF BISCAY, FRANCE. USS Reprisal, Capt. Lambert Wickes, captured 2 British ships.					
	SOUTH ATLANTIC. USS Independence, Capt. John Young, captured a British merchantman.					
Nov. 10 -30	NORTH ATLANTIC. USS Alfred, Capt. John Paul Jones, and Providence, Capt. Hoysted Hacker, captured 10 British ships.					

DATE	ENGAGEMENT	AMERICAN LOSSES				
		K	W	C	M	D
Nov. 25	ATLANTIC. Mass. Independence, Capt. Simeon Sampson, was taken by HMS Hope, Capt. George Dawson.			95		
Dec.	OFF NEW ENGLAND. USS Wasp, Capt. John Baldwin, captured a British ship and recaptured a French ship.					
Dec. 5	OFF CAPE BRETON ISLAND. USS Alfred, Capt. John Paul Jones, captured Betty.					
Dec. 8	WEST INDIES. USS Andrew Doria, Capt. Isaiah Robinson, captured HMS Racehorse, Lt. William Jones, who was killed along with several others.	4	8			
Dec. 16	OFF LONG ISLAND, N.Y. USS Alfred, Capt. John Paul Jones, lost prize when attacked by HMS Greyhound, Capt. Archibald Dickson.			6		
Dec. 18	OFF NEWPORT, R.I. USS Alfred, Capt. John Paul Jones, lost the Betty, taken on Dec. 5, to HMS Preston, Capt. Samuel Appleby.					
Dec. 20	OFF DELAWARE. USS Lexington, Capt. William Hallock, was captured by HMS Pearl, Capt. Thomas Wilkinson, but was retaken the next night from the British prize crew.					
Dec. 25	ATLANTIC. USS Thorn, Capt. Daniel Waters, battled long in capturing HMS Erskine. The British suffered 20 casualties.	(6)	(12)			
	TOTALS for the year 1776:	29	69	224		

| DATE | ENGAGEMENT | AMERICAN LOSSES | | | | |
		K	W	C	M	D
Feb.	OFF CAPE BRETON ISLAND. USS Providence, Capt. Hoysted Hacker, captured a British ship but suffered several wounded.		(10)			
	OFF FRANCE. USS Reprisal, Capt. Lambert Wickes, captured a British ship.	1	2			
Mar.	EASTERN ATLANTIC. Mass. Freedom, Capt. John Clouston, took 3 prizes.					
Apr. 2	OFF DELAWARE. S.C. Defence, Capt. Thomas Pickering, was captured by HMS Roebuck, Capt. Andrew S. Hamond, and Perseus, Capt. George Elphinstone.			87		
	NORTH ATLANTIC. Mass. Tyrannicide, Capt. Jonathan Harraden, and Massachusetts, Capt. John Fisk, captured the British Chaulkly.					
Apr. 5	OFF DELAWARE. USS Sachem, Capt. James Robinson, was taken by HMS Roebuck and Perseus (see above).					
Apr. 6	OFF NOVA SCOTIA. USS Cabot, Capt. Joseph Olney, was driven ashore by HMS Milford, Capt. Henry Mowat, and abandoned. She was later recovered.					
Apr. 8	NORTH ATLANTIC. Mass. Tyrannicide, Capt. Jonathan Harraden, took the British Lonsdale.					
Apr. 11	DELAWARE BAY. USS Morris, Capt. James Anderson, was forced ashore by HMS Roebuck and Perseus (see above) and was blown up.	1				
Apr. 12	OFF VIRGINIA. USS Trumbull, Capt. Dudley Saltonstall, battled 2 British transports into submission.	7	8			
Apr. 13	NORTH ATLANTIC. USS Lee, Capt. John Skimmer, captured fishing schooner Hawke.					
Apr. 26	OFF CAPE HENRY, VA. Va. Raleigh, Capt. Edward Travis, was captured by HMS Thames, Capt. Tyringham Howe.					
Apr. 27	OFF CAPE FLORIDA USS Hornet, Capt. James Nicholson, was captured by HMS Porcupine, Capt. Thomas Cadogan.			35		
May 3	OFF NEWFOUNDLAND. USS Lee, Capt. John Skimmer, captured fishing sloop Betsey.					

DATE	ENGAGEMENT	AMERICAN LOSSES				
		K	W	C	M	D
May 4	OFF THE NETHERLANDS. USS Surprise, Capt. G. Cunningham, captured Prince of Orange and Joseph, but they were released at Dunkirk.					
c. May 10	OFF NEWFOUNDLAND. USS Lee, Capt. John Skimmer, captured fishing brig Charles.					
May 19	BAY OF BISCAY, FRANCE. USS Lynch, Capt. John Adams, was captured by HMS Feudroyant, Capt. John Jervis.					
May 27	CHESAPEAKE BAY. Six British vessels captured 5 men from Md. Independence.			5		
Late May	OFF MASSACHUSETTS. USS Lee, Capt. John Skimmer, captured 2 fishing brigs Capelin and Industry.					
May 30	NORTH ATLANTIC. USS Hancock, Capt. John Manley, and Boston, Capt. Hector McNeill, exchanged shots with HMS Somerset, but did not continue the battle.					
June	OFF MASSACHUSETTS. USS Providence, Capt. Hoysted Hacker, escaped from a battle with 3 British ships.	1	3			
	BAY OF BISCAY AND ENGLISH CHANNEL. Three U.S. ships-- Reprisal, Capt. Lambert Wickes, Lexington, Capt. Henry Johnson, Dolphin, Lt. Samuel Nicholson--captured 15 vessels by June 26.					
	OFF NEW YORK. Mass. Tyrannicide, Capt. Jonathan Harraden, and Massachusetts, Capt. John Fisk, captured 2 transports carrying Hessian soldiers.					
June 4	OFF BARBADOS. Va. Mosquito, Capt. John Harris, was taken by HMS Ariadne, Capt. Thomas Pringle.			(75)		
June 7	OFF NEWFOUNDLAND. USS Hancock, Capt. John Manley, and Boston, Capt. Hector McNeill, captured HMS Fox, Capt. Patrick Fotheringham.	4	6			
July	OFF FLORIDA. S.C. Notre Dame, Capt. Stephen Seymour, captured merchantman Judith.					
July 7 -8	OFF NOVA SCOTIA. USS Hancock, Capt. John Manley, and Boston, Capt. Hector McNeill, were engaged by HMS Rainbow, Capt. Sir George Collier, and Flora, Capt. John Brisbane. The Hancock was taken.	1		188		
July 20	NEW LONDON, CONN. Conn. Spy, Capt. Robert Niles, was chased into the harbor by several British ships firing.					

DATE	ENGAGEMENT	AMERICAN LOSSES				
		K	W	C	M	D
Aug. 29 -30	OFF NEWFOUNDLAND. USS Lee, Capt. John Skimmer, captured 2 provision ships, Industrious Bee and Lively.					
Sep. 4	CARIBBEAN SEA. USS Raleigh, Capt. Thomas Thompson, shattered but did not capture HMS Druid, Capt. P. Carteret, which lost 6 K and 26 W.	1	2			
	OFF CHARLESTON, S.C. USS Randolph, Capt. Nicholas Biddle, captured 2 transports, True Briton and Charming Peggy.					
Sep. 7	OFF CAPE BRETON ISLAND. USS Providence, Capt. John P. Rathburne, was damaged in battle with 3 British ships but got away.	1	3			
Sep. 10	POWNALBORO, ME. HMS Rainbow, Capt. Sir George Collier, tried to capture Mass. Gruel before it put to sea.			3		
Sep. 16	OFF CAPE HENRY, VA. Mass. Freedom, Capt. John Clouston, was captured by HMS Apollo, Capt. Philip Pownall.			101		
Sep. 19	OFF FRENCH COAST. USS Lexington, Capt. Henry Johnson, was captured by HMS Alert, Capt. John Bazely, which had 3 K and 2 W.	7	11	77		
Early Oct.	SOUTH ATLANTIC. USS Lee, Capt. John Skimmer, captured merchantman Dolphin.					
Oct.	GULF OF MEXICO. S.C. Notre Dame, Lt. William Hall, captured 2 merchantmen, John and Jemmy and Sally.					
Oct. 4 -26	DELAWARE RIVER. On several days American galleys fired on British ships trying to get up to Philadelphia. They forced HMS Augusta, Capt. F. Reynolds, and Merlin, Capt. Samuel Reeve, aground and burned them.					
Nov. 3 -5	DELAWARE RIVER. HMS Pearl, Capt. J. Linzee, and Isis finally drove the U.S. galleys up the river.					
Nov.	OFF SOUTH CAROLINA. USS Providence, Capt. John P. Rathburne, captured an unidentified British ship which lost 1 K and 5 W.					
	NORTH ATLANTIC, NEAR FRANCE. USS Ranger, Capt. John Paul Jones, captured 2 British merchantmen.					

116

DATE	ENGAGEMENT	AMERICAN LOSSES				
		K	W	C	M	D
Dec. 22	OFF CAPE ANTHONY. S.C. Comet, Capt. Joseph Turpin, was captured by HMS Daphne, Capt. St. John Chinnery.			100		
	TOTALS for the year 1777:	24	45	671		

DATE	ENGAGEMENT	AMERICAN LOSSES				
		K	W	C	M	D
Jan.	OFF CAPE FRANCOIS, SAN DOMINGO. USS <u>Horn Snake</u>, Capt. Moore, was captured by 2 British ships.					
Jan. or Feb.	OFF CAPE RACE, NEWFOUNDLAND. USS <u>Reprisal</u>, Capt. Lambert Wickes, was sunk, with but one man rescued.	129				
Mar. 4	OFF MARTINIQUE. USS <u>Resistance</u>, Capt. Chew, engaged a British privateer but did not capture it.	4	12			
Mar. 6	OFF BARBADOS. USS <u>Randolph</u>, Capt. Nicholas Biddle, with 4 other U.S. ships engaged HMS <u>Yarmouth</u>, Capt. Nicholas Vincent, which lost 4 K and 12 W. Then the <u>Randolph</u> blew up, killing all but 4 of its crew.	301				
Mar. 7	DELAWARE BAY. Capt. John Barry with 7 U.S. boats captured 2 forage boats and transport <u>Alert</u>.					
Mar. 9	OFF BARBADOS. USS <u>Alfred</u>, Capt. Elisha Hinman, and <u>Raleigh</u>, Capt. Thomas Thompson, were attacked by HMS <u>Ariadne</u>, Capt. Thomas Pringle, and <u>Ceres</u>, Capt. Samuel Warren. <u>Raleigh</u> sailed away in an unsuccessful effort to draw off one of the enemy, but they concentrated on <u>Alfred</u> and captured it.			181		
Mar. 27	OFF POINT JUDITH, R.I. To avoid capture, USS <u>Columbus</u>, Capt. Abraham Whipple, was run ashore. British marines on HMS <u>Spitfire</u> closed in despite firing and set <u>Columbus</u> ablaze.					
Apr.	OFF CUBA. S.C. <u>Notre Dame</u>, Capt. William Hall, <u>General Moultrie</u>, Capt. Sullivan, <u>Polly</u>, Capt. Anthony, and <u>Fair American</u>, Capt. Morgan, who had been with the ill-fated <u>Randolph</u> on Mar. 6, captured 11 British merchantmen.					
Apr. 14	OFF IRELAND. USS <u>Ranger</u>, Capt. John Paul Jones, captured a merchantman and sank her.					
Apr. 15	NEAR THE BAHAMAS. Conn. <u>Defence</u>, Capt. Samuel Smedley, and <u>Oliver Cromwell</u>, Capt. Timothy Parker, captured 2 British privateers, <u>Cyrus</u> and <u>Admiral Keppel</u>.	2	5			
Apr. 17	OFF IRELAND. USS <u>Ranger</u>, Capt. John Paul Jones, captured British merchantman <u>Lord Chatham</u>.					
Apr. 19 -20	OFF IRELAND. USS <u>Ranger</u>, Capt. John Paul Jones, captured and sank 2 British merchantmen.					

DATE	ENGAGEMENT	AMERICAN LOSSES				
		K	W	C	M	D
Apr. 23	ST. MARY'S ISLE, SCOTLAND. USS Ranger, Capt. John Paul Jones, landed to seize Lord Selkirk, but he not being there the sailors looted his house. Jones returned the silver to Lady Selkirk.					
	WHITEHAVEN, ENGLAND. Capt. John Paul Jones landed and burned one ship in port, but failed to set fire to others.				1	
Apr. 24	OFF CARRICKFERGUS, IRELAND. USS Ranger, Capt. John Paul Jones, was attacked by HMS Drake, Capt. Burdon, but after the loss of 42 K and W, Drake surrendered to Ranger.	2	6			
Apr. 30	NARRAGANSETT BAY. Trying to get to sea, USS Providence, Capt. Abraham Whipple, was cannonaded by several British ships. Whipple returned the fire and damaged HMS Lark and got through the blockade.					
May 2	OFF CAPE HENLOPEN, DEL. HMS Zebra, Capt. John Orde, tried to drive rebels from 2 grounded ships but failed to dislodge them.					
May 7	DELAWARE RIVER. Five British ships set fire to USS Washington and Effingham before they got to sea, along with a score of other ships.					
May 10	HUNTINGTON BAY, LONG ISLAND. HMS Raven fired at a rebel galley.					
June	CHARLESTON HARBOR, S.C. Conn. Defence, Commo. Gillon (loaned to S.C.) and S.C. Volant, Capt. Oliver Daniel, engaged 3 British ships and captured 2: Ranger and Governor Tonyn's Revenge.					
Summer	NORTH ATLANTIC. Conn. Spy, Capt. Robert Niles, was captured on its return from France.					
Aug. 27	OFF SANDY HOOK, N.J. USS Resistance, Capt. William Burke, was captured and burned by HMS Ariel, Capt. Charles Phipps.					
Sep. 27	NEAR PENOBSCOT BAY, ME. USS Raleigh, Capt. John Barry,	16		134		

DATE	ENGAGEMENT	AMERICAN LOSSES				
		K	W	C	M	D
Sep. 27	NEAR PENOBSCOT BAY, ME. (cont.) engaged HMS Unicorn, Capt. John Ford, and Experiment, Capt. James Wallace. Damaged, Barry ran his ship on to Seal Island and escaped with a few of his crew; the rest surrendered.					
Oct.	OFF CAPE HENRY, VA. Va. Patriot, Capt. Richard Taylor, was in a fight with a British privateer, Lord Howe.	1	9			
Oct. 29	NARRAGANSETT BAY. R.I. Hawke, under Maj. Silas Talbot, and mixed crew of sailors and soldiers, captured HMS Pigot and a crew of 45.					
Autumn	OFF TANGIER ISLAND, CHESAPEAKE BAY. Va. Dolphin, Capt. John Cowper, engaged 2 British barges.	5	7			
	TOTALS for the year 1778:	460	39	315		

DATE	ENGAGEMENT	AMERICAN LOSSES				
		K	W	C	M	D
Mar.	OFF CAPE HENRY, VA. USS Warren, Commo. J. B. Hopkins, Ranger, Capt. Thomas Simpson, and Queen of France, Capt. Joseph Olney, captured a British privateer.					
	OFF CAROLINA AND GEORGIA. S.C. squadron of Notre Dame, Eagle, Hornet, General Moultrie, Sally, and Family Trader captured 3 ships in 10 days.		1			
Mar. 16	OFF ST. THOMAS, VIRGIN ISLANDS. USS General Gates, Capt. Daniel Waters, and Mass. Hazard, Capt. John F. Williams, captured a British privateer, Active, after killing 3 and wounding 20.	3	(6)			
Mar. 21	SAVANNAH RIVER. S.C. Congress fought several British galleys.		1			
Mar. 26	LONG ISLAND SOUND. USS Hancock, Capt. Elisha Hinman, battled a privateer.		1			
Apr.	OFF CAROLINA COAST. S.C. Hornet was captured by HMS Daphne, Capt. St. John Chinnery.					
	OFF GEORGIA COAST. Ga. Congress, Capt. Campbell, and Lee, Capt. Milligan, were captured by HMS Greenwich and 3 galleys. Lee carried French crew of 130.			100		
	OFF CHARLESTON, S.C. S.C. Notre Dame, Capt. William Hall, Beaufort, and Bellona captured 3 vessels taking supplies to the British at Savannah.					
Apr. 6	OFF CAPE HENRY, VA. USS Warren, Commo. J. B. Hopkins, Ranger, Capt. Thomas Simpson, and Queen of France, Capt. Joseph Olney, captured British Hibernia.					
Apr. 7	OFF CAPE HENRY, VA. Same 3 ships above captured HMS Jason, Capt. Porterfield, and 6 other ships with supplies for the British at Savannah.					
Spring	OFF CAPE HENRY, VA. Va. Dolphin, Capt. John Cowper, was sunk by 3 British ships.	76				
May	NORTH ATLANTIC. Conn. Oliver Cromwell, Capt. Timothy Parker, captured HMS York.					
Early May	ELIZABETH RIVER, VA. Va. Blacksnake was captured by HMS Cornwallis and boats after the British took Norfolk. Some rebel casualties occurred.					
May 7	OFF MASSACHUSETTS. USS Providence, Capt. Hoysted Hacker, captured HMS Diligence, Lt. T. Walbeoff, after 8 were killed and	4	10			

DATE	ENGAGEMENT	AMERICAN LOSSES				
		K	W	C	M	D
May 7	OFF MASSACHUSETTS (cont.) 19 wounded.					
June	OFF CHARLESTON, S.C. S.C. Rattlesnake, Capt. Friskie, captured a British ship.					
June 5	OFF SANDY HOOK, N.J. Conn. Oliver Cromwell, Capt. Timothy Parker, was captured by HMS Daphne, Capt. St. John Chinnery.	3	7	118		
June 6	ATLANTIC. USS Boston, Capt. Samuel Tucker, and Confederacy captured 3 British ships.					
June 7	OFF CAPE HENLOPEN, DEL. Pa. General Greene, Capt. James Montgomery, captured a privateer.					
Late June	CHESAPEAKE BAY. Md. Chester, Commo. Thomas Grason, engaged an enemy vessel which got away.		1			
July 15	OFF NEWFOUNDLAND. USS Providence, Capt. Abraham Whipple, Ranger, Capt. Thomas Simpson, and Queen of France, Capt. John P. Rathburne, captured 10 merchant ships from a large convoy.					
Aug. 7	NORTH ATLANTIC. USS Argo, Capt. Silas Talbot, captured a British ship.					
Aug. 12	NORTH ATLANTIC. USS Deane, Capt. Samuel Nicholson, and Boston, Capt. Samuel Tucker, captured HMS Sandwich, Capt. Hill.					
Aug. 25	NORTH ATLANTIC. Same 2 ships as above captured HMS Thorn, Capt. Wardlow.					
	NORTH ATLANTIC. USS Argo, Capt. Silas Talbot, and Saratoga, Capt. James Munro, attacked an enemy ship that got away.	1	6			
Aug. 31	OFF BRITISH COAST. USS Bonhomme Richard, Capt. John Paul Jones, captured British privateer Union.					
Sep.	NORTH ATLANTIC. USS Deane, Capt. Samuel Nicholson, and Boston, Capt. Samuel Tucker, captured 4 privateers.					
Sep. 23	OFF ENGLISH COAST. USS Bonhomme Richard, Capt. John Paul Jones, and Pallas, Capt. Denis Cotteneau, captured HMS Serapis, Capt. Richard Pearson, and Countess of Scarborough, Capt. T. Piercy. The Serapis had 49 K, 68 W, and 203 C; the	165	137			

DATE	ENGAGEMENT	AMERICAN LOSSES				
		K	W	C	M	D
Sep. 23	OFF ENGLISH COAST (cont.) <u>Countess</u> 4 K, 20 W, and 126 C.					
Nov.	OFF SANDY HOOK, N.J. Mass. <u>Pickering</u>, Capt. Jonathan Harraden, engaged 3 British privateers.		8			
Nov. 13	OFF SABA, WEST INDIES. USS <u>Eagle</u>, Capt. John Ashmead, was chased into the harbor and seized by 2 British privateers despite Dutch protest.					
	TOTALS for the year 1779:	252	178	218		

DATE	ENGAGEMENT	AMERICAN LOSSES				
		K	W	C	M	D
Jan. 23	OFF CHARLESTON, S.C. The tender of USS Ranger, Capt. Thomas Simpson, captured a British ship.					
Jan. 26	OFF CHARLESTON, S.C. USS Ranger, Capt. Thomas Simpson, and Providence, Commo. Abraham Whipple, captured 2 British transports, Henry and Swift.					
Apr. 9	CHARLESTON HARBOR, S.C. Some U.S. galleys exchanged fire with 4 British ships at close range.					
May 18	NORTH ATLANTIC. USS Trumbull, Capt. James Nicholson, captured a British ship.					
June 1	NORTH ATLANTIC. USS Trumbull, Capt. James Nicholson, battled the British privateer Watt, but could not take it. Watt lost 13 K and 79 W.	17	31			
Summer	ATLANTIC. Va. Pocahontas, Capt. Eleazer Callender, was captured by HMS Alcide.			58		
July 9	CARIBBEAN SEA. Mass. Protector, Capt. John F. Williams, engaged the British merchantman Admiral Duff, which blew up.	1	5			
Sep. 3	OFF NEWFOUNDLAND. USS Mercury, Capt. William Pickles, with Henry Laurens aboard, was captured by HMS Vestal, Capt. George Keppel.					
Sep. 9	SOUTH ATLANTIC. USS Saratoga, Capt. John Young, was engaged in a long battle with HMS Keppel, Capt. John Steel, with extensive damage to both. Steel had 1 K and 3 W.					
Sep. 13	SOUTH ATLANTIC. USS Deane, Capt. Samuel Nicholson, and Trumbull, Capt. James Nicholson, captured the British Admiral Barrington, only to lose it later.					
Oct. 8	ATLANTIC. USS Saratoga, Capt. John Young, captured the British Charming Sally, but lost it next day.					
Oct. 9	ATLANTIC. USS Saratoga, Capt. John Young, took 3 British ships, but lost them to HMS Intrepid. Saratoga was not seen again.					

DATE	ENGAGEMENT	AMERICAN LOSSES				
		K	W	C	M	D
Dec.	SOUTH ATLANTIC. USS _Ariel_, Capt. John Paul Jones, battled HMS _Triumph_, Capt. John Pindar, which surrendered and then escaped.					
	TOTALS for the year 1780:	18	36	58		

DATE	ENGAGEMENT	AMERICAN LOSSES				
		K	W	C	M	D
Feb.	ATLANTIC. USS <u>Alliance</u>, Capt. John Barry, captured British privateer <u>Alert</u>.					
Apr. 2	ATLANTIC. USS <u>Alliance</u>, Capt. John Barry, captured British privateers <u>Mars</u> and <u>Minerva</u>.					
Apr. 7	JAMES RIVER, VA. Va. <u>Patriot</u>, Lt. James Watkins, was captured.			31		
Apr. 14	OFF VIRGINIA. USS <u>Confederacy</u>, Capt. Seth Harding, was captured by HMS <u>Roebuck</u>, Capt. Andrew Douglas.			290		
May 2	ATLANTIC. USS <u>Alliance</u>, Capt. John Barry, captured 2 merchantmen.					
May 6	OFF SANDY HOOK, N.J. Mass. <u>Protector</u>, Capt. John F. Williams, was captured by HMS <u>Roebuck</u>, Capt. Andrew Douglas.			180		
May 28	NORTH ATLANTIC. USS <u>Alliance</u>, Capt. John Barry, captured HMS <u>Atalanta</u>, Capt. Edwards, and <u>Trepassy</u>, Capt. Smyth. The British lost 12 K, 29 W, and 169 C.	8	19			
Late July	OFF NOVA SCOTIA. R. I. <u>Aurora</u> was captured by HMS <u>Royal Oak</u>, Adm. Marriot Arbuthnot.					
Aug. 8	OFF DELAWARE. USS <u>Trumbull</u>, Capt. James Nicholson, was captured by HMS <u>Iris</u> and <u>General Monk</u>, Capt. Rogers.	5	11	175		
Oct.	OFF MADEIRA ISLANDS. S.C. <u>South Carolina</u>, Commo. Alexander Gillon, captured <u>Venus</u>.					
Nov. 30	JONES CREEK, DELAWARE BAY. An enemy barge fired on a Del. ship containing 37 Continentals.		1			
Dec. 5	DELAWARE BAY. Col. Charles Pope, who commanded the Del. navy, and the <u>Vigilant</u> exchanged fire with the <u>Fox</u>, Capt. Joseph Burton.					
	TOTALS for the year 1781:	13	31	675		

DATE	ENGAGEMENT	AMERICAN LOSSES				
		K	W	C	M	D
c. Apr. 8	DELAWARE BAY. Pa. Hyder Ally, Capt. Joshua Barney, captured HMS General Monk, Capt. Rogers. The British lost 20 K and 33 W.	3	12			
Apr. 12	SOUTH ATLANTIC. USS Deane, Capt. Samuel Nicholson, captured HMS Jackall, Lt. Logie, and crew of 52.					
May	CARIBBEAN SEA. USS Deane, Capt. Samuel Nicholson, captured 4 British ships.					
May 5	NEAR EGG HARBOR, N.J. USS Enterprize, Capt. Hand, forced a British ship ashore.					
c. May 25	BLOCK ISLAND, R.I. Two galleys from Boston captured HMS Terrible, taking 14 prisoners, and destroyed another galley.					
July 6	SOUTH ATLANTIC. USS General Washington, Capt. Joshua Barney, fought off 2 British ships.					
Early Oct.	NORTH ATLANTIC. Mass. Tartar captured a privateer.					
Nov. 30	CAGEY'S STRAIT, CHESAPEAKE BAY. A Md. barge Protector, Commo. Hedekiah Whaley, was engaged by 6 British barges and captured. The enemy suffered about 25 K and W.	25	29	40		
Dec. 20	OFF NORTH CAROLINA. S.C. South Carolina, Capt. John Joyner, was chased by 3 British warships and after a battle was captured.	(3)	(3)	450		
	TOTALS for the year 1782:	31	44	490		

DATE	ENGAGEMENT	AMERICAN LOSSES				
		K	W	C	M	D
Early Jan.	GUADALOUPE. USS Hague, Capt. John Manley, was forced ashore by HMS Dolphin, but escaped after repairs were made under enemy fire.		1			
Late Feb.	DUCK CREEK, KENT CO., DEL. Capt. Snyder in a Pa. naval ship captured a Loyalist galley, Lady's Revenge, but the crew escaped.					
Mar. 10	OFF FLORIDA. USS Alliance, Capt. John Barry, and Duc de Lauzun, Capt. John Green, were chased by 3 British ships. HMS Sybil, Capt. James Vashon, opened fire on Green, but was driven off much damaged by Barry.	1	9			
Mar. 21	DEVIL'S ISLAND, CHESAPEAKE BAY. A Md. naval ship under Capt. John Lynn captured some enemy barges.					
	TOTALS for the year 1783:	1	10			

SUMMATIONS AND IMPLICATIONS

Summations and Implications

DATE	SUMMATIONS	AMERICAN LOSSES				
		K	W	C	M	D
1775	Casualties in 143 military engagements	323	436	519	5	57
	Casualties in 14 naval engagements	4	5	74		
1776	Casualties in 252 military engagements	604	562	5165	1	
	Casualties in 66 naval engagements	29	69	224		
1777	Casualties in 265 military engagements	1389	2253	2169	38	2
	Casualties in 42 naval engagements	24	45	671		
1778	Casualties in 138 military engagements	753	443	1212	139	20
	Casualties in 26 naval engagements	460	39	315		1
1779	Casualties in 127 military engagements	659	829	859	18	
	Casualties in 29 naval engagements	252	178	218		
1780	Casualties in 152 military engagements	984	1886	4661	9	20
	Casualties in 13 naval engagements	18	36	58		
1781	Casualties in 196 military engagements	1003	1454	761	1216	
	Casualties in 12 naval engagements	13	31	675		
1782	Casualties in 53 military engagements	277	124	80		
	Casualties in 9 naval engagements	31	44	490		
1783	Casualties in 5 military engagements		1	1		
	Casualties in 4 naval engagements	1	10			
	Totals for 1331 military engagements	5992	7988	15427	1426	99
	Totals for 215 naval engagements	832	457	2725		1
	Grand total of battle casualties	6824	8445	18152	1426	100
	Estimate of those who died in camp	10000				
	Estimate of prisoners who died	8500				
	Probable deaths in service	25324				

SUMMATIONS AND
IMPLICATIONS

☆

The foregoing casualty lists represent the fruits of our long investigation. The known battle casualties have simply been added up, but the totals do not, we are sure, measure up to the true numbers. As mentioned in the Introduction, for some battles no report of American casualties could be found; casualty figures for a few others may have been incomplete; and for several naval battles and ship sinkings no figures on losses were available. Our own suspicion, for what it is worth, is that the total killed-in-action number is probably a thousand short of the true total.

As for our estimate of those who died in camp of disease or wounds, we should explain that the military returns available account only for those troops (Continental, state, and militia) who were actually serving, at the time of the return, with the main Continental Army or its detachments and divisions. Many of the actions listed in this volume, on the other hand, were fought by state and militia troops remaining near their homes throughout the rebelling colonies and unattached to the main army. Nevertheless, we have used the returns to project a rough estimate of all deaths in camp. First we deducted those killed in actions which involved the main army (and thus would have shown up in the total death figures on the returns) to arrive at some estimate of true deaths in camp for that army. In the period covered by monthly returns made to headquarters, February 1778 through May 1783, we deduced a total of 4,328 who died in camp. Unaccounted for are those who died in the first two months at Valley Forge, the rest of 1777, and all of 1776. We have projected a total of 3,200 for this period and added 600 for the eight months of war in 1775. Thus the new total is 8,128 deaths in camp. However, not yet counted are those who were not reported to the adjutant general because they died in state regiments and militia units in other areas or because they were on the ill-fated Canadian expedition of 1775-76. Nor have we usually found figures for the Southern Department of the Continental Army or the free-flowing Southern militia who came and went under Marion, Sumter, Pickens, Clarke, and others. A total of 1,872 deaths in camp would seem not to be exaggerated for these unreported categories. Thus we wind up with an estimate of 10,000 deaths in camp, a figure we believe to be defensible.

The prisoners of war who died before release or exchange presented an even more thorny problem. George Washington protested repeatedly about their inhumane treatment. Colonel Ethan Allen, himself a prisoner for a time in England and New York City, accused the British of "murdering premeditately [sic] (in cold blood) near or quite 2,000 helpless prisoners, and that in the most clandestine, mean and shameful manner." Dr. James Thacher, who served in the Continental Army, estimated in his *Military Journal* (Boston: Richardson and Lord, 1823) that the number of American prisoners who died was "no less than eleven thousand." However, his figure for total American deaths in action, camp, and prison (70,000) is so far wrong that it casts doubt on this component. David Ramsay, in his *History of South Carolina* (Charleston: D. Longworth, 1809), declared that over 800, or a third of those held on prison ships in Charleston harbor, perished within a year.

Limiting herself to the prisons and prison ships around New York City, Danske Dandridge, in *American Prisoners of the Revolution* (Charlottesville: Michie Co., printers, 1911), lists 8,000 Americans held at one time or another aboard the prison ship *Jersey*, but she did not know their fate or how many other prisoners perished. In *The Spirit of Seventy-Six* (Indianapolis: Bobbs-Merrill, 1958) Henry S. Commager and Richard B. Morris counted 4,000 Americans taken in the fighting around New York in the summer and fall of 1776, over 5,000 captured at Charleston in 1780, and about 2,000 seamen and fishermen seized. More significant is their estimate that "7,000 Americans perished on the notorious prison ships in the Hudson." Of course, there were other prisons, in England as well as America, so Dr. Thacher may not be too far off with his figure. Father Charles H. Metzger, in his *The Prisoner in the American Revolution* (Chicago: Loyola University Press, 1971), went into considerable detail about treatment and exchange, but hazarded no guess about total numbers or total deaths. To keep to a conservative guess, we adopted the figure of 8,500 for American prisoners who died in confinement.

The grand total of the killed and died in service (25,324) represents 0.9 percent of the American population of 2,781,000 white and black in 1780. The Mexican War produced deaths amounting to 0.06 percent of the population; the Civil War, nearly 1.6 percent of the population; the first World War, 0.12 percent; and World War II, 0.28 percent. Thus the Revolution was second only to the Civil War in deaths relative to population. More arresting would be the percentage of those who lost their lives in relation to the total number who bore arms, but as yet we have no figure for the latter. Utilizing a tentative guess of 200,000 men in service at one time or another, the percentage of deaths in the Revolution is 12½ percent of the participants. This loss is very close to the almost 13 percent suffered by Union troops in our bloodiest war.

The tabulations also reveal that New Jersey was first in number of engagements (238), and that New York was second, with 228.

The information provided in this book has been gathered from source materials. It has not been weighed for causes or effects. Our purpose was simply to bring together the scattered facts of engagements and their cost in human lives and injuries. It is unanalyzed raw data for others to make use of in various investigations. The figures, of course, can tell us more than the mere number of casualties. They give us some human dimensions of the war. They not only invite comparisons with other wars, our own and European, but they also raise some significant questions. What assumptions about our Revolution must we now reexamine? What are the implications for future research? We can suggest a few lines of inquiry.

Initially most of the American colonies easily broke away from British rule by expelling their British governors and judges, and ignoring the royally appointed councillors. The burden of restoring and maintaining British authority fell on the mother country, which meant that British arms had to assume the offensive and defeat or destroy the Colonial army and navy. A review of the engagements listed will indicate how forcibly, how frequently, and how wisely Great Britain pursued this end. Did she maximize her strength in various tactics, or did she thrust and parry, or fritter away her strength in inconclusive actions?

The numerous small actions during the Revolution may suggest at first glance that it was largely guerrilla warfare, but closer examination casts doubt on this characterization of the hostilities; small harassments are not the same as hit-and-run tactics. Moreover the frequency of engagements dispels the view that the Revolution was entirely seasonal, with long lulls of inaction. Of course, the big campaigns were planned for good weather. Was that a characteristic of an agricultural society?

In this connection, who seemed to emerge first from their winter quarters: Americans from their rural camps, or British from their city barracks?

After the Revolution rolled out of New England in the spring of 1776, where was the action hottest in terms of highest casualties? Are the best remembered battles necessarily those costing the most casualties? Why are some costly engagements largely overlooked? Classifying the actions and casualties in various ways will provoke other questions.

The many ship-to-shore actions of individual British warships, compared to ship-versus-ship conflicts, affect assumptions made about the role of the British navy. Was it utilized as effectively as it might have been? Was it supposed to assist the army or to pursue an independent course, or both?

The immense theater of war and the limited mobility of armies raise questions about the scope of actions in some regions, the absence of engagements in other regions, and the importance of possessing ground or cities compared to defeating armies in determining the outcome of the war. The relation of this latter strategic concept to the utilization of the Loyalists also bears reconsideration, and the tables reveal when and where Loyalists were used. Such a study might resolve the contemporary argument arising from the charge that the Loyalists did very little and the defense that Loyalist strength was great but ill-managed.

Similarly, our figures might reopen consideration of the role of Indians. Which side made the most or best use of them? How much frontier hostility between reds and whites was inspired by the war?

In regard to types of military confrontation, how often did cavalry function as cavalry? Were mounted men primarily the eyes of the infantry in the absense of aerial observation? Were horses best used to transport infantry in a hurry? By reviewing the casualties in relation to the size of the forces engaged, military technicians may be able to estimate the effectiveness of fire power. The expenditure of powder, bullets, and cannon balls seems prodigious, even with the acknowledged deficiencies of aiming.

If we cannot offer the final word on casualties of the American Revolution, we hope that we can at least elevate the discussion of those losses by the addition of figures that have heretofore been unknown or unavailable.

BIBLIOGRAPHY

☆

The scope and sweep of this investigation precluded its being a one-man operation. Our research team searched for Revolutionary War records in fourteen state archives of the thirteen original states plus Vermont, as well as in the National Archives. In addition, the libraries of the state historical societies in those states were visited. We were assisted by the efforts of the New Jersey and South Carolina state archives to compile lists of engagements for their own states. We express our thanks to all these institutions for various courtesies.

Many secondary works merely repeated the casualty figures we had already found in contemporary manuscript sources, but occasionally they helped us with a more precise date or a location we lacked. We would like to think that we have not missed anything relevant and reliable, but that remains only a hope. In spite of the fact that some records have been burned or lost, the literature of the American Revolution is much larger than the nonspecialist suspects of an event now nearly two hundred years old.

MANUSCRIPTS

Manuscript collections having some bearing on the American Revolution are voluminous. What follows are some of those depositories and collections most useful for engagements and casualty figures.

Connecticut Historical Society
  Farmington manuscripts
  Hoadley collection
  Jeremiah Wadsworth papers
  Oliver Wolcott manuscripts
  American Revolution collection
Connecticut State Library
  Connecticut Archives, Revolutionary War (3 series)
  William Boardman collection
  Nathaniel Fitz-Randolph manuscripts
  Jonathan Trumbull papers
  Jonathan Trumbull, Jr., papers

Henrietta W. Hubbard collection
Kilbourn collection
Governor Joseph Trumbull collection
Cornwall Revolutionary papers (photostats)
Delaware Hall of Records
  Executive papers, military correspondence
  John Dickinson collection (photostats)
  Legislative papers
Historical Society of Delaware
  Captain William Dansey letters

Allen McLane papers
W. S. Morse collection
Rodney papers
George Read papers
H. F. Brown collection
National Archives
Papers of the Continental Congress
Navy Department, Office of Naval History
Revolutionary War records
Library of Congress
George Washington papers (microfilm)
Georgia Historical Society
Bevan collection
John Houston papers
University of Georgia Library
Cuyler collection
Hargrett collection
Keith Read collection
Maryland Historical Society
Carroll papers
Revolutionary War collection
Otho Holland Williams papers
Military collection, miscellaneous
Maryland Hall of Records
Rainbow series
Revolutionary War papers
American Antiquarian Society
War Diary of John Smith of Bristol, Rhode Island
Boston Public Library
See *Manuscripts of the American Revolution in the Boston Public Library* Boston: Hall, 1964.
Massachusetts Historical Society
General William Heath papers
General Benjamin Lincoln papers
General Henry Knox papers
Solomon Lovell papers
General John Thomas papers
Miscellaneous papers, 1774-75
Letter books of General John Sullivan
Timothy Pickering papers

Artemus Ward papers
Massachusetts State Archives
Volumes 145, 146, and 193-205 were the most useful.
William L. Clements Library
Sir Henry Clinton papers
General Nathanael Greene papers
General Thomas Gage papers
Frederick Mackenzie papers
New Hampshire Historical Society
Cornish Town papers
John Stark papers
Morris papers
New Hampshire State Archives
Weare papers
Miscellaneous Revolutionary War documents
Province and Revolutionary papers
"New Hampshire Archives"
Morristown National Park
Lloyd Smith collection
Archives Division, New Jersey State Library
Revolutionary War collection
Rutgers University Special Collections
Israel Shreve papers
New York Public Library
Livingston papers
Philip Schuyler papers
New York State Library
See their forthcoming published calendar of Manuscripts of the Revolutionary Period (1765-83).
New York Historical Society
Horatio Gates papers
North Carolina Department of Archives and History
Board of War journal and correspondence, 1780-81
Abner Nash papers
Thomas Burke papers
Richard Caswell papers
Dickson manuscripts
English records
John A. Robeson collection

BIBLIOGRAPHY

David Schenck papers
Miscellaneous Revolution papers,
1776-83
Secretary of State's Office papers
Military History Research Collection
at Carlisle Barracks
Sol Feinstone Collection
(microfilm)
Historical Society of Pennsylvania
Elias Boudinot papers
Dreer collection
General John Lacey
correspondence
Gratz collection
Edward Hand papers
Anthony Wayne papers
William Irvine papers
Jacob Weiss family correspondence
Miscellaneous Revolutionary War
papers
Major William Armstrong papers
Pennsylvania State Archives
Edward Hand papers
Rhode Island Historical Society
Nathanael Greene papers
Revolutionary Correspondence,
1775-82
Ward manuscripts
Rhode Island State Archives

Revolutionary War papers
South Carolina State Archives
Gibbes collection
South Carolina Historical Society
Middleton collection
Pinckney papers
South Caroliniana Library at University of South Carolina
Aedanus Burke manuscripts
William Butler manuscripts
Stephen Dayton manuscripts
Oliver Hart manuscripts
John Laurens manuscripts
Francis Marion manuscripts
Mayes family records
Charleston Library Society
John Rutledge manuscripts
Vermont Historical Society
Revolutionary War papers
Vermont State Archives
Stevens papers
Virginia Historical Society
Dabney papers
Virginia State Library, Archives
Division
State papers
Miscellaneous Revolutionary
manuscripts
Cabell papers

NEWSPAPERS

The following newspapers, published during the war years, were examined for reports of land and sea battles:

Connecticut Courant (Hartford)
Connecticut Gazette (New London)
Connecticut Journal (New Haven)
Essex Journal (Newburyport, Mass.)
Freeman's Journal (Philadelphia)
Independent Chronicle (Boston)
Maryland Gazette (Annapolis)
Massachusetts Spy (Boston)
New England Chronicle (Boston)
New Jersey Gazette (Burlington and
Trenton)
New-York Gazette (New York)

New-York Mercury (New York)
Newport Mercury (Newport, R.I.)
North Carolina Gazette (New Bern)
Pennsylvania Gazette (Philadelphia)
Pennsylvania Packet (Philadelphia)
Rivington's New York Gazette
(New York)
Royal Gazette (Charleston, S. C.)
Royal Georgia Gazette (Savannah)
Virginia Gazette (Williamsburg and
Richmond)

BIBLIOGRAPHY

PRIMARY PRINTED SOURCES

Albany Co. Committee of Correspondence. *Minutes of the Albany Committee of Correspondence, 1775-78.* Edited by James Sullivan. 2 vols. Albany: University of the State of New York, 1923,1925.

Allen, Ethan. *A Narrative of Col. Ethan Allen's Captivity, from the Time of His Being Taken by the British . . . . Written by Himself, and Now Published for the Information of the Curious, in All Nations.* Newbury [Mass.]: John Mycall, 1779.

André, John. *André's Journal: An Authentic Record of the Movements and Engagements of the British Army in America from June 1777 to November 1778 as Recorded from Day to Day by Major John André.* Edited by Henry Cabot Lodge. 2 vols. Boston: Bibliophile Society, 1903.

Angell, Israel. *The Diary of Colonel Israel Angell, Commanding the Second Rhode Island Continental Regiment During the American Revolution, 1778-1781; Transcribed from the Original Manuscript, Together with a Biographical Sketch of the Author and Illustrative Notes.* Edited by Edward Field. Providence, R. I.: Preston & Rounds, 1899.

Baurmeister, Carl von. *Revolution in America: Confidential Letters and Journals 1776-1784 of Adjutant General Major Baurmeister of the Hessian Forces.* Translated and annotated by Bernhard A. Uhlendorf. New Brunswick, N. J.: Rutgers University Press, 1957.

Burgoyne, John. *A State of the Expedition from Canada, as Laid Before the House of Commons, by Lieutenant-General Burgoyne, and Verified by Evidence: with a Collection of Authentic Documents, and an Addition of Many Circumstances Which Were Prevented from Appearing Before the House by the Prorogation of Parliament. Written and Collected by Himself.* London: J. Almon, 1780.

Clark, George Rogers. *George Rogers Clark Papers 1771-1783.* Edited by James Alton James. Collections of the Illinois State Historical Library, Virginia Series, vols. 3-4. 2 vols. Springfield, Ill.: Illinois State Historical Library, 1912,1924.

Clinton, George. *Public Papers of George Clinton, First Governor of New York.* War of the Revolution Series. 10 vols. Albany: State Printers, 1899–1914.

Clinton, Sir Henry. *The American Rebellion: Sir Henry Clinton's Narrative of His Campaigns, 1775-1782, with an Appendix of Original Documents.* Edited by William B. Willcox. New Haven: Yale University Press, 1954.

Condict, Jemima. *Jemima Condict, Her Book; Being a Transcription of the Diary of an Essex County Maid During the Revolutionary War.* Newark, N. J.: Carteret Book Club, 1930.

Dearborn, Henry. *An Account of the Battle of Bunker Hill, Written for the Port Folio, at the Request of the Editor.* Philadelphia: Harrison Hall, 1818.

— — —. *Revolutionary War Journals of Henry Dearborn 1775-1783.* Edited by Lloyd A. Brown and Howard H. Peckham. Chicago: Caxton Club, 1939.

BIBLIOGRAPHY

A Detail of Some Particular Services Performed in America, During the Years 1776, 1777, 1778, and 1779, Compiled from Journals and Original Papers, Supposed to be Chiefly Taken from the Journal Kept on Board of the Ship Rainbow . . . . New York: Ithiel Town, 1835.

Digby, William. *The British Invasion from the North: The Campaigns of Generals Carleton and Burgoyne, from Canada, 1776-1777, with the Journal of Lieut. William Digby, of the 53rd, or Shropshire Regiment of Foot.* Edited by James Phinney Baxter. Albany: J. Munsell, 1887.

Force, Peter, editor. *American Archives: Consisting of a Collection of Authentick Records, State Papers, Debates, and Letters and other Notices of Publick Affairs* . . . . 4th ser. 9 vols. Washington: M. St. Clair Clarke and Peter Force, 1837-53.

Gibbes, Robert Wilson, editor. *Documentary History of the American Revolution: Consisting of Letters and Papers Relating to the Contest for Liberty, Chiefly in South Carolina, from Originals in the Possession of the Editor, and Other Sources.* 3 vols. New York: D. Appleton & Co., 1853-57.

Graves, Thomas. *The Graves Papers and Other Documents Relating to the Naval Operations of the Yorktown Campaign, July to October, 1781.* Edited by French Ensor Chadwick. Publications of the Naval History Society, vol. 7. New York: De Vinne Press, 1916.

Hadden, James Murray. *Hadden's Journal and Orderly Books: A Journal Kept in Canada and upon Burgoyne's Campaign in 1776 and 1777, by Lieut. James M. Hadden, Roy. Art. Also Orders Kept by Him and Issued by Sir Guy Carleton, Lieut. General John Burgoyne and Major General William Phillips, in 1776, 1777 and 1778. With an explanatory chapter and notes by Horatio Rogers.* Albany, N. Y.: Joel Munsell's Sons, 1884.

Hall, Edwin, compiler. *The Ancient Historical Records of Norwalk, Connecticut, with a Plan of the Ancient Settlement, and of the Town in 1847.* Norwalk, Conn.: James Mallory & Co., 1847.

Haskell, Caleb. *Caleb Haskell's Diary, May 5-May 30, 1776: A Revolutionary Soldier's Record before Boston and with Arnold's Quebec Expedition.* Edited by Lothrop Withington. Newburyport [Mass.]: W. H. Huse & Co., 1881.

Heath, William. *Memoirs of Major-Gen. William Heath, By Himself* . . . . *To Which is Added the Accounts of the Battle of Bunker Hill by Generals Dearborn, Lee, and Wilkinson.* Edited by William Abbatt. New York: William Abbatt, 1901.

Heckewelder, John Gottlieb Ernestus. *A Narrative of the Mission of the United Brethren Among the Delaware and Mohegan Indians, from its Commencement, in the Year 1740, to the Close of the Year 1808, Comprising All the Remarkable Incidents Which Took Place at Their Missionary Stations During That Period, Interspersed with Anecdotes, Historical Facts, Speeches of Indians, and Other Interesting Matter.* Edited by William Elsey Connelley. Cleveland: Burrows Brothers, 1907.

139

Historical Manuscripts Commission. *Report on American Manuscripts in the Royal Institution of Great Britain.* 4 vols. London: His Majesty's Stationery Office, 1904-9.

Hoadly, Charles Jeremy, editor. *The Public Records of the State of Connecticut . . . with the Journal of the Council of Safety . . . and an Appendix.* 3 vols. Hartford: Case Lockwood & Brainard, 1894-1922.

[Jones, Charles Colcock, editor and translator]. *The Siege of Savannah, in 1779, As Described in Two Contemporaneous Journals of French Officers in the Fleet of Count d'Estaing.* Albany: J. Munsell, 1874.

Kellogg, Louise Phelps, editor. *Frontier Advance on the Upper Ohio, 1778-1779.* Publications of the State Historical Society of Wisconsin. *Collections,* vol. 23. Madison: State Historical Society of Wisconsin, 1916.

— — —. *Frontier Retreat on the Upper Ohio, 1779-1781.* Publications of the State Historical Society of Wisconsin. *Collections,* vol. 24. Madison: State Historical Society of Wisconsin, 1917.

Kinnaird, Lawrence, editor. *Spain in the Mississippi Valley, 1765-1794: Part I, The Revolutionary Period, 1765-1781.* Annual Report of the American Historical Association for the Year 1945, vol. 2. Washington: U. S. Government Printing Office, 1949.

Lauber, Almon Wheeler, editor. *Orderly Books of the Fourth New York Regiment, 1778-1780; The Second New York Regiment, 1780-1783, by Samuel Tallmadge and Others with Diaries of Samuel Tallmadge, 1780-1782, and John Barr, 1779-1782.* Albany: University of the State of New York, 1932.

Lee, Henry. *Memoirs of the War in the Southern Department of the United States.* Washington: P. Force, 1812.

Lincoln, Rufus. *The Papers of Captain Rufus Lincoln of Wareham, Mass.* compiled by James Minor Lincoln. [Cambridge, Mass.: Riverside Press], 1904.

A List of the Names of the Provincials Who Were Killed in the Late Engagement with His Majesty's Troops at Concord, &c. [Boston: Edes and Gill, printers, 1775].

Mackenzie, Frederick. *Diary of Frederick Mackenzie, Giving a Daily Narrative of His Military Service as an Officer of the Regiment of Royal Welch Fusiliers During the Years 1775-1781 in Massachusetts, Rhode Island, and New York.* 2 vols. Cambridge, Mass.: Harvard University Press, 1930.

Massachusetts (Colony) Provincial Congress. *The Journals of Each Provincial Congress of Massachusetts in 1774 and 1775, and of the Committee of Safety . . . ,* Edited by William Lincoln. Boston: Dutton and Wentworth, 1838.

Morris, Margaret Hill. *Margaret Morris, Her Journal, With Biographical Sketch and Notes . . . .* Edited by John W. Jackson. Philadelphia: G. S. MacManus Co., 1949.

New York (State), Secretary of State. *Calendar of Historical Manuscripts Relating to the War of the Revolution, in the Office of the Secretary of*

State, Albany, N. Y. 2 vols. Albany: Weed, Parsons and Co., 1868.

– – –. *Journals of the Military Expedition of Major General John Sullivan Against the Six Nations of Indians in 1779 With Records of Centennial Celebrations, Prepared Pursuant to Chapter 361, Laws of the State of New York of 1885.* Auburn, N. Y.: Knapp, Peck & Thomson, 1887.

New York (State) State Historian. *The Sullivan-Clinton Campaign In 1779: Chronology and Selected Documents.* Prepared by the Division of Archives and History in connection with the Sesquicentennial of the American Revolution. Albany: University of the State of New York, 1929.

O'Callaghan, E. B., and Fernow, B., editors. *Documents Relative to the Colonial History of the State of New York.* 15 vols. Albany: Weed, Parsons and Co., 1853-87.

Powell, Leven. *A Biographical Sketch of Col. Leven Powell, Including His Correspondence During the Revolutionary War,* Edited by Robert C. Powell. Alexandria, Va.: G. H. Ramey & Son, 1877.

Robertson, Archibald. *His Diaries and Sketches in America, 1762-1780.* [New York]: New York Public Library, 1930.

Ryden, George Herbert, editor. *Letters to and from Caesar Rodney, 1756-1784, Member of the Stamp Act Congress, and the First and Second Continental Congresses; Speaker of the Delaware Colonial Assembly; President of the Delaware State; Major General of the Delaware Militia; Signer of the Declaration of Independence.* Philadelphia: Historical Society of Delaware, University of Pennsylvania Press, 1933.

Simcoe, John Graves. *Simcoe's Military Journal: A History of the Operations of a Partisan Corps, Called the Queen's Rangers, Commanded by Lieut. Col. J. G. Simcoe, During the War of the American Revolution . . . With a Memoir of the Author and Other Additions.* New York: Bartlett & Welford, 1844.

Stark, Caleb. *Memoir and Official Correspondence of Gen. John Stark, with Notices of Several Other Officers of the Revolution. Also, a Biography of Capt. Phinehas Stevens and of Col. Robert Rogers, with an Account of His Services in America During the "Seven Years' War."* Concord: Edson E. Eastman, 1877.

Steele, Zadock. *The Indian Captive; or, A Narrative of the Captivity and Sufferings of Zadock Steele, Related by Himself, To Which is Prefixed an Account of the Burning of Royalton.* Montpelier, Vt.: E. P. Walton, 1818.

Stevens, Benjamin Franklin. *B. F. Stevens's Facsimiles of Manuscripts in European Archives Relating to America, 1773-1783, With Descriptions, Editorial Notes, Collations, References and Translations.* 24 vols. London: Malby & Sons, 1889-95.

Sullivan, John. *Letters and Papers of Major-General John Sullivan, Continental Army.* Edited by Otis G. Hammond. New Hampshire Historical Society, *Collections,* vols. 13-15. Concord, N. H.: New Hampshire Historical Society, 1930-39.

Tallmadge, Benjamin. *Memoir of Col. Benjamin Tallmadge.* Edited by Henry Phelps Johnson. Publications of the Society of the Sons of the Revolution in the State of New York. New York: Gillis Press, 1904.

Tarleton, Lt. Col. Banastre. *A History of the Campaigns of 1780 and 1781, in the Southern Provinces of North America.* London, 1787.

Thacher, James. *A Military Journal during the American Revolutionary War, from 1775 to 1783, Describing Interesting Events and Transactions of This Period, with Numerous Historical Facts and Anecdotes, from the Original Manuscript, To Which is Added an Appendix, Containing Biographical Sketches of Several General Officers.* Boston: Richardson and Lord, 1823.

Thwaites, Reuben Gold, and Kellogg, Louise Phelps, editors. *Frontier Defense on the Upper Ohio, 1777-1778, Compiled from the Draper Manuscripts in the Library of the Wisconsin Historical Society and Published at the Charge of the Wisconsin Society of the Sons of the American Revolution.* Madison: Wisconsin Historical Society, 1912.

— — —. *The Revolution on the Upper Ohio, 1775-1777, Compiled from the Draper Manuscripts in the Library of the Wisconsin Historical Society and Published at the Charge of the Wisconsin Society of the Sons of the American Revolution.* Madison: Wisconsin Historical Society, 1908.

Uhlendorf, Bernhard A., translator and editor. *The Siege of Charleston, With an Account of the Province of South Carolina: Diaries and Letters of Hessian Officers From the von Jungkenn Papers in the William L. Clements Library.* Ann Arbor: University of Michigan Press, 1938.

U. S. Naval History Division. *Naval Documents of the American Revolution.* Edited by William Bell Clark (vols. 1-4) and William James Morgan (vols. 5-). Washington: U. S. Government Printing Office, 1964-.

Washington, George. *The Writings of George Washington from the Original Manuscript Sources, 1745-1799, Prepared under the Direction of the United States George Washington Bicentennial Commission and Published by Authority of Congress.* Edited by John C. Fitzpatrick. 39 vols. Washington: U. S. Government Printing Office, 1931-44.

Webb, Samuel Blachley. *Correspondence and Journals of Samuel Blachley Webb.* Edited by Worthington Chauncey Ford. 3 vols. New York, [Lancaster, Pa.: Wickersham Press], 1893.

Williams, Otho Holland. *Calendar of the General Otho Holland Williams Papers in the Maryland Historical Society, Prepared by the Maryland Historical Records Project, Division of Professional and Service Projects, Work Projects Administration.* Baltimore: Maryland Historical Records Survey Project, 1940.

SERIALS

Clark, Walter, editor. *The State Records of North Carolina.* 30 vols. Raleigh: State of North Carolina, 1886-1914.

Connecticut Historical Society. *Collections.* Vols. 1-24. Hartford, 1860-1932.

BIBLIOGRAPHY

Delaware Public Archives Commission. *Delaware Archives.* 5 vols. Wilmington, 1911-19.

Delaware Historical Society. *Papers.* 1st ser., vols. 1-67; 2d ser., vols. 1-3. Wilmington, 1879-1922, 1927-40.

Essex Institute. *Historical Collections.* Vol. 1-. Salem, Mass., 1859-.

Every Evening. Wilmington, Del., 1871-1932.

Georgia Historical Society. *Quarterly.* Vol. 1-. Savannah, 1917-.

——— . *Collections.* Vols. 1-9. Savannah, 1840-1916.

Historical Society of Delaware. *Delaware History.* Vol. 1-. Wilmington: Historical Society of Delaware, 1946-.

Kentucky State Historical Society. *Register.* Vol. 1-. Louisville: Globe Printing Co., 1903-.

Long Island Historical Society. *Memoirs.* Vols. 1-4. Brooklyn, N. Y., 1867-89.

The Magazine of History, with Notes and Queries. Vols. 1-26. 1905-22.

Maine Historical Society. *Collections.* 1st ser., vols. 1-10; 2d ser., vols. 1-10; 3d ser., vols. 1-2. Portland: Maine Historical Society, 1831-87, 1890-99, 1904-6.

Maryland, Hall of Records Commission. *Calendar of Maryland State Papers . . . .* 8 vols. Annapolis, 1943-58.

Maryland Historical Society. *Maryland Historical Magazine.* Vol. 1-. Baltimore, 1906-.

——— . *Archives of Maryland.* 71 vols. Baltimore, 1883-1970.

Massachusetts Historical Society. *Collections.* Vol. 1-. Boston, 1792-.

——— . *Proceedings.* 1st ser., vols. 1-20; 2d ser., vols. 1-20; 3d ser., vols. 1-2; vols. 43-. Boston, 1791-1883, 1884-1907, 1907/8-8/9, 1909/10-.

New England Historical and Genealogical Register. Vol. 1-. Boston, 1847-.

New Hampshire. *Provincial and State Papers.* 40 vols. Concord, 1867-1943.

New Hampshire Historical Society. *Collections.* 15 vols. Concord, N. H., 1824-1939.

——— . *Proceedings.* 5 vols. Concord, N. H., 1872-1912.

New Haven Colony Historical Society. *Papers.* 9 vols. New Haven, Conn., 1865-1918.

New Jersey Historical Society. *Collections.* Vol. 1-. Newark, 1846-.

——— . *Documents Relating to the Revolutionary History of New Jersey . . . Extracts from American Newspapers* [1776-82]. Trenton, 1901-17.

——— . *Proceedings.* 1st ser., vols. 1-10; 2d ser., vols. 1-13; 3d ser., vols. 1-10; new ser., vols. 1-16; vols. 50-. Newark, 1845-66, 1867-95, 1896-1915, 1916-31, 1932-.

New London County Historical Society. *Records and Papers.* Vol. 1-3, no. 2. New London, Conn., 1890-1912.

Palmer, William P., editor. *Calendar of Virginia State Papers and Other Manuscripts* [1652-1869]. 11 vols. Richmond: Superintendent of Public Printing, 1875-93.

Pennsylvania Archives. 1st ser., vols. 1-12; 2d ser., vols. 1-19; 3d ser., vols. 1-

30; 4th ser., vols. 1-12; 5th ser., vols. 1-8; 6th ser., vols. 1-15; 7th ser., vols. 1-5; 8th ser., vols. 1-8; 9th ser., vols. 1-10. Philadelphia and Harrisburgh, 1852-1935.

Pennsylvania Historical Society. *The Pennsylvania Magazine of History and Biography*. Vol. 1-. Philadelphia, 1877-.

Pioneer and Historical Society of the State of Michigan. *Historical Collections*. Vols. 1-40. Lansing, 1874-1929.

Rhode Island Historical Tracts. 1st ser., nos. 1-20; 2d ser., nos. 1-5. Providence, 1877-96.

South Carolina Historical Association. *Proceedings*. Vol. 1-. Columbia, 1931-.

Vermont Historical Society. *Collections*. Vols. 1-2. Montpelier, 1870-71.

Virginia Historical Society. *Virginia Magazine of History and Biography*. Vol. 1-. Richmond, 1893-.

Weymouth Historical Society. *Publications*. Vols. 1-3. Weymouth, Mass., 1881-1905.

Wisconsin State Historical Society. *Collections*. Vols. 1-28. Madison, 1854-1920.

SECONDARY WORKS

Of some 250 secondary works consulted on separate campaigns, battles, local sites, or biography, the following were most useful:

Alden, John R. *A History of the American Revolution*. New York: Knopf, 1969.

Allen, Gardner Weld. *A Naval History of the American Revolution*. Boston and New York: Houghton Mifflin Co., 1913.

Arnold, Samuel Greene. *History of the State of Rhode Island and Providence Plantations, 1636-1790*. 2 vols. New York: D. Appleton & Co., 1859, 1860.

Baird, Charles Washington. *Chronicle of a Border Town: History of Rye, Westchester County, New York, 1660-1870, Including Harrison and the White Plains till 1788*. New York: A. D. F. Randolph, 1871.

Barber, John Warner, and Howe, Henry. *Historical Collections of New Jersey, Past and Present, Containing a General Collection of the Most Interesting Facts, Traditions, Biographical Sketches, Anecdotes, etc., Relating to the History and Antiquities, with Geographical Descriptions of All the Important Places in the State, and the State Census of All the Towns in 1865*. New Haven, Conn.: J. W. Barber, 1868.

Barnhart, John Donald, editor. *Henry Hamilton and George Rogers Clark in the American Revolution with the Unpublished Journal of Lieut. Gov. Henry Hamilton*. Crawfordsville, Ind.: R.E. Banta, 1951.

Bass, Robert Duncan. *Gamecock: The Life and Campaigns of General Thomas Sumter*. New York: Holt, Rinehart and Winston, [1961].

― ― ―. *The Green Dragoon: The Lives of Banastre Tarleton and Mary Robinson*, New York: Holt, [1957].

BIBLIOGRAPHY

— — —. *Swamp Fox: The Life and Campaigns of General Francis Marion.* [New York]: Holt, [1959].

Bicknell, Thomas Williams. *The History of the State of Rhode Island and Providence Plantations.* New York: American Historical Society, 1920.

Bliven, Bruce Ormsby, Jr. *Battle for Manhattan.* New York: Holt, [1956].

Boatner, Mark Mayo III. *Encyclopedia of the American Revolution.* New York: David McKay Co., 1966.

Bolton, Robert, Jr. *History of the County of Westchester, From Its First Settlement to the Present Time.* N. Y.: Alexander S. Gould, 1848.

Canada, Department of National Defense, General Staff, Historical Section, editors. *A History of the Organization, Development and Services of the Military and Naval Forces of Canada from the Peace of Paris in 1763, to the Present Time. With Illustrative Documents.* 2 vols. [Ottawa?], 1919-20.

Carrington, Henry Beebee. *Battles of the American Revolution: Battle Maps and Charts of the American Revolution.* New York and Chicago: A. B. Barnes, 1881.

Case, James Royal. *An Account of Tryon's Raid on Danbury in April, 1777, Also the Battle of Ridgefield and the Career of Gen. David Wooster, with Much Original Matter Hitherto Unpublished.* Danbury, Conn.: [Danbury Printing Co.], 1927.

Caughey, John Walton. *Bernardo de Gálvez in Louisiana, 1776-1783.* Berkeley: University of California Press, 1934.

Clark, William Bell. *George Washington's Navy, Being an Account of His Excellency's Fleet in New England Waters.* Baton Rouge: Louisiana State University Press, 1960.

Coburn, Frank Warren. *A History of the Battle of Bennington, Vermont.* Bennington: Livingston Press, 1912.

Coleman, Kenneth. *The American Revolution in Georgia, 1763-1789.* Athens: University of Georgia Press, 1958.

Collins, Lewis. *Historical Sketches of Kentucky, Embracing Its History, Antiquities, and Natural Curiosities, Geographical, Statistical, and Geological Descriptions; with Anecdotes of Pioneer Life, and More than One Hundred Biographical Sketches of Distinguished Pioneers, Soldiers, Statesmen, Jurists, Lawyers, Divines, etc.* Maysville, Ky: Lewis Collins, 1847.

Commager, Henry Steele, and Morris, Richard Brandon, editors. *The Spirit of Seventy-Six: The Story of the American Revolution as Told by Participants.* Indianapolis: Bobbs-Merrill, [1958].

Cooch, Edward Webb. *The Battle of Cooch's Bridge, Delaware, September 3, 1777; Including: Campaigns by which it was Preceded and Followed; Claims as to the First Use of the Stars and Stripes; Traditions Which Surround the Battle; Pencader's Oath of Fidelity of 1778.* Wilmington, Delaware: W. N. Cann Inc., 1940.

145

Cotterill, Robert Spencer. *History of Pioneer Kentucky*. Cincinnati: Johnson & Hardin, 1917.

Cowell, Benjamin. *Spirit of '76 in Rhode Island; or, Sketches of the Efforts of the Government and People in the War of the Revolution, Together with the Names of Those Who Belonged to Rhode Island Regiments in the Army. With Biographical Notices, Reminiscences, &c., &c.* Boston: A. J. Wright, 1850.

Davidson, Chalmers Gaston. *Piedmont Partisan: The Life and Times of Brigadier-General William Lee Davidson*. Davidson, N. C.: Davidson College, [1968].

Davis, Burke. *The Cowpens-Guilford Courthouse Campaign*. Philadelphia: Lippincott, 1962.

Dawson, Henry Barton. *Battles of the United States by Sea and Land, Embracing Those of the Revolutionary and Indian Wars, the War of 1812, and the Mexican War, with Important Official Documents*. 2 vols. New York: Johnson, Fry & Co., 1858.

De Mond, Robert O. *The Loyalists in North Carolina during the Revolution*. Durham, N. C.: Duke University Press, 1940.

Dole, Esther Mohr. *Maryland during the American Revolution*. Baltimore: Waverly Press, 1941.

Draper, Lyman Copeland. *King's Mountain and Its Heroes: History of the Battle of King's Mountain, October 7, 1780, and the Events which Led to It*. Cincinnati: P. G. Thomson, 1881.

Dupuy, Richard Ernest. *The Battle of Hubbardton: A Critical Analysis*. [Cornwall, N. Y.]: State of Vermont Historic Sites Commission, 1960.

Emmons, George Foster, compiler. *The Navy of the United States, from the Commencement, 1775 to 1783; With a Brief History of Each Vessel's Service and Fate as Appears Upon Record . . . From the Most Reliable Sources, Under the Authority of the Navy Department, To Which is Added a List of Private Armed Vessels, Fitted Out Under the American Flag, Previous and Subsequent to the Revolutionary War, With Their Services and Fate; also a List of Revenue and Coast Survey Vessels, and Principal Ocean Steamers Belonging to Citizens of the United States in 1850*. Washington: Gideon & Co., 1853.

Fairfield, Conn. *Centennial Commemoration of the Burning of Fairfield, Connecticut, by the British Troops under Governor Tryon, July 8th, 1779*. New York: A. S. Barnes & Co., 1879.

Federal Writers Project, Kentucky. *Military History of Kentucky, Chronologically Arranged*. The American Guide series, sponsored by the Military Department of Kentucky. Frankfort, Ky.: State Journal, 1939.

Forbes, James Grant. *Sketches, Historical and Topographical, of the Floridas: More Particularly of East Florida*. New York: C. S. Van Winkle, 1821.

Fortier, Alceé. *A History of Louisiana*. New York: Goupil & Co., 1904.

French, Allen, *The Day of Concord and Lexington, the Nineteenth of April, 1775*. Boston: Little, Brown, and Co., 1925.

BIBLIOGRAPHY

— — —. *The First Year of the American Revolution*. Boston and New York: Houghton Mifflin Co., 1934.

Frothingham, Richard. *History of the Siege of Boston, and of the Battles of Lexington, Concord and Bunker Hill Monument. With Illustrative Documents.* Boston: Little, Brown, 1849.

Gilchrist, Helen Ives. *Fort Ticonderoga in History*. Ticonderoga: Fort Ticonderoga Museum, 192?.

Gordon, William. *The History of the Rise, Progress and Establishment of the Independence of the United States of America: Including an Account of the Late War; and of the Thirteen Colonies, from their Origin to that Period.* London, 1788.

Greene, George Washington, *The Life of Nathanael Greene, Major-General in the Army of the Revolution*. 3 vols, New York: Hurd and Houghton, 1871.

Greenwood, Isaac John. *Captain John Manley, Second in Rank in the United States Navy, 1776-1783*. Boston: C. E. Goodspeed & Co., 1915.

Gruber, Ira D. *The Howe Brothers and the American Revolution*. New York: Atheneum, 1972.

Hall, Charles Samuel. *Life and Letters of Samuel Holden Parsons, Major-General in the Continental Army and Chief Judge of the Northwestern Territory, 1737-1789*. Binghamton, N. Y.: Otseningo, 1905.

Hanson, Willis Tracy, Jr. *A History of Schenectady during the Revolution, to which is Appended a Contribution to the Individual Records of the Inhabitants of the Schenectady District During that Period.* [Brattleboro, Vt.: E. L. Hildreth & Co.], 1916.

Hardin, George Anson, editor. *History of Herkimer County, New York, Illustrated with Portraits of Many of its Citizens*. Syracuse, N.Y.: D. Mason & Co., 1893.

Harris, William Wallace. *The Battle of Groton Heights: A Collection of Narratives, Official Reports, Records, etc., of the Storming of Fort Griswold, the Massacre of its Garrison, and the Burning of New London by British Troops under the Command of Brig.-Gen. Benedict Arnold, on the Sixth of September, 1781.* New London, Conn.: Charles Allyn, 1882.

Heitman, Francis Bernard. *Historical Register of Officers of the Continental Army during the War of the Revolution, April, 1775, to December, 1783*. Washington, D. C.: Rare Book Shop Pub. Co., 1914.

Hinman, Royal Ralph. *A Historical Collection from Official Records, Files, &c., of the Part Sustained by Connecticut, during the War of the Revolution With an Appendix, Containing Important Letters, Depositions, &c. Written During the War.* Hartford: E. Gleason, 1842.

Hough, Franklin Benjamin, editor. *The Northern Invasion of October, 1780: A Series of Papers Relating to the Expeditions from Canada under Sir John Johnson and Others Against the Frontiers of New York, Which were Supposed to Have Connection with Arnold's Treason; Prepared from Originals.* New York: Bradford Club, 1866.

— — —. *The Siege of Savannah, by the Combined American and French Forces,*

147

under the Command of Gen. Lincoln and the Count d'Estaing, in the Autumn of 1779. Albany: J. Munsell, 1866.

Howe, Henry. *Historical Collections of Ohio, Containing a Collection of the Most Interesting Facts, Traditions, Biographical Sketches, Anecdotes, Etc., Relating to Its General and Local History, With Descriptions of its Counties, Principal Towns and Villages.* Cincinnati: Derby, Bradley & Co., 1847.

— — —. *Historical Collections of Virginia, Containing a Collection of the Most Interesting Facts, Traditions, Biographical Sketches, Anecdotes, &c. Relating to its History and Antiquities, Together with Geographical and Statistical Descriptions, To Which is Appended, an Historical and Descriptive Sketch of the District of Columbia.* Charleston, S. C.: W. R. Babcock, 1852.

Hufeland, Otto. *Westchester County during the American Revolution 1775-83.* White Plains, N. Y.: Westchester Co. Hist. Soc., 1926.

Johnson, Cecil. *British West Florida. 1763-1783.* New Haven: Yale University Press, 1943.

Johnson, Joseph. *Traditions and Reminiscences Chiefly of the American Revolution in the South, Including Biographical Sketches, Incidents and Anecdotes, Few of which Have Been Published, Particularly of Residents in the Upper Country.* Charleston, S. C.: Walker & James, 1851.

Johnston, Henry Phelps. *The Battle of Harlem Heights, Sept. 16, 1776; with a Review of the Events of the Campaign.* New York: Columbia University Press and Macmillan Co., 1897.

— — —. *The Yorktown Campaign and the Surrender of Cornwallis, 1781.* New York: Harper & Brothers, 1881.

Jones, Charles Colcock, Jr. *The History of Georgia.* Boston: Houghton, Mifflin & Co., 1883.

Kegley, Frederick Bittle. *Kegley's Virginia Frontier: The Beginning of the Southwest; the Roanoke of Colonial Days, 1740-1783.* Roanoke, Va.: Southwest Virginia Historical Society, 1938.

Ketchum, Richard M. *The Winter Soldiers.* Garden City, N. Y.: Doubleday & Co., 1973.

Kidder, Frederic, editor. *Military Operations in Eastern Maine and Nova Scotia During the Revolution, Chiefly Compiled from the Journals and Letters of Colonel John Allen, with Notes and a Memoir of Col. John Allen.* Albany: Joel Munsell, 1867.

Landrum, John Belton O'Neall. *Colonial and Revolutionary History of Upper South Carolina, Embracing for the Most Part the Primitive and Colonial History of the Territory Comprising the Original County of Spartanburg with a General Review of the Entire Military Operations in the Upper Portion of South Carolina and Portions of North Carolina.* Greenville, S. C.: Shannon & Co., 1897.

Lawrence, Alexander A. *Storm over Savannah: The Story of Count d'Estaing*

148

and the Siege of the Town in 1779. Athens, Ga.: University of Georgia Press, 1951.

Leiby, Adrian Coulter. *The Revolutionary War in the Hackensack Valley: The Jersey Dutch and the Neutral Ground, 1775-1783.* New Brunswick: Rutgers University Press, 1962.

Lossing, Benson John. *The Pictorial Field-Book of the Revolution; or, Illustrations, by Pen and Pencil, of the History, Biography, Scenery, Relics, and Traditions of the War for Independence.* New York: Harper & Brothers, 1851-52.

Lundin, Charles Leonard. *Cockpit of the Revolution: The War for Independence in New Jersey.* Princeton: Princeton University Press, 1940.

McCall, Hugh. *History of Georgia, Containing Brief Sketches of the Most Remarkable Events up to the Present Day (1784).* Atlanta, Ga.: A.B. Caldwell, 1816.

McCrady, Edward. *The History of South Carolina in the Revolution, 1775-1783.* 2 vols. New York: Macmillan, 1901-2.

Metzger, Charles H. *The Prisoner in the American Revolution.* Chicago: Loyola University Press, 1971.

Middlebrook, Louis Frank. *History of Maritime Connecticut during the American Revolution, 1775-1783.* Salem, Mass.: Essex Institute, 1925.

Mills, Robert. *Statistics of South Carolina, Including a View of its Natural, Civil, and Military History, General and Particular.* Charleston, S. C.: Hurlbut and Lloyd, 1826.

Montross, Lynn. *Rag, Tag and Bobtail: The Story of The Continental Army 1775-1783.* New York: Harper & Brothers, 1952.

Moore, Frank, compiler. *The Diary of the American Revolution, 1775-1781.* New York: Charles T. Evans, 1863.

Mowat, Charles Loch. *East Florida as a British Province 1763-1784.* Gainesville, Fla.: University of Florida Press, 1943.

Neeser, Robert Wilden. *Statistical and Chronological History of the United States Navy, 1775-1907.* New York: Macmillan Co., 1909.

Peckham, Howard Henry. *The War for Independence: A Military History.* The Chicago History of American Civilization. Chicago: University of Chicago Press, 1958.

Purviance, Robert. *Narrative of Events which Occurred In Baltimore Town during the Revolutionary War, To Which Are Appended Various Documents and Letters, the Greater Part of Which Have Never Been Heretofore Published.* Baltimore: Joseph Robinson, 1849.

Quaife, Milo Milton. "Detroit Battles: The Blue Licks." *Burton Historical Collection Leaflet.* Vol. 6, no. 2 (November 1927).

— — —. "When Detroit Invaded Kentucky." *Burton Historical Collection Leaflet.* Vol. 4, no. 2 (November 1925).

Ramsay, David. *The History of the Revolution of South-Carolina, from a*

BIBLIOGRAPHY

British Province to an Independent State. Trenton: Isaac Collins, 1785.
Rankin, Hugh F. *The American Revolution.* New York: Putnam, 1964.
— — —. *The North Carolina Continentals.* Chapel Hill: University of North Carolina Press, 1971.
Report of the Commission to Locate the Site of the Frontier Forts of Pennsylvania. N.p.: Clarence M. Busch, 1896.
Roberts, Kenneth Lewis, editor. *March to Quebec: Journals of the Members of Arnold's Expedition, Compiled and Annotated by Kenneth Roberts during the Writing of Arundel.* New York: Doubleday, Doran & Co., 1938.
Roe, Clara Goldsmith. "Major General Nathanael Greene and the Southern Campaign of the American Revolution, 1780-83." Ph. D. dissertation, University of Michigan, 1947.
Sabine, Lorenzo. *Biographical Sketches of Loyalists of the American Revolution.* Boston: Little, Brown & Co., 1864.
Schenck, David. *North Carolina, 1780-81, Being a History of the Invasion of the Carolinas by the British Army Under Lord Cornwallis in 1780-81, With the Particular Design of Showing the Part Borne by North Carolina in that Struggle for Liberty and Independence, and To Correct Some of the Errors of History in Regard to that State and Its People.* Raleigh, N. C.: Edwards & Broughton, 1889.
Siebert, Wilbur Henry. *Loyalists in East Florida, 1774 to 1785: The Most Important Documents Pertaining Thereto, Edited with an Accompanying Narrative.* 2 vols. DeLand, Fla.: Florida State Historical Society, 1929.
Smith, Charles. *The Monthly Military Repository, Respectfully Inscribed to the Military of the United States of America.* 2 vols. New York, 1796, 1797.
Starr, Joseph Barton. "Tories, Dons, and Rebels: The American Revolution in British West Florida." Ph. D. dissertation, Florida State University, 1971.
Stewart, Robert Armistead. *The History of Virginia's Navy of the Revolution.* [Richmond: Mitchell & Hotchkiss, 1934.]
Stryker, William Scudder. *The Battle of Monmouth.* Edited by William Starr Myers. Princeton: Princeton University Press, 1927.
— — —. *The Battles of Trenton and Princeton.* Boston: Houghton, Mifflin and Co., 1898.
— — —. *The Forts on the Delaware in the Revolutionary War.* Trenton, N. J.: J. L. Murphy, 1901.
Ward, Christopher Longstreth. *The Delaware Continentals, 1776-1783.* Wilmington, Del.: Historical Society of Delaware, 1941.
— — —. *The War of the Revolution.* Edited by John Richard Alden. New York: Macmillan, 1952.
Weigley, Russell Frank. *The Partisan War: The South Carolina Campaign of 1780-1782.* Columbia: University of South Carolina Press, [1970].
Williams, Samuel Cole. *Tennessee during the Revolutionary War.* Nashville: Tennessee Historical Commission, 1944.

INDEX

☆

In this index all battle locations, ships, and commanders on either side are listed. Officers carry the rank they held when first mentioned. Men without first names are identified as American (Amer.), British (Brit.), or Loyalist (Loy.). Ships are similarly identified as to ownership. Under the name of each state, capitalized, are references to all engagements that occurred in that state. Forts, lakes, rivers, and mountains are alphabetized under their individual names.

169